NOLO *and* USA TODAY

 ## NOLO
YOUR LEGAL COMPANION

For more than 35 years, Nolo has been helping ordinary folks who want to answer their legal questions, create their own documents, or work with a lawyer more efficiently. Nolo.com provides quick information about wills, house buying, credit repair, starting a business—and just about anything else that's affected by the law. It's packed with free articles, legal updates, resources, and a complete catalog of Nolo books and software.

To find out about any important legal or other changes to this book's contents, sign up for our free update service at nolo.com/legalupdater or go to nolo.com/updates. And to make sure that you've got the most recent edition of this book, check Nolo's website or give us a call at 800-728-3555.

 ## USA TODAY
The Nation's Newspaper

USA TODAY, the nation's largest circulation newspaper, was founded in 1982. It has nearly 3.9 million readers daily, making it the most widely read newspaper in the country.

USATODAY.com adds blogs, interactive graphics, games, travel resources, and trailblazing network journalism, allowing readers to comment on every story.

First-Time Landlord

Your Guide to Renting Out a Single-Family Home

by Attorney Janet Portman,
Marcia Stewart, and Michael Molinski

First Edition	FEBRUARY 2009
Editors	ILONA BRAY, ALAYNA SCHROEDER
Cover Design	JALEH DOANE
Book Design	SUSAN PUTNEY
Proofreading	ANI DIMUSHEVA
Index	BAYSIDE INDEXING SERVICE
Printing	DELTA PRINTING SOLUTIONS, INC.

Portman, Janet.
    First-time landlord : your guide to renting out a single-family home / by Janet Portman,
Marcia Stewart, and Michael Molinski. -- 1st ed.
        p. cm.
    Includes bibliographical references.
    ISBN-13: 978-1-4133-0911-9 (pbk.)
    ISBN-10: 1-4133-0911-9 (pbk.)
    1. Real estate management--United States. 2. Rental housing--United States--
Management. 3. Landlord and tenant--United States. I. Stewart, Marcia. II. Molinski,
Michael, 1963- III. Title.
    HD1394.5.U6P67 2009
    333.33'8--dc22
                                            2008037030

For information on bulk purchases or corporate premium sales, please contact Nolo's Special Sales
Department. For academic sales or textbook adoptions, ask for Academic Sales. Call 800-955-4775
or write to Nolo, 950 Parker Street, Berkeley, CA 94710.

Acknowledgments

We couldn't have written this book without our editor Ilona Bray. Every page reflects Ilona's outstanding editing and writing skills, great ideas, and constant support and enthusiasm for the project. Nolo legal editor Alayna Schroeder was also invaluable, supplying information on the technical aspects of buying and selling and the financial and legal fine points of ownership, and coming through for us cheerfully and skillfully. Both Ilona's and Alayna's contributions were so great, we consider them more co-authors than editors.

Also integral to this book were contributions from the many first-time or accidental landlords who provided stories from around the country, including Amy Benton, Catherine Berryessa, Danielle Bray, Phil Cunliffe, Dennis Deen, Kathy Eldridge, Lisa Guerin, Stuart Jacobsen, Darren Johnston, John Lindenmeyer, Laura Macht, Sergio Raddavero, Amy Shelf, Kyung Yu, Sharon Vallejo, Gordon and Connie Finwall, and others who wished not to be named.

Thanks also go to Nolo authors and editors Steve Fishman and Diana Fitzpatrick for their help regarding the tax deductions associated with owning rental property, Richard Stim for contributions regarding the small business aspects of being a landlord, Mary Randolph and Emily Doskow for their advice on taking title and co-owning rental property, and Stan Jacobsen for research help. Finally, thanks to the ever-helpful Mike Mansel, certified insurance counselor (see www.insuranceadvisor. pro), for providing tips on converting homeowners' insurance when a home is converted to rental use.

None of this information would help anyone if it weren't laid out attractively, so hats off to Nolo's production team for their fine efforts and patience, including Jaleh Doane, Susan Putney, Emma Cofod, and Emilie Guttner.

About the Authors

Janet Portman is an attorney and a nationally recognized expert on residential and commercial landlord/tenant law, including legal issues related to courts, landlords and tenants, and neighbor disputes. A syndicated columnist with Inman News, Portman's column, "Rent It Right," appears regularly in the Chicago Tribune, Los Angeles Times, Yahoo!, and other prominent newspapers and websites. Portman is the author or co-author of *Every Landlord's Legal Guide, Every Landlord's Guide to Finding Great Tenants, Every Tenant's Legal Guide, Renters' Rights, Negotiate the Best Lease for Your Business, Leases & Rental Agreements, The California Landlord's Law Book: Rights & Responsibilities,* and *California Tenants' Rights.*

Marcia Stewart writes and edits books on landlord-tenant law, real estate, and other consumer issues. She is the co-author of *Nolo's Essential Guide to Buying Your First Home, Every Landlord's Legal Guide, Every Tenant's Legal Guide, Leases & Rental Agreements,* and *Renters' Rights.* She has edited dozens of Nolo books, including *How to Buy a House in California.*

Michael Molinski is a long-time landlord, with homes in various U.S. cities. His properties range from single-family homes to four-plex apartment buildings. Molinski is a veteran writer, having spent 15 years as a reporter, editor, and foreign correspondent at Bloomberg News, MarketWatch, and United Press International. Molinski is a former director of investment research and publications at Charles Schwab & Co., and is a founding partner of a business communications company, IAB Media (iabmedia.com). He is the author and co-author of several books about small business, real estate, and entrepreneurship, including *Small Business in Paradise* (Nolo).

Table of Contents

Your First-Time Landlord's Companion

This book is for the millions of people who rent out (or want to rent out) a single-family house or condo, and who might want to do much of the work themselves. You may not consider yourself a "real" landlord—you may not even like the term. Yet you no doubt want to make money and avoid legal hassles.

If you're balancing a day job and a family, taking on the tasks of being a landlord can actually seem overwhelming, especially if it's not a role you actively chose. An increasing number of landlords are the "accidental" sort, having come into their rental property in one of the following ways:

- **Inheritance.** Many people become accidental landlords by inheriting a property (usually a single-family home) from a family member or friend. You may be deciding whether to sell or keep the place.

- **Divorce.** When couples separate, they often agree—or a court decides—that one or the other gets to keep a property, whether a family home or investment or vacation property. And if two divorcing parties decide to share a property, renting it out can actually help them recover from the financial difficulties of the split.

USA TODAY Snapshots®

Passing on
Greatest sources of conflict in dealing with parents' legacy:

Distribution of personal possessions of emotional value	15%
Fulfilling the last wishes and instructions of your parents	15%
Distribution of real estate/property	11%
The choice of the executor	8%
Distribution of financial assets	3%

Source: The Allianz American Legacies Study survey of 2,627 adults. Margin of error ±3 percentage points

By Jae Yang and Alejandro Gonzalez, USA TODAY 2005

- **Trading up or moving out of the area.** Perhaps you need more space or are moving to a new location, but aren't prepared to sell your current home, maybe because the housing market is soft or you're thinking your might move back someday.

- **Trading down or fighting foreclosure.** Like many homeowners, you may be having trouble paying the mortgage on your current home—but reluctant to sell if prices are down. Renting out your home, while you live somewhere less expensive, can provide the cushion you need until you're ready to move back or sell.

- **Having extra space.** Perhaps your kids have graduated from college or you've divorced and the extra living space could be rented out. Or you might own a duplex or house with an in-law unit. If there's room for a tenant, you might be looking at a handy way to raise extra cash without much change to your fixed expenses.

- **Caring for a loved one's property.** A close relative or friend may need help renting out a property, for example, because they've moved to a nursing home.

- **Temporary move.** If you're taking an overseas sabbatical, serving in the military, or making some other temporary move, you probably don't want your house sitting empty. You can prevent this, and make money, by renting it out.

In any of these situations, you may be wondering whether to sell the property immediately, rent it out temporarily before selling, or turn it into a long-term investment property. This book will start by helping you make that decision, then orient you to all the financial, legal, and practical rules every landlord needs to know. It will also help you if you're thinking of going out to buy real estate for use as a rental (maybe for your college student child or older parent, or as an investment—but not to "flip" and sell quickly).

We provide nuts-and-bolts information on how to:

- find and choose good tenants (the number one key to your success)—from low-cost ideas for sprucing up a property to writing ads to checking prospective tenants' credit and references

- prepare a solid lease or rental agreement, which will help assure that tenants pay rent on time, respect your property, and cause you little hassle
- make the most of landlord tax deductions, and manage financial recordkeeping
- handle repairs and maintenance legally and efficiently—without driving yourself crazy or going broke
- use careful landlord practices and a good insurance policy to stay out of legal trouble (and limit your liability) when it comes to tenant health and safety, discrimination, and crime on the property
- maintain a good relationship with your tenant, or deal with a tenant who's skipping out on the rent, damaging your property, or otherwise causing you sleepless nights
- manage rental property from a distance
- hire a property manager and other professionals as needed
- share the work (and legal ownership and tax benefits of landlording) with a spouse, relative, or friend—while maintaining your personal relationship
- take over a rental house with tenants in place, and
- get out of the landlording business while maximizing profit and minimizing taxes.

We've tried to concentrate on the things that every first-timer needs to know. We also include lots of hands-on practical anecdotes and advice from real landlords who've come before you—people like Catherine, who rents out a cottage behind her own house, or Laura, who lives in Washington but rents out properties in three states. We hope this book provides a valuable companion on your path to being a successful and satisfied rental property owner.

Other Helpful Nolo Titles for Landlords

Nolo publishes a comprehensive library of books for landlords and rental owners, with all the forms and state-by-state legal information you need. In addition, we offer lots of free information on our website (check out "Landlords and Property Management" under the Property and Money section at www.nolo.com). The Legal Research Center at nolo.com will also help you find federal and state laws that affect your rental property.

And once you've figured out your needs, these Nolo products can help you with tasks like creating an actual lease or rental agreement:

- *Every Landlord's Legal Guide*, a 50-state book with CD-ROM, which provides detailed legal information and forms, from the lease or rental agreement to the documents you'll use at the end of the tenancy, and

- *Every Landlord's Tax Deduction Guide*, a book on how to take advantage of tax deductions and write-offs available to landlords, with instructions on filling out Schedule E.

Nolo also publishes several single-topic books for landlords, including *Every Landlord's Property Protection Guide*, *Every Landlord's Guide to Finding Great Tenants*, and *Leases & Rental Agreements*. And if your property is in California, see *The California Landlord's Law Book: Rights & Responsibilities*, and *The California Landlord's Law Book: Evictions*.

You can order these books from Nolo's website (www.nolo.com) or by phone (800-728-3555). You can also find Nolo books at public libraries and bookstores.

Is Owning Rental Property for You?

Being a landlord may sound appealing in theory—you find a decent tenant, collect a monthly rent check, and celebrate your good fortune. If only it were that simple. Before you start fantasizing about a multi-unit building on Park Place, let's look at what it takes to own and manage rental property, and how to decide whether a particular property is actually going to make you money. Along the way, we'll share some helpful advice from other first-time landlords.

Great Things About Being a Landlord

Owning rental property offers both financial and lifestyle benefits. As Laura, a landlord with properties in Washington, Nevada, and Florida, says, "I like people, and the feeling that I'm doing a good job. In fact, I have to be careful not to get too friendly—I have tenants in Florida with adorable kids, and I'm often tempted to volunteer to babysit, but have to remind myself to keep it all business. Of course, it's also nice to earn money through my efforts, and to be able to take tax-deductible trips. I remember the first time I sold one of my rental properties, and made a nice profit on the sale, it made me very happy."

USA TODAY Snapshots®

Housing: Owning vs. renting
A breakdown of
U.S. households
(in millions):

72.3 — Owner occupied

34.0 — Renter occupied

Source: Census American Housing Survey 2001

By Shannon Reilly and Julie Snider, USA TODAY 2004

Below is an overview of the various benefits that Laura and other landlords enjoy. Try to remember these later, when you're cursing the latest plumbing problem or fretting over how to fill a vacancy.

Appreciation and wealth building

If you hold onto your property long enough, it will almost certainly go up ("appreciate") in value—eventually. Since World War II, real estate prices in America have risen an average of 5% a year (with some nerve-wracking ups and downs in between). And even if the house's value isn't changing much, renting it may allow you to build equity until you own it outright. Owning investment property is a great way to increase your net worth.

Where Are House Prices Going?

In 2008, USA TODAY asked a group of experts and consumers to predict what's ahead in the real estate market. Here is one of their exchanges:

USA TODAY: History shows that over the long run, home-price appreciation barely exceeds inflation and trails the stock market. Given the extraordinary run-up in home prices of the past decade, will price appreciation run below average for the next decade or so?

Dean Baker, codirector of the Center for Economic and Policy Research in Washington, DC: My bet is that prices will fall back to trend levels over the next year or so and from that point forward will again move with inflation.

Mark Zandi, chief economist of Moody's Economy.com: Prices will decline for another year and go sideways early in the next decade. In the longer run, house price growth will equal the growth in household incomes.

Leslie Sellers, vice president, the Appraisal Institute: Remember that real estate has certain advantages that the stock market does not offer. Tax write-offs for certain costs, depreciation deductions, and leverage of the purchase are just a few.

Joel Naroff, president, Naroff Economic Advisors, and chief economist, Commerce Bank: If younger buyers only buy what they can afford, then prices are going to fall for a long time, as the baby boomers will not be able to unload their McMansions.

 "Real Estate Roundtable; Experts, consumers share home market views," by Stephanie Armour, April 29, 2008.

Income

A well-managed investment property, with tenants who pay the rent on time and monthly expenses that are less than the rent, can bring you a steady stream of income. Fifty-one percent of landlords owning single-family homes (surveyed in 2007 by the National Association of Realtors®) bought with this purpose in mind.

Diversification of income

You never know what life is going to throw at you. If you're laid off from your job, or your health takes a turn for the worse, your primary source of income—presumably your salary—could be jeopardized. Owning an investment property diversifies your income stream, and can give you somewhat of a cushion.

Low-risk investment

Unlike more volatile investments, the returns on real estate are fairly steady. While stock values can fall or even disintegrate entirely, land and property won't disappear on you. And history shows us that they almost always hold their value—or at least bounce back after a tumble.

That may sound unduly optimistic given the recent drop seen in many of real estate markets across the country. But notably, 2007 was the first year in the previous 50 in which the average price of U.S. single-family homes did not go up. In late 2008, at the time this book went to print, median prices were still declining. Yet the number of sales was picking up, leading some experts to predict a turnaround.

USA TODAY Snapshots®

Home sweet home
Highest and lowest homeownership rates, by state:

Highest
West Virginia — 81.3%

Lowest
New York — 55.9%

Source: Census Bureau

By David Stuckey and Adrienne Lewis, USA TODAY
2008

Does Owning Real Estate Create Millionaires?

Catherine McBreen and George Walper, authors of *Get Rich, Stay Rich, Pass It On*, are managing director and president, respectively, of Spectrem Group, a research and consulting company that has been studying the affluent since 1991.

Each year, the firm surveys more than 5,000 millionaire and megamillionaire (more than $5 million in assets, not including primary residence) households. While there are many ways to get rich, the authors identified two definitive ways to ensure lasting wealth: owning incoming-producing real estate and investing in an innovative company, product, or service.

In this model for getting rich, just below half of the typical megamillionaire portfolio is invested in marketable assets: stocks, bonds, mutual funds and other securities. The rest of the assets are not so liquid.

If you dream of being really rich, you will need to actively invest in real estate, they write. "Building up a nest egg with the equity in your home is a fine thing. But what distinguishes the model for getting rich, staying rich, and passing it on is its emphasis on investing in current and future income-producing real estate." Look for opportunities initially in areas you know, they advise.

On average, 23% to 29% of your wealth should be allocated to real estate. Here's how it breaks down: 11%–13% of your real estate investments should be equity in your principal home, 3%–6% should be income-producing property, 5%–7% a second home, 3%–5% other real estate holdings such as REITS, 2%–4% undeveloped land, and 2%–4% third or additional homes.

There are a slew of caveats, of course, on top of the myriad decisions that go into selecting the right properties. And yet, for those willing and eager to go the distance, consider the book's parting thought: "Keep in mind that all this is doable."

 "Path to wealth is through real estate holdings," by Kerry Hannon, January 28, 2008.

Investment diversification

Owning property also diversifies your investment portfolio, a cardinal rule of investing. And it's pretty easy to understand, if you get the idea of not putting all your eggs in one basket. Should something unforeseeable happen to your riskier investments, such as stocks, you'll have the backup of a tangible, relatively low-risk asset. As you approach retirement, it's good to start shifting into lower-risk investments, to ensure the cash you need doesn't disappear when you're relying on it.

USA TODAY Snapshots®

'Underpaid' for work we do

When asked whether they, are overpaid, underpaid or paid about right for the work they do, workers say:

Overpaid **3%**

Underpaid **51%**

Paid right amount **46%**

Source: Gallup Poll of 557 adults employed full or part time, Aug. 7-10

By Anne R. Carey and Suzy Parker, USA TODAY 2008

Leverage

Unlike other investments, a little bit of cash will buy a lot of real estate: A down payment of 10% or 20% of the value of the property is usually enough to get you started. You could, for example, buy a $400,000 property with a $40,000 down payment; while that amount will buy you only $40,000 worth of stock. And if the value of that stock were to increase by 10%, you'd have a $4,000 profit, whereas if the value of the property increased 10%, you'd have a $40,000 profit.

This is called being highly "leveraged"—in one sense, deeply in debt, but in another sense, poised to gain high returns based on a relatively small up-front investment. Leveraging your investment allows you to trade up to more profitable properties.

> **EXAMPLE:** Shari is selling a single-family house she bought three years ago for $400,000 with a 20% down payment ($80,000). The property's value has increased to $440,000. If Shari sells for $440,000, she'll recoup her $80,000 down payment plus walk away with a $40,000 profit (not factoring in costs like sales commissions and taxes). That

gives her $120,000 to put down on one or more properties. Assuming she qualifies for a loan, with a 20% down payment, she can now buy property worth $600,000—perhaps a four-unit building that brings in even more income.

Short-term tax advantages

While the rental income from your property is taxable, you can deduct most of the expenses related to owning and maintaining the property. Among these are mortgage interest, insurance, repairs, and upkeep. They also include your business expenses, such as phone calls, office supplies, professional fees (for example, to the accountant who helps you figure out your business taxes), and more.

Another major tax advantage is the ability to "depreciate" your property—to take an annual deduction that reflects the decreased value of the property caused by wear and tear. (In the most literal sense, depreciation is a fiction, because the value of the property will probably go up—but it's a wonderful fiction for tax purposes.) Chapter 6 of this book discusses tax issues in detail.

Long-term tax advantages

Even if your property skyrockets in value on paper, the IRS won't expect you to pay taxes on that increased value until you sell. (Your state and local property taxes may be another matter, however, rising steadily to catch up with the property's value.) And when you do sell, there are several strategies you can use to decrease your tax liability. We'll discuss those in Chapter 11.

Part-time commitment

If you own just one property, and it's not too far from where you live, you can probably handle its management in your spare time, while still working a full-time job. A little job flexibility will help, of course. Although weeks may go by when the property needs little or no attention, there will be times when it will need hours from you, for example, when you're getting the place painted while dealing with the departure of the old tenant and interviewing prospective new tenants.

Your time commitment will be even less if you hire a property management company—though your profits will decrease as well. We discuss the pros and cons of hiring property managers in Chapter 10.

Professional development

Being a landlord and owning property can give you a sense of accomplishment (and some stories to tell at parties). It shows that you've broken out of the mold of the average working stiff, and are willing to take risks and accept major responsibilities—you're learning new skills involving finances, dealing with people, and maybe even home repair, which may help you in other areas of life.

Personal satisfaction

Being a competent and conscientious landlord will pay dividends in other respects, too—you're going to feel pleased about the way you're doing business. As Amy, who lives in Berkeley, California, and rents out her former home in Austin, Texas, puts it: "I've rented from a few crummy landlords myself, so it's very satisfying to be able to give my tenants a positive experience, for example quickly taking care of repairs if something goes wrong."

Tough Parts of Being a Landlord

Landlording is not for everybody, and not every property is worth keeping or buying as an investment. The main reasons that people tend to give up on landlording are the time required to manage a property effectively, the risks involved (such as problem tenants, long vacancies, and legal risks), and the cost. Here's a quick overview of these issues. Later chapters in this book provide detailed advice on preventing and dealing with them.

Time

Even though landlording isn't a full-time job, it will take more than an hour or two of your time every few weeks. For one thing, you'll need to be reachable and available nearly around the clock, to respond to calls from tenants when the plumbing backs up or the neighbor's dog is barking all night. Occasionally, you'll need to put in large chunks of time, for tasks like listing and showing the property during a vacancy, screening and approving tenants, and handling rent checks and deposits, to name a few.

In this book, we'll help you strategize ways to cut down on the time you spend landlording. For example, Chapters 3 and 4 will give you tips on how to market your property, attract and choose the right tenants (who will hopefully stick around for awhile), and list the property so as to fill vacancies quickly and efficiently.

Problem tenants

One of the pitfalls of owning rental property is the possibility that you're going to get that rare "tenant from Hell"—someone who doesn't pay the rent on time, trashes the property, or constantly bugs you about every little thing that goes wrong—all of which can be expensive to remedy. Catherine, who rents out a cottage behind her house in Berkeley, describes often feeling "vulnerable," because someone else has day-to-day control of property she owns and cares about.

It's more likely that your tenants will be perfectly decent, responsible people. Good screening procedures (as described in Chapter 4) will help assure this. Nevertheless, people can change. Catherine's low point as a landlord came, she says, when "one of my tenants, who six months before had a nice job and drove a BMW, developed a crack addiction. The neighbors formed a watch group around my house, and I'd see drug deals going on and find vials in the backyard."

A properly structured lease or rental agreement (as covered in Chapter 5) will help deal with difficult situations like this, and reduce many of the risks associated with problem tenants. And knowing how to deal with bad tenants (Chapter 9) will also help you do damage control when needed.

Difficulty renting

There may be times when the market is soft and it will be difficult to rent your place out. Vacancies are a reality of life for most landlords, but can be made worse by local economic conditions, the need for major repairs in your property, or just sheer bad luck. That's why we'll make sure you factor expected vacancies into your analysis of potential profits on the property, below.

Legal risks

If you really want to talk worst-case scenario, you could worry about the legal risks that come with owning rental property—that is, the possibility that a tenant, prospective tenant, or someone else on your property will sue you over a health, safety, environmental, discrimination or other legal matter. You could even face legal trouble from third parties, stemming from misbehavior of your tenant. For example, if a tenant's drug dealing results in injury to a neighbor, you might be liable if the neighbor can prove that you knew what was going on but failed to take action.

Knowing your own responsibilities and potential liabilities (which we'll describe in Chapter 8) and acting to reduce the risk of problems occuring will limit the chances that you'll face serious legal situations.

Costs

The costs of owning an investment property go well beyond the mortgage. They include property taxes, insurance, utilities, upkeep, repairs, property management costs (if you choose), wages for a handyperson, legal costs when needed, and much more.

As Dennis, a landlord since 1982 describes it, "We haven't had much of a negative cash flow on our properties, but we have sometimes. From a financial point of view, if people are really tight they shouldn't get into the landlord business. There's always the unexpected plumbing problem, or an appliance that wears out."

Reducing costs is one of the keys to being a successful landlord. We'll advise you on how to assess the cost side of your property in Chapter 6.

Landlording Duties

❑ Research and set rental price.

❑ Establish a bookkeeping system for tracking income and expenses.

❑ Participate in a local landlords' association (optional).

❑ Learn the key laws and ordinances that cover residential renting in your state and city.

❑ Advertise property for rent.

❑ Respond to people interested in renting the property.

❑ Clean property in preparation for tenants.

❑ Show property to prospective tenants.

❑ Review tenant applications, obtain credit reports, and conduct reference checks.

❑ Draft and negotiate lease or rental agreement.

❑ Supervise tenant move-in.

❑ Collect and manage security deposit.

❑ Respond to tenant problems or inquiries.

❑ Collect rent.

❑ Respond to late rent and other violations of the rental agreement.

❑ Pay mortgage, utilities, insurance, etc.

❑ Prepare annual tax paperwork.

❑ Evaluate and fix problems and contact maintenance repair people.

❑ Supervise tenant move-out.

❑ Evaluate the condition of the vacated rental, and return tenant security deposit.

❑ Handle disputes among tenants (multi-family rentals) or disputes or complaints from neighbors.

Cute, Cheap, and More: Features of the Ideal Rental Property

Whether you're planning to buy a rental property or deciding whether to keep a property you already own, one of your first considerations should be whether the place is actually suited for renting. Look especially hard at features of the property that can't be changed, like its location and whether it has a yard. Let's consider its suitability from both the tenant's vantage point and yours.

What gives a property "tenant appeal"?

Here are the most important, primarily physical characteristics of a house that will appeal to a wide range of tenants:

- **Size.** This depends on the local population. For example, a house with several bedrooms will be attractive to large families.
- **Location.** Nearby transportation access—particularly public transport, with gas prices setting all-time highs—is a big plus. So is proximity to shopping and commercial areas.
- **Security.** No one likes to live in a high-crime area—and making sure the property is secure enough for your tenants can add to your to-do list as a landlord, too.
- **Good nearby public schools.** A family that wants to make sure their children go to the best schools and finds a good home nearby to rent may settle there for years. But even short-term renters appreciate a good school, and the corresponding community spirit.
- **Affordability.** With rare exceptions, it's difficult to find tenants for large, luxury houses. Any prospective tenant who has the money to afford the monthly rent can probably also afford to buy a house.
- **In good repair.** Even if it's otherwise in good shape, a house with ongoing maintenance issues—perhaps a nearby creek that often floods, or being so old that everything is falling apart—may put off tenants who don't want to be dealing with inconveniences or calling you with numerous repair requests.

- **Layout.** Like everyone, rental tenants want a place that's well-designed. Don't assume, for example, that a renter will be content with a tiny kitchen. And if the house is likely to be shared among roommates, each bedroom should be reasonably private and have bathroom access that doesn't involve invading someone else's room.
- **Charm and aesthetics.** Like homebuyers, renters will be drawn to a place that looks nice. But you can't know every prospective tenant's taste. That's why a house with broad appeal rather than quirky features is your best bet.

Of course, tenants will also be concerned with certain nonphysical parts of the property, like how much rent you charge and whether you allow dogs. However, such policies are largely within your control, and don't affect whether you'll buy or keep the house in the first place, so we'll discuss them in Chapter 3.

When Cheap Houses Make Good Rentals

Most real estate investors would jump at the chance to buy a condo with water views along Florida's Gulf Coast, or a leafy estate in Greenwich, Connecticut.

Not Jonas Lee, managing partner of Redbrick Partners, a firm that runs the only U.S. investment fund dedicated to single-family housing. The 1993 Harvard Business School grad prefers to invest in humble row houses located in working-class neighborhoods in gritty Northeast cities such as Philadelphia, Baltimore, and Trenton, New Jersey.

"It's all about the numbers," Lee said on a recent rainy day while inspecting the electric and heating systems in the wet basement of one of the 99 row houses he's contracted to buy for $5.4 million in the Kensington section of Philadelphia. "You have to keep your emotions out of it. It's not like I drive up to a home and say, 'I love the bricks; they are so red.'"

When Cheap Houses Make Good Rentals, cont'd

Real estate investing isn't as easy as it sounds on those late-night infomercials. Redbrick says residential landlords overestimate how much they will make off rental properties. The "Redbrick Rule" assumes 50% of rental income will get eaten up by expenses, such as vacancies, taxes, fixing leaky faucets, and replacing roofs and furnaces.

So why does Redbrick prefer buying homes in aging industrial towns rather than more desirable locations? The answer: Rental yields, which is how much you actually pocket from rent each year as a percentage of your purchase price. Redbrick uses a simple equation to calculate yield: It takes 50% of annual rental income and divides that by the property's purchase price.

For example, a $1 million home that rents for $6,000 a month, or $72,000 a year, nets a rental yield of 3.6%. In contrast, a $75,000 home that rents for $1,100 a month, or $13,200 annually, delivers a heftier yield of 8.8%.

Most homes yield about 4% but can go as low as 2% and as high as 9%, depending on the market. Redbrick prefers yields at the high end of the range. The most expensive properties do not always translate into the best rental investments. If you strip out potential price appreciation, rents that fail to cover costs result in negative cash flow.

 "Renting out a home 'all about numbers'; Cheaper house might provide better return," by Adam Shell, July 15, 2005.

What makes a good rental from the landlord's point of view?

After thinking about whether your property has sufficient tenant appeal, turn your attention to whether the house you're considering is appropriate for you, given your available time, skills, and interest. In most cases, this is a house that:

- **Requires little fixup and maintenance.** For example, a house that's relatively new isn't likely to need new plumbing or wiring anytime soon. But this doesn't mean a newly built house is necessarily the best. A place that's well constructed but isn't on the verge of becoming "historic" is your best bet.

- **Is close to your own home or work.** Who wants to drive for an hour—or get onto an airplane—every time to interview new tenants or see to a maintenance problem? And even if you hire a property management company, it's good to be able to check on the property yourself from time to time.

CAUTION

Dealing with maintenance gets a lot harder at a distance. As Kyung, who formerly rented out her triplex home in New Haven, Connecticut, explains, "For the ten years we lived in the unit above the rental, we had practically no maintenance problems. But wouldn't you know it, as soon as we moved to Pennsylvania, things started to fail. The tenants were calling in the middle of the night, and I'd have to call some 24-hour service and pay a premium to get the repairs made."

- **Isn't in a heavily regulated city or area.** If your property is in an area with rent control or other restrictions on landlords, take a careful look before you leap. Read the regulations and talk to other local landlords about their experiences. If you'll be buying a property with existing, long-term tenants who show signs of planning to stay there forever, you'll have to make do with below-market rent well into the future. In situations like this, your investment may be a losing proposition.

- **Will attract long-term renters.** For example, a house near a vacation resort or a college might not be optimal if you're hoping for year-round tenants. (Students tend to leave at the summer break and often switch housing every year, which means regular turnover and repairs.) If there's high turnover, you'll at least want correspondingly low vacancy rates and high rents.

- **Is convenient to commercial supply sources and repair people.** In other words, avoid houses in remote locations where you'll have to struggle to get to a hardware store or find high-quality help for maintaining or improving the property.

- **Is in a strong rental market.** Ideally, you're looking for a property that's cheaper to buy than to rent, so you can bring in income. But you're also looking for a market with lots of would-be renters: Otherwise, you'll find profits eaten up by vacancy periods.

> *Among investment properties bought in 2007, 61% were detached single-family homes, 20% were condos, 11% were townhouses or row houses, and 8% were other types.*

Special concerns when renting out a condo or co-op

Whether you already own a condominium or other home in a common-interest development (CID) or are thinking of buying one, you need to be aware of how the property's unique features impact its suitability as a rental property.

Condos and townhomes are the most common types of homes in CIDs. Renting them offers special advantages, including:

- **Less maintenance responsibility.** The homeowners' association will take care of common areas, freeing you from hands-on responsibilities like tending the garden or (in most cases) repairing the roof. (Of course, you pay to get these things done via your association dues.)

- **Affordability.** A condo or townhouse is usually cheaper than a single family home, because you own less—you own your particular unit, and own common areas jointly. And the maintenance can be less expensive too, since costs that might otherwise be individually paid—like landscaping and insurance—are instead shared.

- **Amenities to attract tenants.** Without having to buy a whole apartment building, you may be able to offer your tenants access to a pool or other recreational or meeting spaces.

But let's not forget the disadvantages:

- **Community rules and regulations.** In a CID, residents typically must agree to live by a set of rules. These may govern everything from the size of residents' dogs to whether they can hang clothes on the line, add a spare room, smoke in the unit, change the color of the curtains, or change the color of the outside paint. Getting your tenants to read and abide by these rules, when they don't have a long-term stake in the community, can be challenging.

- **Restrictions on renting.** Possibly the most significant rule in a CID is a restriction on renting. Some CIDs place numerical limits on how many units can be rented, or ban renting altogether. Although the association is unlikely to weigh in on your choice of tenants (which would expose it to liability for discrimination and the like), it may insist that you put certain clauses in your lease (for example, committing the tenant to abide by community rules), or exert other oversight.

- **Community fees and costs.** Every CID charges a monthly fee for maintenance and shared costs, and the rules typically also allow special assessments for major expenses like a new roof on the property or dealing with a flood or other emergency. These can run into the hundreds, even thousands of dollars per month, which you'll need to figure into your budget. (The landlord is normally responsible for making these payments, not the tenant.)

- **Slow property appreciation.** Historically, condos and townhomes have appreciated in value at a slower rate than single-family homes.

We've given a broad description of CIDs, which can vary immensely in physical features and character. Your job, before deciding to buy or rent out one of these properties, will be to fully research its costs, rules (often in a document called Covenants, Conditions, and Restrictions, or "CC&Rs"), and current community concerns. Read the CC&Rs and recent meeting minutes thoroughly, talk to neighbors, and investigate the reputation and financial strength of the property's builder or owner.

Thinking About Buying an Investment Property?

Not all landlords are accidental landlords. You may be thinking about buying a property so that you can rent it out. (If not, and you already own a property, skip down to the next section, "What Will Your Monthly Profit Be?") In fact, a survey by the National Association of Realtors® showed that 1.35 million second homes, or 22% of all new home sales in 2007, were for investment purposes.

Before you make that decision, you'll want to do a careful analysis of the costs and potential returns of your investment. Keep in mind that real estate is not a get-rich-quick business. You'll have to invest some significant cash upfront. And while your rental income may be a source of ongoing profit (we'll help you calculate how much below), a large portion of the financial gain will come about as time passes and the value of the property increases. And you won't actually realize that benefit until you sell (though you could use your increased equity as collateral for a loan).

While some people have gotten rich in real estate, you've probably seen the headlines about the many who've been disappointed— the would-be house "flippers" who, during the recent real estate downturn, found they couldn't buy and sell property for quick profits as they'd planned, and ended up in foreclosure or bankruptcy. For many of them, turning their house into a rental property wasn't an option—their carrying costs were too high compared to the rents they could charge, and they faced a long road of losses ahead.

Where are people buying investment properties?

In 2007, 23% of properties purchased were in the Northeast, 19% in the Midwest, 38% in the South, and 21% in the West. And 39% of these investment homes were purchased in a suburb, 20% in an urban or central city area, 21% in a small town, 15% in a rural area, and 5% in a resort area. (Source: National Association of Realtors®.)

We're going to assume you don't have aspirations toward house flipping, but are looking to invest in rental property over the long term, and ride out the inevitable ups and downs of the market. Or perhaps your ultimate goal isn't to sell, but to live in the home yourself, after you've retired. Let's evaluate your budget and how buying a rental property will fit in, both as a short- and long-term investment.

> **RESOURCE**
> **This book doesn't attempt to present a complete guide to choosing a house to buy or financing investment property.** Some good resources for that include:
> - *Real Estate Investing for Dummies*, by Eric Tyson and Robert S. Griswold (Wiley Publishing, Inc.)
> - *Buying a Second Home: Income, Getaway or Retirement*, by Craig Venezia (Nolo)
> - *Nolo's Essential Guide to Buying Your First Home*, by Ilona Bray, Alayna Schroeder, and Marcia Stewart.

How much cash you can put down

To determine whether buying an investment property is even a financial possibility for you, let's start with a simple calculation: How much cash can you free up for a down payment, and how much house will that buy? Most lenders require at least 10% to 20% down, especially on an investment property. (The days of zero down payments are gone, victims of the bursting real estate bubble and subsequent foreclosure crisis.) A quick visit to the real estate section of your local paper, or to an online

USA TODAY Snapshots®

Investors say real estate is best investment

■ African-American ■ White

	African-American	White
Real estate	61%	51%
Mutual funds	21%	30%
Stocks	7%	8%
Bonds	3%	3%
Whole life insurance	5%	3%
Not sure	3%	5%

Source: Ariel Mutual Funds/Charles Schwab 2004 Black Investor Survey of 1,000 respondents. Margin of error ±4 percentage points.

By Darryl Haralson and Marcy E. Mullins, USA TODAY 2004

site like www.realtor.org, will show you typical prices in the location where you're interested in buying.

USA TODAY Snapshots®

Neighborhood street vs. Wall Street
Which do you think is the better investment?

Real estate market

Street 69%

Stock market

24%

Don't know

7%

Source: TIAA–CREF survey of 1,001 investors ages 30 and older who help make household financial decisions. Margin of error: ±3 percentage points.

By Jae Yang and Julie Snider, USA TODAY
2006

You'll also need to budget around 2%–3% of the house's price for closing costs, depending on what state you live in, what kind of mortgage you get, and what you can expect to pay in escrow fees, title fees, real estate agent commissions, and taxes and insurance at closing. So if you can put down $80,000 plus pay $12,000 in closing costs, you're well on your way to buying a $400,000 property. If your cash on hand will likely buy a worthwhile rental in your area, keep reading.

> **CAUTION**
> **Looking at a fixer upper?** In that case, you'll need even more cash on hand. Major home improvements always seem to take more time and money than originally expected, so think twice about this strategy if you're not experienced with home repairs or construction.

How high a loan you'll qualify for

You'll probably be taking out a loan with which to buy your property (unless you're among the approximately 35% of real estate investors who pay all cash). That means you'll need to show a lender that you can afford the monthly payments. One of the tests that lenders use is your credit history and score, or your record of paying debts on time. We're not going to discuss credit scores in detail here—for more information, see the free articles in the Nolopedia at www.nolo.com.

The other test that lenders use is the comparison between your income and your debt load, called your "debt-to-income" ratio. The more debt obligations you already have hanging over you, the less likely the lender is to let you take on more. In fact, the lender may be stricter than when you bought your first home, because lending practices have tightened and mortgages on investment properties are considered riskier.

> **CAUTION**
> **Evaluate your monthly expenses even more strictly than your lender.** What we're discussing here is how much mortgage you'll qualify for. But if you tend to spend everything you earn each month—and perhaps aren't even sure where the money is going—you need to get your first house in order before taking on a second one. For help with household budgeting, see *The Busy Family's Guide to Money*, by Sandra Block, Kathy Chu, and John Waggoner (Nolo).

The concept of "debt-to-income ratio" isn't as complicated as it sounds. The lender looks first at your household's gross monthly income (the amount you earn before taxes and other monthly withdrawals, plus income from all other sources, like rents, royalties, alimony, or investments). Then it makes sure that your combined minimum debt payments on the property—for your PITI (principal, interest, taxes, and insurance), plus any community association fees, credit card payments, car debt, student loans, and more—don't eat up more than a certain percentage of that gross income. See the sample Debt-to-Income Ratio Worksheet below.

Debt-to-Income Ratio Worksheet		
Gross monthly income:	$4,000	
Gross monthly income x .28	$1,120	Maximum monthly PITI payment
Gross monthly income x .36	$1,440	Maximum monthly debt overall

How high can your debt-to-income ratio go? Traditionally, lenders have said that your PITI payment shouldn't exceed 28% of your gross monthly income, and your overall debt shouldn't exceed 36%. Although that formula was largely tossed out during the real estate boom of the early 2000s, it's back in full force. With that ratio in hand, the lenders set your maximum monthly mortgage payment. Using the calculators listed below, you can arrive at roughly the same figure—and then decide whether that amount is enough to buy a rental property in your chosen area.

RESOURCE

Ready to run some real numbers? Find online affordability calculators at www.nolo.com/calculator, www.hsh.com, and www. interest.com. Make sure any calculator you use factors in the amount of your down payment, your income and your debts, and your estimated taxes and insurance.

Keep in mind that interest rates are higher on investment properties, so don't run your calculations on the assumption that you'll qualify for the rock-bottom rate offered to buyers with stellar credit who are buying primary residences. You won't be offered these rates, because lenders know they're in a riskier position when their borrower is paying two mortgages: If you hit hard financial times, you'll pay the mortgage on your primary residence first.

Some investors with lots of equity in their primary residences get around these higher rates by doing a cash-out refinance (drawing out cash from their main home to pay for a second) or taking out a home equity loan. This strategy is beyond the scope of this book; in general, while you can use it to get a lower interest rate, the lender will subject you to the same financial evaluation discussed above.

USA TODAY Snapshots®

Using the Net to buy a home
How did you use the Internet for your first home purchase?

Search listings — 41%
Research values — 18%
Research location — 8%
Research schools and city/county — 6%

Source: RealEstate.com survey of 2,000 first-time home buyers. Margin of error: ±3 percentage points.

By Jae Yang and Karl Gelles, USA TODAY 2005

Fortunately, lenders will allow you to include your expected income from the property in your calculations. This is helpful because it will increase your overall income and help you qualify for a bigger loan. However, lenders will probably be conservative in estimating your likely income, for example by figuring a higher-than-expected vacancy rate.

You'll need to know how much loan you qualify for so you can estimate what kind of property you can buy, how much it will cost you each month, and how much you can expect it to bring in. Later in this chapter, we'll cover whether it's profitable to buy based on these factors.

What Will Your Monthly Profit Be?

Earning steady profits from the rent stream should be at the top of your goals list. So don't just guesstimate or hope for the best. Do the research and run through the analysis below to determine whether you'll make money each month.

Calculate rental income

Wouldn't it be nice if you could just add up your expenses for the property, tack on a little extra for profit, and call the result your monthly rental amount? Unfortunately, it doesn't work that way (except by coincidence). The local rental market largely sets the prices, based on how many properties are available and what amount tenants are willing and able to pay. That's why many landlords must settle for rental amounts that don't actually cover their costs, hoping that long-term appreciation in property value will make their investment worthwhile.

As a first-time landlord, your safest bet is to rent out your property only if the rent you can charge will cover your expenses (unless you have no other realistic choice). To figure out whether that's feasible, look at local ads for comparable properties of the same size and condition, in the same neighborhood and school district.

If the house is already being rented, the existing landlord will of course tell you what the monthly rent has been—and will continue to be, if the tenant has a lease that lasts beyond the property transfer. (You can't raise the rent until you renew the lease.) But if the tenant will be leaving, your outside research will come in handy, because the landlord may have kept the rent below market rates, perhaps in order to keep a good tenant. And even a tenant who wants to stay may have only a month-to-month rental agreement, which you are free to either terminate or renegotiate (unless your state or local laws add restrictions).

For more on rentability, see "What gives a property 'tenant appeal'?" above. And see Chapter 3 for ideas on how to spiff up your house for added appeal. When setting your rental policies (which we'll detail in Chapters 3 and 5), consider whether you might be willing to, say, allow pets or charge a lower security deposit in trade for a higher rent. Depending on who your likely tenants are, a furnished property might also allow you to raise the rent—for example, if you'll be renting out a downtown condo to busy young professionals. This will be particularly handy if you inherited a fully furnished property.

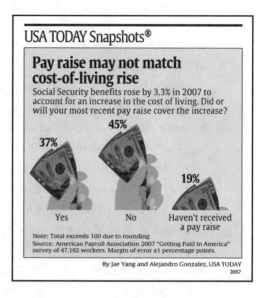

USA TODAY Snapshots®

Pay raise may not match cost-of-living rise

Social Security benefits rose by 3.3% in 2007 to account for an increase in the cost of living. Did or will your most recent pay raise cover the increase?

- 45%
- 37%
- 19%

Yes — No — Haven't received a pay raise

Note: Total exceeds 100 due to rounding
Source: American Payroll Association 2007 "Getting Paid in America" survey of 47,192 workers. Margin of error ±1 percentage points.

By Jae Yang and Alejandro Gonzalez, USA TODAY 2007

Also visit other rentals (say, during open houses) to see how yours stacks up. There's no need to be undercover about it—identify yourself as a new landlord researching the market, and you may find a fellow landlord who's eager to share tips and stories.

TIP

Consider setting your rent slightly below market rates. In the experience of Gordon, a landlord with a single-family property in San Jose, California, "It's important to not charge as much as you can get away with. If you charge top dollar, you're more likely to have a tenant not take care of it. But if you give them a fair rent and they feel you're treating them fairly, they'll return the favor by taking care of the place."

When Will You Be Able to Raise the Rent?

After you're in full swing as landlord, keep an eye on changes in your local rental rates, by watching the ads and talking to local real estate management experts. If rents go up, then you may be able to renegotiate a raise at the next lease renewal, or, if you have a month-to-month rental agreement, within the next month or two (depending on your state's requirements for giving the tenant advance notice). Local rent control laws, if any, will also affect when and by how much you can raise the rent.

The next question is whether you'll want to raise your rent. Dennis (the long-time landlord mentioned earlier), says, "I usually don't raise the rent on anyone in the property. I raise it when I rent to someone new. Maybe I can save 50 bucks a month by raising the rent, but I can save thousands by not having it vacant. I have one set of tenants whose rent I haven't raised in 12 years. They're the nicest, neatest people. They put in their own blinds, they garden and mow."

After figuring out a likely market rent, your next task is to check into the local vacancy rate, usually expressed as a percentage. A real estate or property management company should be able to tell you how many rental houses like yours are sitting empty. You can also get a sense of likely demand for your house by considering factors such as whether your area is growing economically (so that new employees need housing), whether there's a steady stream of likely renters (such as students), and whether home prices are out of reach for the average local resident, who will turn to renting instead. Nationwide, a vacancy rate of up to 10% of the year is not uncommon, according to U.S. Census Bureau figures. Of course, this is just a ballpark, and you can lower this rate by using some of the methods in this book to find and keep long-term tenants.

Putting it all together, you should be able to come up with a monthly and annual dollar figure that your rental is likely to command—the monthly rent figure times twelve, minus expected vacancies. Assume that your vacancy rate will be the same as the average where you live, even if you expect to have a long-term renter.

Subtract expenses

If you're already a homeowner—most people are before becoming a landlord—you know that keeping up a home isn't cheap. Your regular annual expenses will include the mortgage (both principal and interest, assuming it hasn't already been paid off), homeowners' insurance, property and other taxes, and property management services if you decide to use them. You'll also face less predictable or lower expenses, such as maintenance and improvements, accounting fees now that you're in business, and more.

Now's the time to draw up a budget, estimating what it will cost to keep your property. The worksheet below will help with this task. We've broken it down so that you enter monthly figures—of course, you'll need to fiddle with some of the numbers, for example dividing your annual property tax payment by 12.

CAUTION
Double the amount you think you'll spend on maintenance.
If you base your likely maintenance figures on what you usually spend on your own home, you'll probably come out low. Tenants tend to be harder on houses than owners, and blind to minor maintenance issues until they become major.

If the property is already being rented, the last owner is a valuable source of financial information. Ask for:

- a copy of the lease or rental agreement
- details on security deposits (location, amount, and whether the old owner will be returning them to tenants, in which case you'll need to recollect them)

- service contracts (such as for gardening—these can be canceled, but you might not want to if the seller is getting a good bargain)
- utility bills and maintenance and repair records for at least the last year (preferably longer), and
- all other paperwork relevant to the property.

And if the current tenant plans to stay, figure out which expenses you can cut out of your budget accordingly. Advertising and screening are the obvious ones, but you may be able to reduce the number of repairs and improvements you otherwise would have done before a new tenant moved in.

TIP

If you want existing tenants to stay, encourage them. During a transfer, tenants may worry that the new landlord will be difficult to work with and will raise the rent or change other lease or rental agreement terms as soon as legally possible. Some will start looking for a new place, just in case. As soon as you can, meet with the tenants to explain your policies and establish some personal rapport.

Our expense worksheet also includes some categories that you may not be able to estimate yet, such as gifts (for example, flowers to your tax accountant for dealing with your shoebox of receipts). Leave these blank if you can't imagine paying them—but use them as a reminder of possible unexpected expenses.

Monthly Property Expense Estimate	
Expense Description	**Amount**
Advertising and tenant screening	$
Local transportation	$
Out-of-city travel, meals, lodging	$
Cleaning and maintenance	$
Homeowners' insurance (if not included in mortgage payment)	$
Legal and other professional fees (accountant, property manager)	$
Mortgage payment (principal and interest, plus property taxes and insurance, if included)	$
Other loan payments	$
Repairs	$
Appliances and furnishings (irregular, but major expenses such as a refrigerator)	$
Supplies (for office and rental property)	$
Income tax	$
Property tax (if not included in mortgage payment)	$
Utilities and phone (if not covered by tenant)	$
Gifts and entertainment	$
Licenses	$
Homeowners' association dues (in condos and some developments)	$
Landlords' association dues, if you choose to join one	$
Educational publications, subscriptions, and memberships	$
Tools and equipment	$
Construction and improvements	$
Other, miscellaneous expenses	$
Total estimated expenses	$

CAUTION
Costs can mount if you're unable to make regular visits to the property. Amy explains, "My property tax bill recently went up significantly, and I decided it wasn't worth the time and expense to fly from California to Texas to appeal it. But if more surprise costs like this come along, I'll probably have to either raise the rent or sell."

Estimate short-term profits

Continuing with the simple calculations, let's say you can afford to buy—or you already own—a house that's suitable for renting. Now you need to estimate whether the rent will cover your costs. Do that by filling in the chart below:

Estimated Monthly House Profit or Loss	
Expected rental income (based on "Calculate rental income," above)	$
– Estimated costs (based on "Monthly Property Expense Estimate" worksheet, above)	$
= Profit or loss (expected income minus estimated costs)	$

This chart will tell you whether you stand to make money on such a property in the short term. If the income comes out ahead of the costs, great. But remember that if you're buying, you'll probably have put in a large down payment, and may eventually want to sell the place. That's why it's worth figuring out the ultimate return on your investment, which we'll discuss next.

If the property's expected income isn't enough to cover its costs and more, we recommend walking away (if you can—see our discussion for people trying to avoid foreclosure, below). Sure, the place might make a good long-term investment if and when property values rise, but that's a different ballgame—we're assuming you picked up this book because you wanted to earn regular money as a landlord, not aim for one-time profits.

CAUTION

This calculation doesn't include tax benefits. These benefits—depreciation and other tax deductions—can reduce your tax liability by thousands of dollars. If your calculations look borderline, skip ahead to Chapter 6, where you'll learn more about what these tax benefits are and how they help you increase your profits.

Another thing worth considering is the value of your own time. We can't calculate that for you, but we will discuss some of the tasks that go into being a landlord in this book.

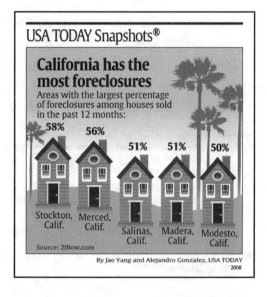

USA TODAY Snapshots®

California has the most foreclosures

Areas with the largest percentage of foreclosures among houses sold in the past 12 months:

58% — Stockton, Calif.
56% — Merced, Calif.
51% — Salinas, Calif.
51% — Madera, Calif.
50% — Modesto, Calif.

Source: Zillow.com

By Jae Yang and Alejandro Gonzalez, USA TODAY 2008

Added financial concerns when trying to avoid foreclosure

It may be that you aren't trying to make a profit, but are just trying to avoid losing a home that has become unaffordable—perhaps one you don't think you can sell for what you owe on it. In that case, you might avoid foreclosure by renting the place to someone else. Most likely, you'll rent another place of your own until the situation changes.

In that case, you should continue your calculations as follows:

Profit or loss from rental (from above)	$
– Cost of renting another house	$
= Total cash you'll need to spend on housing (after paying other bills)	$

EXAMPLE: Samuel's monthly mortgage is $1,000, but after paying his other bills, he has only $800 with which to make the payment. By renting out his house for $1,200, he covers the mortgage and other expenses so that he breaks even, neither profiting nor losing money on the rental itself. If he can find a smaller place to rent for $800 a month, he may be able to pay the bills and keep his house.

Added financial concerns when buying for a college student

Buying a house for a college-bound child has become an increasingly popular option, with dorm costs often prohibitively high. The average annual room and board for public, four-year schools rose to $7,404 in 2007–2008 (up 5.3% over the previous school year), while private school room and board averaged $8,595, (up 5%). (Source: the College Board.) But before you assume buying a place for your college kid will be cheaper, make sure you'll truly come out ahead.

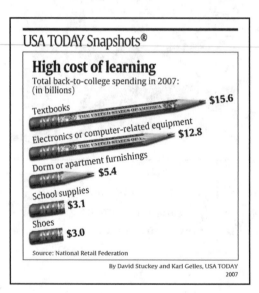

USA TODAY Snapshots®

High cost of learning

Total back-to-college spending in 2007: (in billions)

Textbooks — $15.6

Electronics or computer-related equipment — $12.8

Dorm or apartment furnishings — $5.4

School supplies — $3.1

Shoes — $3.0

Source: National Retail Federation

By David Stuckey and Karl Gelles, USA TODAY
2007

Step one is to find out what the actual room and board at your child's college will likely be. Then research both the rental and the real estate market in the area. If you're lucky, your child will be attending school in an area where average rentals are high enough to offset average mortgages and other costs (the reverse may be true, although the demand for housing in college towns has a tendency to drive up rents). By renting out some rooms to other students, you may come out ahead even before your child graduates. When this book went to print, for example, parents of children going to school in Lawrence, Kansas were looking at a potentially good market to buy into, with average single-family home rentals at $1,162 and average monthly house payments at $859.

Of course, citywide averages may not be enough. You'll need to look at property values right around the college, which will naturally be affected by student demand for housing. With a couple of sample home prospects in mind, run the profit-or-loss calculation described under "Estimate short-term profits," above, then compare it to how much you'd be spending on room and board. If it comes out about the same, then you should buy the property only if you like the idea of a long-term investment, or think it will bring in a high return when you sell (as discussed next).

What Will Your Long-Term Gain Be?

Whether you're an accidental landlord or are actively looking to buy a house to rent out, your research so far will help you analyze your house's worth as a long-term investment—taking into account upfront costs, ongoing costs versus income, property appreciation, and profits from the sale. Now you can:

- estimate the house's likely appreciation, or increase in value over time, and
- calculate the likely return on your investment (ROI), or the expected value of your investment in your property.

Appreciation: Will your rental property rise in value?

We've already discussed the general tendency for homes to rise in value over time. But to get a true picture of your home's prospects, you'll need to look at local home prices. Ask your real estate agent to calculate the change in median prices for the past ten or more years, or call or visit the town clerk or assessor. The more local your research, the better— one neighborhood's house values may rise or remain steady while another one's drop.

If the price trend looks to be heading upward, you're probably on safe ground buying. If it's heading downward, you'll have to make a tougher decision—will you be getting a bargain just before prices tick upward again, or will you be entering a depressed housing market in which you'll have little choice but to hang onto the property for years trying to make the most of your rental income? Talk to your real estate agent and read the local media before making your decision.

Also remember that falling real estate markets sometimes increase demand for rental units, since people are skittish about buying, or have left a house due to foreclosure. And if you can charge enough rent to offset the purchase price from the beginning, it's a solid investment by any measure.

To figure out the actual amount by which your house is likely to go up in value year by year, take the appreciation rate that you researched above and use it to create an analysis like the one in the chart below. (It looks complicated at first, but is actually quite obvious when you follow it line by line.) The example shows the projected appreciation of a $400,000 house over a five-year period in an area with 5% appreciation.

Sample Projected Appreciation on $400,000 House								
Year	Current house value		Local appreciation rate		Appre-ciation amount		Current house value		Appreciated house value
1	$400,000	x	5% (or 0.05)	=	$20,000	+	$400,000	=	$420,000
2	$420,000	x	5% (or 0.05)	=	$21,000	+	$420,000	=	$441,000
3	$441,000	x	5% (or 0.05)	=	$22,050	+	$441,000	=	$463,050
4	$463,050	x	5% (or 0.05)	=	$23,153	+	$463,050	=	$486,203
5	$486,202	x	5% (or 0.05)	=	$24,310	+	$486,203	=	$510,513

Return on investment: How much will you get back?

Let's look years down the road, to estimate whether your total investment in the property will be worth it after paying all the associated expenses. The term to describe this is "return on investment," or "ROI." It's usually expressed as a percentage. You can calculate ROI on other investments as well (such as stocks and bonds), and see how they're all doing relative to one another.

The basic idea is to take your estimated annual profits (including rents plus home appreciation—which are only paper profits until you sell, but that's okay), and divide it by your total investment in the property (down payment, annual costs, total mortgage principal paid that year, and anything you spent for major home improvements). That means filling in the following calculation (simplified to leave out tax deductions and depreciation):

> Annual profit after expenses ($____)
> + annual appreciation ($____)
> = total annual gain or loss $____
> ÷ annual investment
> = ____% ROI.

EXAMPLE: Kira bought a house for $400,000 (putting $80,000 down), and began renting it out immediately. In her first year she earned $2,000 in income (after expenses including mortgage interest, plus maintenance, utilities, and the rest), plus another $5,000 in home appreciation (paper profits until she sells). Dividing that by her investment amount (her $80,000 down payment plus $5,000 in mortgage principal payments over the year), her ROI would be approximately .082 or 8%.

So, what does the ROI percentage mean? It means that, continuing with our example, if Kira sold her home after the first year, she'd have earned an 8% return on her initial investment. She's probably doing pretty well compared to the returns on her stocks and other investments. Of course, we're using artificial numbers, and your returns may be far less.

At this point, we suggest you do the ROI calculation using projected numbers, for the first year as well as later years that you plan to own the property. If it's positive, that's another green light—but again, don't be too swayed by the prospect of home appreciation if your actual profits are negative. An ROI that's lower than you could get with other investments after several years may be a sign to look elsewhere.

USA TODAY Snapshots®

Small, single-family homes lose least

Value changes in the past 12 months:

Small single-family (less than 1,200 s.f.)

Midsize single-family (1,200 to 1,900 s.f.)

Large single-family (more than 1,900 s.f.)

Condo-minium

All homes

-1.0%

-3.1%

-2.8%

-2.8%

-5.2%

1 - From June 2006 to June 2007

Source: Zillow.com   By Jae Yang and Karl Gelles, USA TODAY
2007

Return to the ROI calculation once you have actual numbers, to see how reality compares with your projections. It might actually be a source of comfort if you're not earning a profit on your rents but home prices are appreciating. You may still come out ahead.

Setting Your Goals

It's decision time: Having explored some of the basics of owning rental property, you must decide whether it's truly right for you. To help you in this process, answer the following questions:

- **How committed are you to holding onto the property?** If you're hoping for, say, a year's trial run, it's safest if you already own the property. Buying a property that you might not keep for at least three to five years is a recipe for loss (especially because of the transaction costs: 5%–6% for the real estate agent's fees alone).

- **What are your short-term financial goals?** After running the calculations above, decide what amount of property income will make it worth your while to pursue this project. Balance this against your long-term goals, below.

- **What are your long-term financial goals?** At some point, you may want—or need—to sell the house. What amount of profits are you expecting or hoping to make? If your sales profits aren't likely to be high, then it's even more important that you're satisfied with the anticipated monthly rental income.

- **How much time are you willing to put into this project?** If being a landlord will take precious hours you can't spare, then it may not be worth prioritizing right now.

Take a careful inventory of your objectives as a landlord and property owner, both in the short-term and the long-term. Discuss them with your family, especially if you expect them to help maintain the property, deal with your absences, or travel with you for that purpose. Then keep track of where you are vis-à-vis those goals from year to year. We'll help you track your profits and expenses in Chapter 6.

So Happy Together:
Landlording With Family or Friends

After evaluating all the pros and cons of being a landlord, you may feel like it's too much for any one person to handle. Good news! You don't have to do it alone. Today, many people share the responsibilities and benefits of co-ownership with family members, friends, or professional associates.

In this chapter, we'll talk about investing together and divvying up the responsibilities of being a landlord, including:

- the pros and cons of landlording together
- how to decide whether co-landlording is right for you
- ways to take title together, and
- what to cover in a co-ownership agreement.

Whether you're undertaking these responsibilities with your spouse, your sister, a long-time professional associate, or a distant cousin with whom you've inherited a property, this information will help you decide how to manage the property and finances.

The Pros and Cons of Landlording Together

Sharing the experience of being a landlord with someone else is like any situation with multiple cooks in the kitchen—some things are easier to do with the help of another person, and some things just seem to get more complicated. Here are some of the advantages you can expect:

- **Fewer responsibilities.** As we'll discuss in the next section, you and your co-owner may choose to divvy up landlording responsibilities according to your skills. Working on projects you're good at should mean that you can accomplish them efficiently and quickly. You may be able to avoid—or at least share—some of the tasks you don't like, if your co-owner is willing to do them.

- **Lower expenses.** You and your co-owner can share expenses, most likely in proportion to your ownership interest. For example, if you own 50%, you would only pay 50% of the replacement cost if the water heater broke.

- **Greater buying power.** You may be able to increase your buying power by co-owning with someone else. For example, by pooling resources you might purchase a more expensive and lucrative property, such as a multi-unit building instead of a single-family house.

- **Lower risk of vacancy.** If a tenant doesn't pay the rent or the unit sits vacant for a month or two, the loss won't fall entirely on you—you'll share it with your co-owner.

But before you start scouting around for a co-owner, consider these drawbacks:

- **Less income.** As nice as it may be to share the responsibilities of landlording, you also have to share the proceeds. If you each own 50% and split profits that way, you'll get half as much as you would otherwise. You'll also make less when you sell.

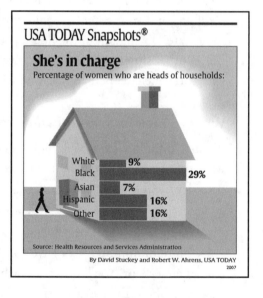

USA TODAY Snapshots®

She's in charge
Percentage of women who are heads of households:

White 9%
Black 29%
Asian 7%
Hispanic 16%
Other 16%

Source: Health Resources and Services Administration

By David Stuckey and Robert W. Ahrens, USA TODAY
2007

- **Less independence.** When you're the only landlord, you can decide who moves in, how much rent they pay, who will do repairs, and more. You'll probably lose some of this autonomy, and you and your co-owner may even disagree about some issues.

- **Less stability.** When you own with someone else, you must rely on that other person to do a designated share of the work—and pay a share of the bills. If your co-owner doesn't pay the appropriate share of the mortgage, for example, you may have to pay the whole thing or risk being foreclosed on.

- **Difficulty selling.** Depending how you and your co-owner take title (discussed further below), you may each be free to sell your interest in the property at any time. But because there isn't a huge market in partial ownership shares, it may be difficult to sell only your share.

Having a Compatible Co-Owner

Whether sharing the risks and responsibilities of landlording is right for you depends on more than the objective pros and cons. The biggest predictor of success is your ability to actually work with a co-owner to accomplish your goals. You'll want to co-own with someone who sees things the same way you do.

Of course, your choice may have already been made for you, for example if you and your sister have jointly inherited a house, or you and your spouse are moving out of the house you already own but plan to rent. But in other situations, you may actively decide to co-buy and co-own with someone else, perhaps even someone you don't know very well.

What to look for in a co-owner

If you're thinking about looking for a co-owner—or just want to know what to expect if you're planning to work with your spouse—carefully consider the following factors:

- **Finances.** You and your co-owner should be willing to share the minute details of your finances with each other, including the amount of money you have coming in and where it's currently being spent. You'll probably each want to know as much as you can about the past, current, and anticipated debts, income, and expenses of your co-owner.

- **Location.** It will be much easier to share the experience of landlording if you're both near the property in question. If you're both far away, you may want to discuss hiring a property manager, covered in Chapter 10.

- **Goals.** It's best if you and any co-owner have the same goals in mind. Do you want to buy a house your college kids can share, then sell it when they're done with school? What if your son decides to stick around a few extra years? Or are you hoping to buy out the co-owner's share in a few years, so you can retire in the place? You'll need to make sure you are on the same page about both short- and long-term goals.

USA TODAY Snapshots®

Traveling together
When it comes to vacationing, Americans say yes to traveling with someone. Favorite companions:

55% Spouse
37% Children
13% Friends
7% Parents
8% Alone

Source: Travel Industry Association telephone survey of 1,300 adults, April 7-17. The margin of error is ±3 percentage points.

By Mary Cadden and Alejandro Gonzalez, USA TODAY 2005

- **Personality.** You'll want to choose a co-owner who you're sure you can get along with professionally. That may mean that you don't discuss the possibility with your best friend, who's a great pal but absentminded and has trouble balancing a checkbook.

Finding a co-owner

To find a co-owner, start by making your intentions known. If you have a particular co-owner in mind, you can approach that person with your proposition. It may be a vague idea about an eventual purchase or a specific plan to buy a property you've already identified. The more detail you provide, the more likely you are to look like—and find—a serious investor. If you don't have anyone in particular in mind, you can discuss your ideas more generally with people you know, getting the word out that you're looking.

If you're willing to work with someone you don't know, ask local real estate professionals whether they know others interested in similar investments. Buying with someone you don't know is beyond the scope of this book, but suffice it to say that all the factors above—finances, location, goals, and personality—become even more important when the person isn't someone you're already acquainted with.

Sharing duties with your co-owner

Early on, you and your co-owner should talk about the various duties that co-owning a rental property will require, and who will do them. You may decide on a formal arrangement where each of you takes on certain tasks, perhaps using the "Overview of Landlording Duties" list in Chapter 1. Or you may decide to be more flexible ("If you can handle maintenance problems on the weekdays, I'll take them on the weekends"). And married couples can take flexibility to the extreme, like Sarah, a San Francisco landlord, who explains, "I'll generally say to my husband something like, "The doorbell's not working, do you wanna call Tom or shall I?" In any case, it's a good idea to discuss the different possibilities so you can decide how to proceed before you make a purchase together.

Once you've decided who will do what, each of you should stick to your responsibilities and give each other the freedom to handle the assigned tasks as desired (unless it's going to have major negative effects, such as decreasing the property value or subjecting the tenant to uninhabitable conditions). For example, while Amy attended school in Berkeley, California, her partner Phil remained in Texas for awhile, and agreed to help manage her rental property in Austin. However, Amy explains, "After a hailstorm, Phil said he'd take care of communicating with the insurance company and the roof repairperson. But I got so anxious, I kept stepping in, which only caused confusion. Finally Phil had to remind me of our agreement."

There may also be some tasks you handle together. Gordon and Connie, for example, who co-own a house in San Jose, California, always make a point of interviewing potential tenants together. They find they each recognize different flaws and strengths in the applicants. Gordon, a lawyer, pays more attention to whether the applicants appear willing to abide by contractual obligations and can afford the rent. Connie tends to focus on whether people will pay on time, regardless of whether they can afford it, and whether they'll care for the property as if it were their own. Working together, they're able to select better tenants than if they worked singly, and they are less apt to lay blame if one of the tenants doesn't work out.

How to Take Title

When you own property with another person, you'll need to decide how you take title—that is, how you own the property together. This isn't a decision to procrastinate or flip a coin over, because it needs to be stated on your deed. Unless you're married, you have two main options for taking title in your own names: as tenants in common or as joint tenants. A third alternative is to form a business entity, such as an LLC, which will take title to the property in its name.

> CAUTION
>
> **How you hold title affects your rights to use, rent, and sell the property.** The information provided here will give you some basic information about your choices, but it's a good idea to talk to your attorney or tax adviser about your own situation before deciding which form of ownership is right for you.

Tenants in common

A tenancy in common (TIC) is probably the most popular way for unrelated co-owners to take title. As a tenant in common, you and your co-owner can own unequal shares of the property—for example, you could own 40% and your co-owner 60%. (You can also have more than one co-owner, with each of you owning different shares.) This is a big advantage if you have different amounts of cash to invest or are looking for different levels of return.

Owning a share doesn't mean you own a particular slice of the pie, however. Your portion is called an "undivided interest," which means all co-owners have the right to use and enjoy the entire property. Let's say, for example, that you and your friend decide to split your ownership 60/40, and you'd like to apply your 40% share toward ownership of the smaller downstairs unit, while your co-owner owns the more spacious upstairs unit. That's not going to work in terms of legal ownership rights. If you ever want to separate your ownership share and your co-owner disagrees, you'll have to request that a court "partition" the property—that is, legally split it into separate parcels, owned individually. Because physically dividing property isn't feasible in most cases, the usual result is that the property is sold and the proceeds split. It's a lengthy and expensive process, which you're better off avoiding.

Another potential problem with owning as tenants in common is that either you or your co-owner can transfer your interest at any time. That means that your friend might suddenly decide to sell that 60% interest in the property—and can legally do so without your consent, to any interested buyer.

And then there's the matter of what happens if one of you dies. In a tenancy in common, a deceased person's share passes under the terms of that person's will or, if there isn't one, the inheritance laws of the state. You could find yourself sharing with a new co-owner (your current co-owner's long-lost daughter in Africa, for example).

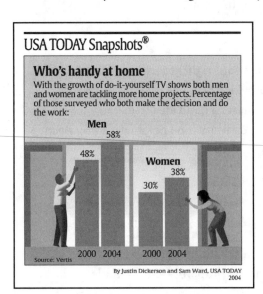

USA TODAY Snapshots®

Who's handy at home

With the growth of do-it-yourself TV shows both men and women are tackling more home projects. Percentage of those surveyed who both make the decision and do the work:

Men: 2000 48%, 2004 58%
Women: 2000 30%, 2004 38%

Source: Vertis

By Justin Dickerson and Sam Ward, USA TODAY 2004

Perhaps even more troublesome, co-ownership gives owners the right to "encumber" the property, which means take out loans against it. If your co-owner takes out a large equity loan against the property and doesn't pay it back, he or she can put your ownership at risk. You could get stuck making payments to stay out of foreclosure, even if your co-owner has taken the cash and skipped town.

Fortunately, you can draft an agreement to deal with some of these possibilities before they ever happen, which we'll discuss later in this chapter.

Joint tenants with right of survivorship

Another way to take title is as joint tenants with right of survivorship (JTWROS). Like tenants in common, joint tenants own an undivided interest in the entire property, and can't, for instance, draw a line down the middle. However, unlike tenants in common, joint tenants in most states must own equal shares—that is, if there are two of you, you each own 50%.

The other main difference between joint tenants and tenants in common is that if a joint tenant dies, the property immediately passes to the other tenant, even if the person's will says otherwise. That means you should own property this way only if you want your co-owner to own the entire property if you die. This is a common way for married couples, domestic partners, and those in committed relationships to take title. It's probably not the best option if you're buying with an unrelated investor, however.

Other options for married couples

In addition to the ownership methods described above, married couples have a few more options when it comes to taking title. In several states (Alaska, Arizona, California, Idaho, Louisiana, Nevada, New Mexico, Texas, Washington, and Wisconsin), married couples (and in some states, registered domestic partners) can own community property. Couples

USA TODAY Snapshots®

Money and relationships

In a recent survey respondents said managing their finances is the biggest strain on their relationships. Complaints of respondents with financial issues:

Not being able to control partner's spending habits **44%**

Repeated questions about my spending habits **21%**

Partner not sticking to agreed-upon budget **17%**

Not agreeing on long-term savings goals **14%**

Partner is hiding money from me **5%**

Source: Quicken survey of 631 respondents. Margin of error ±4 percentage points.

By Darryl Haralson and Suzy Parker, USA TODAY 2005

who own property this way each own half the property, which they can pass to whomever they please through their wills. While living, they can't sell or give away their share unless the other spouse consents.

A few states (Alaska, Arizona, California, Nevada, and Wisconsin) offer the additional advantage of community property with the right of survivorship. Property held this way doesn't have to pass through probate when one spouse dies, but instead goes straight to the other spouse (or, if the state allows, the registered domestic partner).

Finally, about half the states allow married couples (and sometimes, those in registered domestic partnerships or other "official" relationships) to take title as tenants by the entirety. In this case, you and your spouse or partner each own the entire property and can sell it only with the other's consent. In most states, if one of you is in debt, creditors can't come against that person's share of the property. Like joint tenancy, if one spouse dies, the other gets the property without probate hassles.

Married Couples, Title, and Estate Planning: The Quick Lowdown

The most common types of property ownership:

Joint tenancy: Available in nearly every state, this form of ownership is used for everything from homes to bank accounts. Its biggest advantage is that when the first owner dies, jointly owned property doesn't go through probate, the sometimes costly procedure by which the court distributes your assets after you die, says Mary Randolph, author of 8 Ways to Avoid Probate (Nolo). You can enter into a joint tenancy with anyone.

But joint tenancy has some serious drawbacks. If your spouse or other co-owner slides into debt, creditors could file liens against that owner's share of the home.

Tenancy by the entirety: This type of title is similar to joint ownership, but offers better protection if one spouse is in debt or files for bankruptcy, Randolph says.

Married Couples, Title, and Estate Planning: The Quick Lowdown, cont'd

While laws vary among states, creditors usually can't come after the indebted spouse's portion of the property, as is the case with joint ownership. If your spouse has a lot of debts or is planning to launch a business, tenancy by the entirety "can be a powerful protection," Randolph says. Creditors "can't force the split of the property to get at one spouse's half."

Tenancy by the entirety may not protect you if your spouse is in trouble with the IRS. The Supreme Court ruled in 2002 that the IRS can place tax liens against a home for one spouse's unpaid taxes, even if the property is held in tenancy by the entirety.

Most states that offer tenancy by the entirety limit it to married couples. Like joint ownership, property automatically reverts to the survivor when one spouse dies, bypassing probate.

Community property: If you're married and live in a community property state, most property is automatically considered jointly owned. There are exceptions for inheritances and gifts.

Unfortunately, debt is also considered community property, and it's more difficult to protect your home from your spouse's creditors, says Emily Doskow, an attorney and legal editor for Nolo.

Community property states have different rules governing probate, so it's important to understand your own state's rules when planning your estate.

While reviewing your title is a good idea for all couples, it's particularly important for couples with large or complicated estates that could be subject to estate taxes.

 "Check home's title to make sure all owners are protected," by Sandra Block, September 16, 2003.

Holding property as a business entity

One final option for co-owners is to form a separate business entity and take title in its name. All co-owners would, in turn, own shares or a membership interest in the business.

Probably the most popular choice for those interested in forming a business entity is the limited liability company, or LLC. An LLC combines some of the best features of corporations and partnerships, offering these advantages:

- **Limited liability.** The LLC protects your personal assets (your house, car, and such) from business debts. That means a creditor claiming to be owed money by the business (the rental property) won't be able to come after you personally. Similarly, if a tenant is injured on the property, the tenant will be able to recover only from the LLC, not from you.

- **Tax benefits.** LLCs benefit from what's called "pass through" tax status. That means the business's tax liabilities are paid directly by the members. The entity itself does not separately pay taxes.

- **Less formality than other business entities.** Relatively speaking, LLCs have to comply with fewer paperwork and meeting formalities than other business entities, such as regular "C" corporations.

- **No right of partition.** A property held in an LLC cannot be partitioned—the LLC owns it fully. You can decide in your operating agreement how any individual's membership interest can be sold, but you are protected from a partition action.

However, LLCs also have disadvantages, such as:

- **Complex tax rules.** If you form an LLC with another person, you will be treated as a partnership for tax purposes. Tax rules governing partnerships are significantly more complicated than rules for individuals. You will need to hire a tax professional to help you deal with these complexities.

- **Cost.** Forming an LLC will take extra cash. You'll have to follow the process outlined in your state, and spend as much as several hundred dollars for filing fees alone. Costs will be even greater if you get the help or advice of a professional.

- **Formalities.** Although the formalities associated with forming and running an LLC are fewer than with a corporation, they're still more than with a simple co-ownership agreement between two people. For example, you must file some paperwork to form the LLC (usually called the articles of organization), and then will want to prepare an operating agreement (covering a lot of the same topics a co-ownership agreement normally would).

- **Difficulty obtaining financing.** You may find it difficult—and more expensive—to find a lender willing to loan money to your LLC. Even if you find a willing lender, you'll probably have to provide a personal guarantee (undercutting the limited liability that made an LLC attractive in the first place). Some people get around this by taking title in their own names, then transferring title to the LLC. But most mortgages have a "due on sale" clause, making the mortgage fully payable when the property is sold. You risk the mortgagor "calling" your loan as a result of the transfer, forcing you to repay it in full or refinance the property.

> **CAUTION**
>
> **If you operate as a business entity, you may not be able to do a 1031 exchange.** A 1031 exchange, discussed further in Chapter 11, is a tax strategy that allows you to defer capital gains taxes when you sell investment property and purchase other investment property with the proceeds. If you think you may want to do a 1031 exchange in the future, discuss the possibility with your tax adviser.

Because limited liability is one of the primary benefits of forming an LLC, you should consider forming one if you are particularly concerned about protecting your assets. Another way to protect yourself is to purchase an umbrella insurance policy. Unless you own several rental properties, adequate insurance will probably be the more cost-effective way to deal with the risk of being sued. For more information on obtaining insurance, see Chapter 8.

If you've inherited property with family members and keeping the property in the family is a primary goal, you might also consider an LLC. In that case, an LLC can protect the property, because your co-owners won't be able to sell or encumber it. If interested, talk to your attorney about how to best convert ownership into an LLC.

> **RESOURCE**
> **Need to form an LLC?** To form an LLC online right now, use Nolo's Online LLC formation service. You complete a comprehensive interview online, and Nolo will create a customized LLC operating agreement and file your articles of organization with the state filing office. Your LLC will come into existence the day the articles are filed. See www.nolo.com/llc.cfm.

Creating a Co-Ownership Agreement

As we've already explained, there are many logistics involved in working with another person to co-own and manage rental property. Many of these details can be worked out—and potential problems can be avoided—if you and your co-owner start out with an agreement that specifies what each of you will be responsible for.

If you form an LLC, much of this will probably be covered in your organization's operating agreement. And if you're taking title in a form available only to married couples, you and your spouse may not face the same legal risks of other forms of shared ownership. Here, we're assuming you're taking title as tenants in common or joint tenants with a co-owner you aren't married to. A good co-ownership agreement should address:

- **How you'll choose tenants.** As co-owners, each of you has a right to use the property. Technically, each of you could rent it out to whoever you'd like. But to avoid stepping on each other's toes, create a system for choosing tenants. You may set certain (non-discriminatory) criteria (such as income, job stability, or lease length minimums), or provide a system for reviewing applications (each person gets the right to veto one applicant who otherwise meets all minimum stated requirements).

- **Whether each of you will have the right to use the property personally.** Ownership as a tenant in common or joint tenant also entitles you to use of the property in question—if one of you occupies the place, the law won't assume that your possession is "adverse" to the rights of the other owner (in other words, your occupancy will be assumed legal). But neither of you want your co-owner, or your co-owner's best friend, moving in rent free. Make sure the agreement specifies what happens if one of you wants to use the property personally.

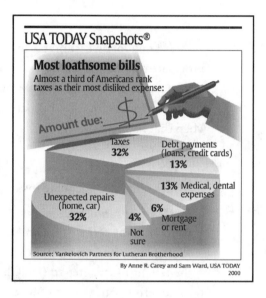

USA TODAY Snapshots®

Most loathsome bills
Almost a third of Americans rank taxes as their most disliked expense:

Taxes **32%**

Debt payments (loans, credit cards) **13%**

13% Medical, dental expenses

Unexpected repairs (home, car) **32%**

6%

4% Mortgage or rent

Not sure

Source: Yankelovich Partners for Lutheran Brotherhood

By Anne R. Carey and Sam Ward, USA TODAY 2000

- **The responsibilities each of you will handle.** As discussed above, you and your co-owner will want to lay out the exact duties each of you will be responsible for. The more detail you provide, the less there will be to disagree about later.

- **How you'll divide expenses and profits.** Make sure the agreement specifies that you'll split expenses and profits in relation to your ownership shares. (If you want another arrangement, discuss it with a tax adviser first—it could mean you're functioning as a partnership for tax purposes.)

- **Improvements.** Unlike regular maintenance expenses, you may not be legally entitled to reimbursement from your co-owner if you make any improvements to the property. Address how you will decide to make improvements and how you will pay for them.

- **Responsibility for the mortgage.** Usually but not always, co-owners purchase with a single mortgage. You must decide what to do if one of you does not pay the promised share. For example, you may agree that the non-paying party must make up payments with interest and is not allowed to participate in decisions about managing the property until current.

TIP

Look for an assumable loan. If you have a joint loan and anticipate that one of you might sell before the loan is paid off, consider getting an assumable loan. This will allow a subsequent purchaser to take the seller's place with the loan, meaning you won't have to refinance when that happens.

- **Making sure the property is adequately insured.** Agree that you will always maintain adequate insurance (discussed in Chapter 8).

- **The lease or rental agreement.** Your lease or rental agreement will contain many terms you choose—for example, whether you will allow pets, when rent will be collected, and how long a lease term the tenant must agree to (see Chapter 5). You may wish to discuss these terms with your co-owner first, then agree how you'll handle any changes.

- **What to do if one of you wants to sell.** To avoid getting stuck in business with a complete stranger (since either of you may have the right to sell your interest to whomever you please), spell out what you will do if one of you wants to sell. For example, you might determine that each of you has the "right of first refusal"—that is, the right to purchase the other's share before it's offered to anyone else. You'll have to determine how to value the property if you go this route—to keep things simple, you might agree to pay to have the property appraised, and for the purchasing party to pay the fair market value as determined by the appraiser.

- **What to do if one of you dies.** If you own property as joint tenants and one of you dies, the other will own the property. But if you are tenants in common, ownership will pass according to the terms of the deceased person's will or trust (or state inheritance laws, if there is no will or trust). In your agreement, you can specify that if either of you dies, the other has the right to purchase the deceased owner's share from the estate, and that each of you will add this to your will or trust documents.

- **How you will resolve disputes.** Even if it's hard to anticipate now, it's possible that you and your co-owner won't always agree. If that happens, you may want to try to resolve problems without going to court, for example using mediation. You can set up the requirements for this in your agreement.

Inherited a House? Watch Out for Flying Apples

How wrenching is it to let go of the family homestead? Anne Hyde Hyland, the youngest of five siblings, is finding out. The home in question is a rambling seaside house near Bath, Maine, used as a summertime gathering place for four generations. It is rife with memories and in grave need of repair.

When the family matriarch died last summer, the house was left to the eldest sister, who plans to rent it out this summer for the first time to pay for a new furnace and roof.

"My kids don't get it," says Hyland, who, as the only sibling living nearby, is being hit the hardest. "They say, 'What do you mean we can't come to our house anymore?'"

As the generation that produced the baby boomers dies or downsizes, people are increasingly likely to inherit a home.

The Hydes' mother had hoped to prevent disputes among her children, reasoning that leaving the home to one child, who could share it with the others, was more harmonious than splitting it five ways.

Inherited a House? Watch Out for Flying Apples, cont'd

Unfortunately, "our mother was thinking about it in a fairy-tale sense," says Hyland. One brother feels disenfranchised. Another objects to renovating the antiquated kitchen. Hyland was alarmed to find her sister had locked away a ship painting that hung above the fireplace, fearing it might be stolen. The siblings are "struggling" to schedule use of the house around the renters, and to negotiate a family rate, says Hyland.

Elizabeth Arnold, a lawyer in San Francisco who specializes in estate planning, tells of one family with a vacation home in the Pocono Mountains that squabbled after one in-law painted the bare two-by-fours on the walls. Later, at a family meeting, "two wives started voicing all their frustrations," and one pelted the other with apples from the fruit bowl.

It was the wake-up call they needed.

Arnold helped resolve disputes about the broken burner on the stove (fixed), the buck's head on the wall (removed), the newly painted two-by-fours (covered with paneling) and the lime-green shag carpeting (replaced by hardwood floors).

The family also started a new tradition: gathering one night each summer "to share memories and talk about what the place meant to them," says Arnold.

"This stuff is completely avoidable if the families get together and talk about it," she says.

 "Inheriting a house, but not the squabbles," by Joyce Cohen, April 11, 2003.

As you can see, the issues you will need to cover in a co-ownership agreement are many. "The most challenging part of drafting a co-ownership agreement is anticipating issues while everything looks rosy," says Craig Venezia, an expert on private mortgages and author of *Buying a Second Home* (Nolo). "Most people enter into co-ownership with the friendliest of intentions, thinking they can work out any unforeseen questions later. But with big dollars and possibly your leisure or retirement time at stake, fundamental disagreements can arise—and be tough to work out." Because these agreements can get complicated, we suggest you hire an attorney to help you draft one or review one you've drafted. Better to spend a little upfront, if it helps save money and hassle in the long term.

USA TODAY Snapshots®

All in the family
Do you plan to bring your children into the family business?

No **43%**

Undecided **31%**

Yes **26%**

Source: SunTrust Bank Private Wealth Management survey of 201 business owners of companies with revenue of $10 million or more.

By Jae Yang and and Bob Laird, USA TODAY
2007

Making It Work Over the Long Haul

Managing a property with a co-owner takes a lot more than just similar goals and objectives, and a good solid contract. It takes patience, understanding, and a longstanding relationship that is nurtured over time. For example, Sergio Raddavero and his co-owner have owned a single-family home in Burlingame, California, for 20 years. They have an oral agreement that has never been put on paper. Sergio says the secret to their success is that "we understand each other and complement each other."

"He does more on the handyman side. I do more on the management side," says Sergio. "I'm better at managing the rentals, and I organize the finances. Every month, I print out a financial statement and send it to him. Keeping your partner informed and in the loop makes him feel comfortable and secure." The fact that they have had positive cash flow for most of those 20 years has also made it easier. They repaint the house every six years, put on a new roof every ten years or so, and remodeled the kitchen once—always using a reserve account set aside for such repairs, and never having to dip into their own pockets.

The point is, while we highly recommend having a written co-ownership agreement, sometimes the mutual understanding and respect you have for each other is enough to create a good property management relationship. Regardless, being aware of your expectations before crafting an agreement, and having a clear understanding of each other's strengths and weaknesses, are keys to making the rental property business a success.

Preparing and Marketing Your Rental Property

Before you open the doors to prospective renters, you'll need to make sure the rental home is ready for showing. Particularly in competitive markets, your place should look as good as it can, to attract the best tenants at the best price. As John, who's been a landlord since 1975 explains, "It took me many years to discover that there's competition among landlords for the good tenants. The good tenants take away all your problems—they aren't breaking things and making up stories—and they let you stay ahead of the game."

This chapter explains the prep work involved, from scrubbing the toilet to painting the living room to making sure the house is fully up to code. Particularly if you're renting out a house that you or your parents have lived in for many years, you may have a lot of work to do.

This chapter also covers your choices for advertising and marketing your rental house and how to deal with renting out property that's still occupied. We'll also discuss why it's important to make a number of key decisions—such as how much rent you'll charge or whether you allow pets—before you run your first ad or talk with potential tenants.

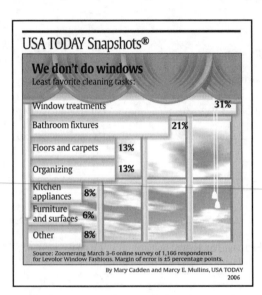

USA TODAY Snapshots®

We don't do windows
Least favorite cleaning tasks:

Window treatments	31%
Bathroom fixtures	21%
Floors and carpets	13%
Organizing	13%
Kitchen appliances	8%
Furniture and surfaces	6%
Other	8%

Source: Zoomerang March 3–6 online survey of 1,166 respondents for Levolor Window Fashions. Margin of error is ±5 percentage points.

By Mary Cadden and Marcy E. Mullins, USA TODAY 2006

Make Sure Everything Is Up to Code

Your first order of business is to make sure your house complies with all local and state housing codes. Chapter 7 discusses your legal duty to rent out habitable housing and your repair and maintenance obligations, and explains how to find out the extent of your responsibilities.

If you recently bought the property, you doubtless have an inspection report, which hopefully chronicled the structure's condition and repair needs. But if you're about to rent out a home that hasn't been inspected recently, you may not be sure what kind of shape it's in, or what repairs it could use. It's worth hiring a professional inspector—just like you'd do when buying a house—to check the place out and identify potential problems such as a leaky roof or faulty electrical circuits.

Look for an inspector who will give you a written, narrative report that helps you understand which issues need immediate attention and which you'll need to follow up on in the future. Common and significant code compliance issues include insufficient smoke detectors and the absence of ground-fault circuit interruption (GFCI) outlets.

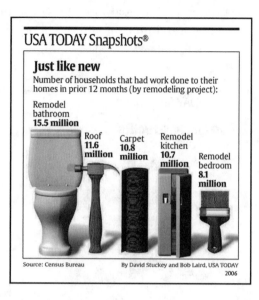

USA TODAY Snapshots®

Just like new

Number of households that had work done to their homes in prior 12 months (by remodeling project):

Remodel bathroom
15.5 million

Roof
11.6 million

Carpet
10.8 million

Remodel kitchen
10.7 million

Remodel bedroom
8.1 million

Source: Census Bureau   By David Stuckey and Bob Laird, USA TODAY 2006

Should You Make Major Repairs or Improvements?

If your property is in really bad shape (perhaps you've inherited your parents' 75-year-old house), it might be easier to sell it than to turn it into a rental. At the very least, preparation for renting means making sure that the house is safe and habitable. And, particularly in competitive markets, you may need to spend some big bucks on optional upgrades (such as on modernizing the kitchen or bathroom) before finding a renter. Unless you have the cash to pay for such upgrades, you may end up having to add repayments on a home equity loan to your monthly expenses—making it even less likely that the rent will cover the costs.

Start by talking to contractors and getting cost estimates. Then look again at the calculations in Chapter 1, to see how your short-term profits and long-term investment prospects will shake out. If you'll be going deep into debt with no hope of profiting until years later when you sell, putting the place up for sale now might make as much sense. (See Chapter 11 for tips on selling your house.)

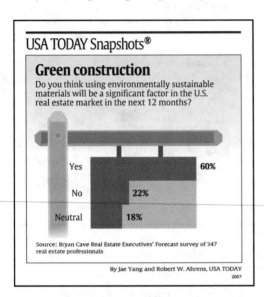

USA TODAY Snapshots®

Green construction

Do you think using environmentally sustainable materials will be a significant factor in the U.S. real estate market in the next 12 months?

Yes 60%
No 22%
Neutral 18%

Source: Bryan Cave Real Estate Executives' Forecast survey of 347 real estate professionals

By Jae Yang and Robert W. Ahrens, USA TODAY 2007

But what if you can't or don't want to sell right now, or think the property won't sell without some improvements anyway? That might change the analysis. After all, a renter might be willing to pay more once the place is improved. And in competitive markets, you may have little choice: If competing rentals (particularly in a planned unit development where units look alike) offer more amenities such as dishwashers, you might need to install one, too.

Do your homework, however, before deciding which improvements to make. Major home improvements almost never return 100% of their value. Remodeled kitchens tend to do the most to boost sales price, but you're still unlikely to recoup the entire amount spent. For a breakdown by project, see the National Association of Realtors® annual "Cost vs. Value" report (go to www.realtor.org and search for "cost vs. value").

Prepare the Rental for an Attractive Showing

First impressions count, and when interested renters first lay eyes on your rental house, you want their reactions to be positive. No amount of, "I'm going to take care of that … and that … and that … in the next few weeks" will dispel the negative impression left by dirty windows, peeling paint, or an unkempt front yard. Basic cleanup doesn't cost much, but it can make all the difference to prospective tenants.

If you're too busy to do the work yourself, hiring a handyperson or cleaning service may well pay for itself, by cutting down the amount of time your place is vacant, and attracting good tenants.

> **TIP**
> **Keep your receipts.** Much of your prep work will be tax-deductible, as discussed in Chapter 6.

Clean up the outside

The true first impression is made while your prospective tenants are getting out of their car or walking up to your property. If it looks run down or bedraggled, some people may just turn around and leave. Make sure your property looks welcoming and demonstrates your attention to maintenance. Here are the basics:

USA TODAY Snapshots®

Who has the best yard in the neighborhood?

A neighbor does **64%**

I do **36%**

Source: Harris Interactive survey for Vigoro of 773 adults (April 21-25). Margin of error is +/- 3.5 percentage points.

By Mary Cadden and Adrienne Lewis, USA TODAY
2008

- Sweep the sidewalk and clear paper and debris from the yard, porch, driveway, and entryways.

- Mow the lawn, prune the shrubs, and pull up weeds.

- Wash all the windows.

- Check that the doorbell works.

- Make sure the property is well lit, and the address is visible from the street. Replace the porch light bulbs, and consider adding lights with sensor detectors that go on automatically when someone approaches the house.

- Add greenery, such as flowering potted plants that you can place strategically.
- Put out a nice welcome mat or add other decorative touches such as a bench on the porch or a birdhouse in the tree.
- Paint the exterior of the house if it's looking bad.

Spruce up the inside

No matter how good the outside looks, tenants will ultimately focus on picturing their daily life inside your property. Here's how to create a clean, tidy, and attractive interior:

- Make sure all rooms (especially the bathroom and kitchen) are spotless (including all appliances, cabinets, and fixtures).
- Clear all hallways and counters.
- Sweep or vacuum the floors or carpets. Replace any flooring that's torn, badly stained, or mildewed. Remove slippery throw rugs.
- Make sure everything works—from the shower to the ceiling fan to the front door lock.
- Replace the window coverings if they're in bad shape. And leave curtains open when prospective tenants visit, to let in lots of light.
- Repaint all rooms, especially if it's been a year or two since the last paint job. As USA TODAY's Noelle Knox found, "Dark walls make the house look smaller. Walls should be off-white, or have earthy tones if the room has lots of light."
- Get rid of ants and any pests that may be roaming the rental.
- Cover electrical outlets, especially if families with small children will be visiting the place. Coil long electrical or phone cords to get them out of the way. Block off or child-proof any dangerous areas for kids, such as pools and stairways.
- Check that smoke detectors and fire extinguishers are in place (and in working order).
- Bring in a few nice pieces of furniture, including a chair or two that will give people a chance to sit down and imagine what it

might be like to live there. A coffee table with flowers and a few magazines or books will make the living room appealing.

- Put fresh towels and a new shower curtain in the bathroom.
- Put a pot of spiced apple cider on the stove, a tried-and-true trick to make the house smell good.

"The rental property should be absolutely spotless," says Sharon, who owns a rental property in Chico, California, and also manages two other properties in Sonoma County. "There should be no litter, no trash that needs to be emptied, no dust, no mildew, no paint that doesn't look fresh, and no lawn that needs mowing. In short, it should look like the kind of place you would live in!"

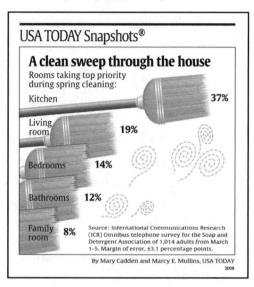

USA TODAY Snapshots®

A clean sweep through the house

Rooms taking top priority during spring cleaning:

Kitchen	37%
Living room	19%
Bedrooms	14%
Bathrooms	12%
Family room	8%

Source: International Communications Research (ICR) Omnibus telephone survey for the Soap and Detergent Association of 1,014 adults from March 1-5. Margin of error, ±3.1 percentage points.

By Mary Cadden and Marcy E. Mullins, USA TODAY 2008

> **TIP**
>
> **Do the work now.** No matter how anxious you are to get new tenants moved in, take the time to repair and refurbish first. By waiting to deal with things like a ratty carpet or a bad paint job, you'll just end up paying bigger bucks later, when the job has gotten bigger. Plus, you'll irritate or inconvenience your tenants.

Set the Rent and Other Important Terms

Before you place your first ad, talk with prospective tenants, or prepare your lease or rental documents, you'll need to make a number of key decisions, including:

- the amount of rent you're going to charge (see Chapter 1)
- your requirements for tenants' minimum income and credit
- how much security deposit you're going to collect
- number of occupants
- whether pets are allowed (and, if so, what kind)
- whether to offer a fixed-term lease or a month-to-month tenancy
- when the rental will be available
- what utilities (if any) you'll pay for, and
- any other important issues, such as whether you'll allow a home business, a cosigner on the lease, or smoking in the rental property.

Good rental policies are a combination of the practical ("What will work for this property?") and the legal ("May I legally require or forbid this?"). Showing your rental property (or even having an initial phone conversation) without a firm idea of how you'll handle these issues is a real mistake, and will waste everyone's time. Plus, you may get into legal trouble, such as a fair housing complaint, if you provide certain terms for some tenants, but not others.

Most of these issues dovetail with writing your lease (a topic we'll cover in Chapter 5).

USA TODAY Snapshots®

The money pit

Given $10,000 to spend on their home or themselves, homeowners say they would choose:

Home **75%**

Self **19%**

Don't know/ no answer **6%**

Source: Caravan survey by Opinion Research Corp. for Minwax of 750 homeowners, taken March 24-27. Margin of error, ± 3.7 percentage points.

By Mary Cadden and Bob Laird USA TODAY 2008

Get to Know the Neighbors

While you're puttering around the property, take the time to introduce yourself to neighbors in the surrounding houses. Some of them may be concerned about the house becoming a rental, given the widespread reputation that renters have for taking worse care of a property than homeowners do.

Reassure them that you're doing your best to find excellent tenants and plan to maintain regular oversight of the property. Sometimes just knowing that the landlord is a real person goes a long way toward making neighbors feel comfortable.

> **CAUTION**
>
> **Let neighbors know how to reach you with complaints about your tenants.** Laura, a Bellevue, Washington landlord, for example, says: "I like to meet the neighbors, give them my phone number, and say, 'If you have a problem, give me a call.' That happened with a Bellevue property—in fact, I wish they'd called me sooner. The tenants were leaving garbage on the back deck, and the neighbors had to look at dirty diapers and stuff. I went and talked to the tenants: problem solved." (If a tenant later does cause trouble, our advice in Chapter 9 will explain how to act swiftly.)

Come on Down! Advertising Your House for Rent

A little word-of-mouth among your friends or colleagues may be all you need to find the perfect tenant, particularly if the market is tight and you have a competitively priced rental. For example, Laura describes how she found one of her best tenants: "The existing tenant (who needed to get out of the lease early), placed an ad in her moms' club's newsletter. I've also heard of landlords offering tenants money if they bring in a good replacement tenant."

For wider choice, however, you'll need to advertise publicly. Possible ways to do that include:

- putting a "House for Rent" sign in front of the property, on a nearby corner or sidewalk, or in one of the windows
- posting flyers on neighborhood bulletin boards
- listing with a local homefinders' service that provides a centralized listing of rental units for a particular geographic area

- advertising in a local newspaper
- working with a local real estate broker who handles rentals, and
- if you live in one of the many areas served by Craigslist (www. craigslist.org), using that free online service (or other local online services you may find).

The method of advertising that will work best depends on your particular rental house (its rent, size, amenities, location), your budget, the saturation of the market, the type of renter who will likely be your tenant (such as students versus families), and whether you're under time pressure to rent your place out. If, for example, your rental is near a popular park or shopping area, a For Rent sign in the window is a must. In an Internet-savvy place like California, long-time landlord Dennis has found that, "What does work is Craigslist. I don't use the newspapers anymore. You don't get many calls from the paper."

> **TIP**
> **A picture really is worth a thousand words.** One of the great advantages of online advertising services is that you can post digital photos of your rental, inside and out.

Your ads should contain a clear (and accurate) description of the property, including basic details, such as:

- rent
- size—particularly number of bedrooms and baths
- location—either the general neighborhood or street address, including proximity to public transportation and shopping areas
- whether you're offering a fixed-term lease or a month-to-month rental agreement
- the date the rental house is available
- special features—such as fenced-in yard, view, washer/dryer, fireplace, remodeled kitchen, furnishings, garage, parking, hardwood floors, wall-to-wall carpeting, or cable TV
- any important rules, such as no pets

- your phone number or email for more information, or the date and time of any open house.

> ! CAUTION
> **Avoid discrimination complaints—or a lawsuit.** Be sure your ad never mentions sex, race, religion, national origin, disability, or age (unless your property meets the legal requirements of senior citizens housing). See Chapter 4 for a discussion of anti-discrimination laws.

How to Show Your Property

Prospective tenants may start phoning as soon as you've advertised your vacancy. Be ready to tell them how they can come for a visit. You have three basic choices:

- individual appointments, in which you meet at the property and conduct a personal tour
- private open houses attended by multiple prospects who have been invited by you, or
- public open houses, where anyone who has seen your ad or knows of the vacancy can show up.

During that first phone call, provide complete details on the property and your policies. Sure, some prospective tenants will say "No thanks" on the spot, but that's fine. You'll avoid wasting your time showing your rental to someone who wouldn't have been interested in it anyway (or won't meet your requirements). Also, as John, an experienced California landlord, reminds us, "Give prospective tenants clear, simple driving directions, so they're not feeling frustrated by the time they arrive—if they find their way there at all."

Your decision whether to show your rental by appointment or by open house depends on market factors and your own time and preferences. For example, in a soft market, where good tenants are hard to find, you'll need to schedule appointments at the prospective tenant's convenience. In a hot market, with lots of interested applicants, one or two open houses may do the job. If you hold an open house, be sure it's at a convenient time, such as during two or three hours on a Saturday afternoon.

> **TIP**
>
> **Prepare the rental unit for a secure showing.** If you'll be allowing strangers into a rental house that no one is currently living in, consider bringing at least one other person with you. If you'll be holding an open house and expect a mob scene, sign up more than one person, ideally people who can answer questions and promote your rental to its best advantage. If someone is still living on the property, ask that they hide all valuables and prescriptions.

As you show your rental to prospective tenants, be polite and informative to everyone, even those whom you're pretty sure are not in the running. For example, after hearing someone's laundry list of needed cosmetic upgrades, you could fairly cross that applicant off your list. Still, while it's fine to tell the person that you won't be making those upgrades anytime soon, beware of doing so in a way that might cause offense. For one thing, you need to preserve (or begin creating) your reputation as a business-like landlord. Perhaps more importantly, you never want to give a disappointed prospect an opening to accuse you of a fair housing violation, as may happen if the demanding prospect concludes that your tone and demeanor had more to do with race, religion, sex, or another protected characteristic than it did with your unwillingness to go along with the demands.

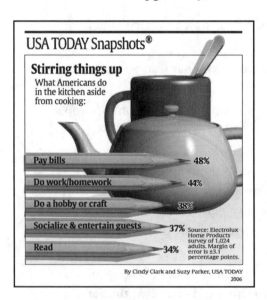

USA TODAY Snapshots®

Stirring things up

What Americans do in the kitchen aside from cooking:

Pay bills — 48%
Do work/homework — 44%
Do a hobby or craft — 38%
Socialize & entertain guests — 37%
Read — 34%

Source: Electrolux Home Products survey of 1,024 adults. Margin of error is ±3.1 percentage points.

By Cindy Clark and Suzy Parker, USA TODAY 2006

While it's important to carefully observe prospects' behavior, don't put too much stock in first impressions. As John (California landlord) has found, "Some people will come in looking sloppy, others come in dressed to the tee. We had some prospective tenants come in wearing suits and black ties, looking very professional—it turned out they were importing heroin from Italy or somewhere. When you get the credit report you'll see who they really are. And you'll probably discover that you're not as good a judge of character as you thought you were."

Pardon Those People: Renting Property That's Still Occupied

Many first-time landlords buy or inherit property with a tenant in place. Hopefully, this will be a good tenant who wants to keep renting. But what if the tenant plans to leave, or you decide not to renew the lease or rental agreement for a tenant who is less than ideal? If possible, wait until the current tenant moves out to show a rental unit to prospective tenants. (This is especially a good idea if your elderly parents are the current renters and they're leaving their long-time home for a nursing home or assisted living.)

Waiting until the place is vacant gives you the chance to spruce it up. It also avoids problems such as promising the house to a new tenant, only to have the existing tenant not move out on time or leave the place a mess.

Nevertheless, to comply with a lease that's still valid for many weeks or months, or to eliminate any gap in rent, you may need to show your property while its current tenants are still there. Follow these suggestions to minimize the disruptions to current tenants and maximize your chances of having a successful showing:

- **Communicate.** Before advertising, discuss your plans with outgoing tenants so you can be as accommodating as possible.

- **Warn tenants about showings.** Give current tenants as much notice as possible before entering and showing a rental house to prospective new tenants. In all states, you have a right to show the still-occupied property to prospective tenants, but your current tenants are still entitled to a reasonable level of privacy and appropriate notice (typically 24 hours—for details, see the discussion of the notice-of-entry clause in leases and rental agreements in Chapter 5).

- **Don't overdo showings.** Try to limit the number of times you show the house in a given week, and make sure your current tenants agree to any evening and weekend visits.

- **Offer something in return.** Consider offering a restaurant gift certificate or other perk. As a last resort, for situations where showing the rental will be a major imposition or the tenants refused to cooperate, you might reduce the rent slightly.

- **Avoid putting a sign on the rental property itself.** This almost guarantees that your existing tenants will be bothered by strangers. Or, if a sign seems like an important advertising method, make sure it clearly warns against disturbing the occupant and includes a telephone number for information: for example, "For Rent: Shown by Appointment Only. Call 555-1700. Do Not Disturb Occupants." If you're using a real estate agent to help with the renting and showing, do not allow the use of a "lockbox," which results in unannounced (and often illegal) property showings.

TIP

You don't want a tenant who violates the "Do not disturb" sign. Catherine, a Berkeley landlord who rents a cottage behind her own house, looked out her window one day to see a woman wandering through her back yard. Catherine says, "It turns out she was a prospective tenant who just chose to ignore the sign. I figured this didn't bode well for her ability to follow my rental agreement terms, so of course I didn't rent the place to her."

If, despite your best efforts, the current tenants are uncooperative or hostile, avoid hassles and wait until they leave before showing the rental. Also, if the current tenant is a complete slob or has damaged the place, you're better off applying paint and elbow grease before trying to re-rent it. Never advertise or rent a unit in which the current tenant is ignoring a termination notice or, worse, fighting an eviction. Better to clear the decks before embarking on your search for a new tenant. ●

Screening and Choosing Good Tenants

After all your work preparing, showing, and marketing your new property, the day will come when a prospective tenant looks around and says, "It's great, I'd like to rent it." Is that your cue to set a move-in date and watch the rent checks start to roll in? Not so fast.

Choosing tenants is the most important decision you'll make. A bad choice can result in damage and lost rent. And tenant turnover is invariably expensive: By the time you factor in lost rental income (depending on how long the property sits vacant), advertising and screening costs, and the value of your time to plan and run the whole tenant selection show, one change of tenants can easily cost two to three times the monthly rent. And nothing can destroy a profitable year more quickly than an eviction lawsuit, even one that you ultimately win.

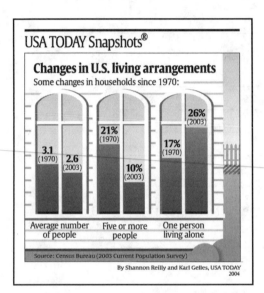

USA TODAY Snapshots®

Changes in U.S. living arrangements

Some changes in households since 1970:

- Average number of people: 3.1 (1970), 2.6 (2003)
- Five or more people: 21% (1970), 10% (2003)
- One person living alone: 17% (1970), 26% (2003)

Source: Census Bureau (2003 Current Population Survey)

By Shannon Reilly and Karl Gelles, USA TODAY 2004

Every landlord we talked to in preparing this book was eager to tell us horror stories about tenants who didn't work out—and how they learned to find the best tenants (and avoid legal hassles) through a fair and thorough screening process. This chapter shows how your common sense and business moxie, coupled with a clear understanding of the law, will keep your rental income steady and safe. It will help you meet the all-important goal of finding (and keeping) good tenants who pay their rent on time, take good care of your property, and are considerate neighbors.

TIP

Lesson learned the hard way: Nice guys aren't always what they seem. As Darla, in Seattle, found, "When I tried to rent my house out, I had plenty of people interested. One guy seemed really nice, and looked good on the application he filled out. So I didn't bother to do a financial background check. Bad move—he was a total loser, with a lousy credit record and past evictions. I wound up with a big utility bill after I evicted him for nonpayment of rent."

Hate to Choose? A Property Manager Could Handle This

Many landlords decide to contract with a property management company, which will take care of advertising your property and screening tenants, as well as collecting rent, handling tenant complaints, arranging repairs and maintenance, and evicting troublesome tenants (usually for an additional fee). But not all management companies will deliver on their promises—like prospects, they too have to be researched and screened. See Chapter 10 for details.

Creating a Rental Application

If you were to ask a group of landlords whether their "gut reactions" to prospective tenants have always panned out, chances are you'd find some whose instincts have never failed them. Alas, you'd also find a fair share of rueful stories, chronicling the disappointments or even disasters that resulted from trusting skin-deep impressions. To avoid being misled, ask each prospective tenant to fill out a rental application that includes:

- the applicant's employment, income, credit, and rental housing history
- up-to-date references from landlords and employers
- identifying information, such as the applicant's Social Security number (SSN), driver's license number, passport, or Individual Taxpayer Identification Number (ITIN) which is issued by the IRS to persons who are required to file income taxes but who can't obtain a Social Security number, and
- details on past bankruptcies, evictions, or criminal convictions (you'll also get much of this information from a credit report, as discussed below).

RESOURCE

Where to find a rental application. Nolo publishes several books, including *Every Landlord's Legal Guide*, which include a rental application and detailed instructions. *Every Landlord's Guide to Finding Great Tenants* focuses specifically on attracting, choosing, and screening the best tenants possible. See www.nolo.com.

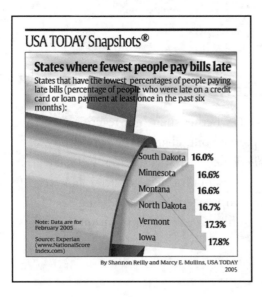

USA TODAY Snapshots®

States where fewest people pay bills late

States that have the lowest percentages of people paying late bills (percentage of people who were late on a credit card or loan payment at least once in the past six months):

South Dakota	16.0%
Minnesota	16.6%
Montana	16.6%
North Dakota	16.7%
Vermont	17.3%
Iowa	17.8%

Note: Data are for February 2005

Source: Experian (www.NationalScore Index.com)

By Shannon Reilly and Marcy E. Mullins, USA TODAY 2005

You can either hand over the blank rental application in person when showing your rental or email a copy to interested applicants. If more than one person plans to live in your property, each one over the age of 18 needs to fill out their own, separate application. This is true whether you're renting to a married couple or unrelated roommates, complete strangers or the cousins of your current tenant.

> ⓘ **CAUTION**
> **Don't pick and choose who gets a rental application.** After explaining the basic terms of the tenancy (such as the length of the rental, the rent, deposit, maximum number of occupants, and pet rules), give a rental application to anyone who appears to be qualified and interested—even if you think they can't afford your place. Be sure applicants understand that they must fully complete the application in order to be considered.

Your prospect's signature at the bottom of the rental application is crucial. It authorizes you to verify the information and references and to run a credit report. (Some employers and banks require written authorization before talking to you about the person.)

Renting to Section 8 Tenants

"Section 8" is a federally run and financed housing assistance program. Private landlords receive roughly two-thirds of the rent from the tenant, and the local housing authority pays the rest. In most states, you aren't obligated to accept a Section 8 tenant, but can choose whether to participate in the program. Your local public housing agency can provide details. If you have property in a low-income neighborhood, you may find that most of your applications are Section 8 renters, and you may need to accept them in order to stay in business.

There are pluses and minuses to participating in Section 8. Although many landlords are leery of accepting tenants whose ability to pay the rent is already marginal, Phil, a first-time landlord who shares his Berkeley triplex with two Section 8 tenants, says, "It's worked out fabulously. The fact that they're getting a rental subsidy helps them pay on time. Plus, it's a good deal for them and they want to keep it that way, so if anything, they're more responsible than regular tenants might be."

Check References and Run a Credit Report

If you're lucky, you may easily find one or more potential tenants whom you like personally, and whose written applications look good. Should you sign one of them up yet? Sorry, those written applications can lie or cover up a rental or financial history that would make the applicant a poor risk. Even after 20 years as a landlord, Dennis says, "It's hard to judge people just by meeting them—are they going to pay bills, are they going to take care of property, are they going to be a nuisance to the neighborhood?" So your next step is to choose your top two or three applicants and confirm the representations on the application.

USA TODAY Snapshots®

The lies have it

Overall, 42% of high school students think a person has to lie or cheat sometimes to succeed. By gender:

Male
50%

Female
33%

Source: Josephson Institute's 2006 Report Card on the Ethics of American Youth, a questionnaire survey of 36,000 high school students ages 14–19 from 114 schools, January–June; margin of error is ±1 percentage point.

By Tracey Wong Briggs and Alejandro Gonzalez, USA TODAY
2006

> 💡 **TIP**
>
> **Best thing I ever did: Weed out tenants by charging first and last months' rent.** Kyung bought a three-family house in New Haven, Connecticut and lived in one of the units (the two rents paid the entire mortgage). "But," she explains, "because we had a small child, and were going to be sharing the driveway and laundry area, we needed tenants we could trust. We not only interviewed people carefully, but we asked them to sign a one-year lease, plus put down first and last months' rent. That ruled out a lot of people who didn't have money or were bad risks. We decided we'd rather go months with no one living there than regret saying yes to someone. It worked out great, we found good, long-term tenants."

Collect Holding Deposits Carefully

Eager applicants will often ask you to accept a holding deposit pending your review of their rental application. (A holding deposit is supposed to guarantee that the applicant will get the rental if his credit and references check out.) These tenants want you to know that their money is where their mouths are—if their rental, employment, and credit histories meet your satisfaction, they'll move in.

Holding deposits should be accepted warily and handled with care. Some states impose disclosure requirements on landlords who collect them, by requiring you to explain the circumstances in which you'll keep or return the deposits (or credit the deposit to the first month's rent). Beyond these technicalities, however, consider the added bookkeeping. Are you prepared to keep track of these deposits? It's generally a bad idea to require holding deposits—many tenants who are otherwise perfectly good candidates will not have cash available to sideline into a holding deposit.

Check with previous landlords

Who better to tell you about a tenant than the person's past landlords? In particular, a former landlord has no reason to paint a deceptively rosy picture of a problem tenant in order to unload that person onto you. When you call, ask targeted questions such as:

- Did this person pay the rent on time (and, if not, what were the circumstances)?
- Did the person ask for repairs when appropriate (but not every time there was a minor problem)?
- How easy was it to communicate with this person?
- Was he or she considerate of neighbors (no loud parties)?
- Did the person take good care of the property?
- Would you rent to this person again?

Assuming you're dealing with a candid, business-like landlord, you want to hear positive answers to your questions. But what if you sense that you're talking to an unreasonable landlord, whom even you wouldn't want to rent from? If so, or if your prospect has alerted you to this possibility, consider the landlord's statements, but be sure to contact other, past landlords to get a more complete picture.

TIP

Check out pets, too. If the prospect has a dog, cat, or other pet, ask landlord references whether the pet caused any damage or problems for other tenants or neighbors. It's also good to meet the pet, so you can make sure that it's well-groomed and well-behaved. That will avoid situations like the one Gordon, with property in San Jose, California, faced: "One tenant told us they had a small dog, and they didn't, they had a big one. And the dog basically killed all the grass in the back yard and destroyed the landscaping." You must, however, accommodate an applicant with a legally recognized disability whose pet serves as a support animal— no matter what your pet policies otherwise might be.

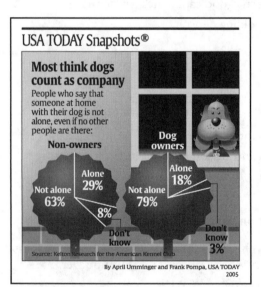

USA TODAY Snapshots®

Most think dogs count as company

People who say that someone at home with their dog is not alone, even if no other people are there:

Non-owners
Alone 29%
Not alone 63%
8%
Don't know

Dog owners
Alone 18%
Not alone 79%
Don't know 3%

Source: Kelton Research for the American Kennel Club

By April Umminger and Frank Pompa, USA TODAY 2005

Verify income and employment

You no doubt want a tenant who will pay the rent each month. That's why you need to find out whether, in raw numerical terms, the tenant has the income with which to do so. Call the prospective tenant's employer to verify income and length of employment. (The employer might require written authorization from the employee, which you'll have on the rental application or on a separate, stand-alone consent form—fax either one to the employer.) You may also ask the prospective tenant to document other sources of income, such as Social Security, disability payments, workers' compensation, welfare, child support, or alimony. Ask self-employed applicants to provide copies of recent tax returns.

How much income is enough? Think twice before renting to tenants where the rent will take more than one-third of their income, especially if they have a lot of debts or financial obligations, if their job is seasonal, or they have a history of bouncing from job to job.

> CAUTION
>
> **Boring tenants can be better than ones you'd want to hang out with.** As Sarah, a San Francisco landlord, explains, "We've rented to people we wanted to give a break to—we identified with them, because they were young and having trouble finding a place. Of course, being young, their plans changed, and they moved on quickly, and broke the lease. If we could do it all over again, we'd choose the boring tenants with the more stable financial situation."

Check credit reports

A handy way to check prospective tenants' financial circumstances (in particular, their debt load) and on-time payment record is to get each person's credit report from at least one credit reporting agency (CRA). John, who's been a landlord since 1975, puts it another way: "If you don't run credit checks, you're crazy."

A good credit report contains a gold mine of information, such as the person's history of paying rent or bills late, past bankruptcies, some criminal convictions, and sometimes past evictions. (Your legal right to get information on evictions, however, may vary from state to state.) Credit reports may also give you a FICO score, which is a number between 300 and 800 that purports to reflect the chances that the consumer will fulfill his or her future financial obligations. A low number indicates a poor risk; most landlords will reject applicants with scores under 550 or 600.

Credit reports usually cover the past seven to ten years. To obtain one, you'll need a prospective tenant's name, address, and Social Security number or ITIN (Individual Taxpayer Identification Number). Technically, as long as you're requesting the report for a valid business reason, which includes evaluating the credit risk of a prospective tenant, you don't need the prospect's consent. But, because many people believe that you need their okay, it's simpler to ask for it (for convenience' sake, get it in writing).

Three CRAs have cornered the market on credit reports:

- Equifax, www.equifax.com
- Experian, www.experian.com, and
- TransUnion, www.transunion.com.

However, you can't order a credit report for someone else directly from one of these big three. Instead, you'll need to work through a credit reporting or tenant screening service (type "tenant screening" or "credit report" into your browser's search box). Look for a company that operates in your area, has been in business for a while, and provides you with a sample report that's clear and informative.

It's legal in most states to charge prospective tenants a fee for the cost of the credit report and your time and trouble. Any credit check fee should be reasonably related to the cost of the credit check itself—$20 to $30 is common. (And you must really run the credit check—you can't just pocket the fee.) Check your state law for any limits.

USA TODAY Snapshots®

Many Americans unprepared

How long could you cover household living expenses with your current liquid savings?

Less than one week	One week to less than one month	One month to less than three months	Three months to less than six months	Six months or more	Declined to answer
17%	14%	24%	10%	19%	17%

Note: Total doesn't add up to 100 due to rounding

Source: LexisNexis Martindale-Hubbell's Lawyers.com survey of 2,318 adults 18 and older. Margin of error ±3 percentage points.

By Jae Yang and Marcy E. Mullins, USA TODAY 2006

Check Database of Sex Offenders

Not surprisingly, most landlords don't want tenants with criminal records, particularly of violent crimes or crimes against children.

Checking a prospective tenant's credit report is one way to attempt to find out about a person's criminal history, but not all convictions will show up on a credit report. Self-reporting is another: Rental applications typically ask whether the prospective tenant has ever been convicted of a crime.

"Megan's Law" databases may also be a useful source of information. Named after a young girl killed by a convicted child molester who lived in her neighborhood, this federal disclosure law charges the FBI with keeping a nationwide database of persons convicted of sexual offenses against minors and violent sexual offenses against anyone. (42 U.S.C. §§ 14071 and following.)

Every state has its own version of Megan's Law, requiring certain convicted sexual offenders to register with local law enforcement officials, who keep a database on their whereabouts. For information on accessing this database, and restrictions on your use of information derived from it, contact your local law enforcement agency or check www.parentsformeganslaw.com.

TIP
Keep good records. Take notes of all your conversations with applicants and references and keep them on file, along with applicants' credit reports. (See our advice on recordkeeping in Chapter 5.) You'll need these records in order to survive a fair housing challenge if a disappointed applicant files a discrimination complaint. Take special care to store credit reports in a safe place, such as a locked filing cabinet, where only you and those who "need to know" can access them. Under the "Disposal Rule" of the Fair and Accurate Credit Transactions Act of 2003, you must destroy the report when you no longer need it.

Check college transcripts

If you'll be renting to college students, the credit reports may not show much—they may be just signing up for their first credit cards! But you can ask to see a copy of a recent school transcript. (If they're freshmen, a high school transcript will do.)

A transcript can reveal a lot. If it shows no "incompletes," a full load, and good grades, you're probably looking at a person who can follow through with a commitment. Even so, you may want to consider requiring a cosigner (as discussed in Chapter 5) if the student depends on parents for substantial support.

Avoiding Illegal Discrimination

Although you can exercise personal choice in deciding who lives in your rental house, there are limits on the reasons for which you can exclude someone. Federal, state, and local laws specify illegal reasons to refuse to rent to a tenant, and limit what you can say and do in the tenant selection process. The federal Fair Housing Act and Fair Housing Amendments Act (42 U.S.C. §§ 3601-3619, 3631) prohibit discrimination on the basis of race or color, religion, national origin, gender, age, familial status (pregnancy or children), and physical or mental disability (including recovering alcoholics and people with a past drug addiction). Many states and cities also prohibit discrimination based on marital status, military status, or sexual orientation.

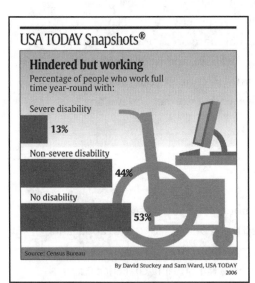

USA TODAY Snapshots®

Hindered but working
Percentage of people who work full time year-round with:

Severe disability
13%

Non-severe disability
44%

No disability
53%

Source: Census Bureau

By David Stuckey and Sam Ward, USA TODAY
2006

The federal anti-discrimination laws mentioned above don't apply to owner-occupied rental housing of four units or less, but they do apply to single-family home rentals, unless you go without advertising or the services of a real estate broker. Don't fasten onto this exception without considering the practicalities involved: Rarely will you be able to rent the home without some sort of advertising or help from a broker. And even if you end up continuously renting via word of mouth, your state or local anti-discrimination laws may cover this loophole in the federal rules. It's far more efficient to comply with fair housing laws from the get-go and not open yourself up to a charge of discrimination which, even if you prevail, will cost you plenty in time, money, and a sullied reputation.

To minimize the chances that you'll need to answer to a fair housing charge, treat all applicants more or less equally. For example, don't set tougher standards (such as a higher income level or a credit score) for renting to a member of an ethnic minority or a single parent. Base your decisions on where you advertise, what you say, and how you screen and choose tenants on sound business reasons, devoid of stereotypes or your personal feelings.

CAUTION
You can't use your property's inaccessibility as an excuse not to rent to a disabled tenant. The Fair Housing Amendments Act requires all landlords to accommodate the reasonable needs of disabled tenants, in many cases at the landlord's expense. (42 U.S.C. § 3604(f)(3)(B).) You're expected to adjust your rules, procedures, or services in order to give a person with a disability an equal opportunity to use and enjoy the house, dwelling unit, or a common space (such as a walkway or yard area). Accommodations include such things as providing a close-in, spacious parking space for a wheelchair-bound tenant (if you provide parking). You aren't, however, required to make accommodations that would pose an unreasonable expense for you. For more on the rights of a disabled tenant, see Chapter 5.

Renting to Undocumented Immigrants

It's not against the law to rent to someone who is in the United States illegally. Then again, it's not against the law to refuse to rent to someone who is here illegally. Some landlords recognize that many undocumented immigrants have been here for years, hold stable jobs, and are unlikely to become the target of hit-or-miss immigration raids. Others assume, whether rightly or not, that people who are here without proper documentation, and subject to deportation, are more likely to skip out on a rental than others.

If you decide to rent to legal residents only, you'll need to advise all applicants that they must supply proof of legal residence. Asking only those who appear to be "foreign" will open you up to a charge of discrimination based on national origin.

Next, you'll have to review and understand the documents that applicants give you. You'll quickly discover that the various visas, work permits, receipt notices, and other documents issued by United States Citizenship and Immigration Services (USCIS) are indecipherable, to say the least. And that's before you deal with the possibility of fake documents. Short of being shown a U.S. passport, many landlords throw up their hands.

In recent years, several localities around the United States have passed ordinances making it illegal to rent to people who aren't legal residents. Every such ordinance has either been withdrawn or struck down by a court. Landlords in California and New York City must heed their state and local rules forbidding landlords from demanding proof of legal residence; but if the landlord learns of an applicant's illegal status through any other means, the landlord may decline to rent on that basis.

For further protection, keep a paper trail (such as copies of all credit reports and references from previous landlords) for all applicants. Be organized about filing the applications and other materials and notes on prospective tenants, and keep these for at least three years after you rent a particular unit.

For information on the rules and regulations of the Fair Housing Act, contact HUD's Housing Discrimination Hotline at 800-669-9777 or check the HUD website at www.hud.gov. For information on state and local housing discrimination laws, contact your state fair housing agency, via www.fairhousing.com, a website maintained by the National Fair Housing Advocate Online.

Is This the One? Characteristics of the Perfect Tenant

Armed with the information you've collected, it's time to see how your top pick or picks match up against the "Checklist of Ideal Tenant Qualities," below.

Checklist of Ideal Tenant Qualities

Any tenant you accept should meet all or most of these criteria:

- ❏ ability to meet your basic rental terms, such as number of people living in your space or length of the rental term
- ❏ sufficient income to pay the rent (the industry standard is a monthly gross income that's triple the monthly rent)
- ❏ satisfactory credit report (debt level and bill-paying history)
- ❏ solid to high credit score
- ❏ positive references from other landlords
- ❏ positive references from current employer
- ❏ no recent terminations or evictions
- ❏ clean criminal record, and
- ❏ complete and accurate rental application.

Of course, intangibles will also come into play. If you communicate well with one prospective tenant and not with another, it makes sense to choose the one whose phone calls you won't soon come to dread. That's doubly true if you're sharing the same property, for example in duplex units.

USA TODAY Snapshots®

Two-parent homes decline

Percentage of children younger than 18 who lived with two parents:

88%

68%

80%

60%

40%

20%

0

'60   '70   '80   '90   '00 '04

Source: National Fatherhood Initiative

By David Stuckey and Marcy E. Mullins, USA TODAY
2007

If you're lucky, you'll find someone who meets all of these criteria and will likely be a good, long-term tenant. Or maybe none of your prospects will seem acceptable—all might have either a troubling rental history, insufficient income, or some other quality (such as immediate and unreasonable requests for upgrades) that would lead most any landlord to reject them. We advise against just swallowing your misgivings and picking the least objectionable.

No matter how urgently you want the rent stream to resume, remember that a bad pick can cost you dearly. Instead, go back to the well, and perhaps advertise in different media, drop the rent, spiff up the rental to make it more attractive, or do something else to enlarge the pool of promising applicants.

But once you've identified a good applicant, your next step is to convey the good news to the lucky person and set a date to sign the lease or rental agreement (discussed in the next chapter).

TIP

Best thing I ever did: Choose a known tenant, despite possible overcrowding. Don, who lives in Philadelphia, says, "When I upgraded to a three-bedroom condo, I decided to rent out my original two-bedroom unit, which included a small den. A hard-working janitor I knew was having trouble finding a place he could afford for his family of five. I let them rent my condo, despite the cramped quarters (they converted the den to a nursery). They were so thrilled, they've taken better care of the place than anyone else would have."

When None of Your Prospects Look Financially Solid

Depending on your rental and the market, the pickings may be slim. If you've held off long enough and simply can't find a financially stable tenant, consider requiring a creditworthy cosigner on the lease. (This approach is often used by landlords renting to college students.) If you're renting to someone with bad credit, be extra sure that their references check out. And consider charging a good-sized deposit—as much as you can collect under state law and the market will bear. For more information on security deposit agreements and cosigners, see Chapter 5.

Whom to Reject

You'll probably have people applying for your rental whom you simply don't want to rent to, even if they're the only applicants. You're legally free to reject people for the following reasons (called your "legitimate business interests"):

- poor credit history
- income that you reasonably regard as insufficient to pay the rent
- negative references from previous landlords indicating problems—such as property damage or consistently late rent payments—that make someone a bad risk
- convictions for criminal offenses of any kind (however, you cannot reject someone with a conviction for drug use; you can, however, reject a person who was convicted of manufacturing or selling drugs, or who currently uses illegal drugs)
- inability to meet the legal terms of a lease or rental agreement, such as someone who can't come up with the security deposit or who wants to keep a pet and your policy is no pets, or
- more people than you want to live in the unit—assuming that your limit on the number of tenants is clearly tied to health and safety or legitimate business needs. (See the discussion of occupancy limits in Chapter 5.)

These are the candidates whom you may safely and legally reject. If you have a bunch of equally qualified applicants and need to pick one, it's safest to choose the person who applied first. You can also apply tie-breaking criteria that are less hard-and-fast. You might, for example, pick the one you feel you'll communicate best with, or who appears to have the skills necessary to take care of your house and garden. But be sure to examine your motives to make sure your preference for one applicant over another isn't based on discriminatory assumptions about people who are in a protected class.

USA TODAY Snapshots®

Pet-friendly homes
Number of pets among owners:

35% — 1
25% — 2
13% — 3
7% — 4
6% — 5
13% — 6 or more

Note: Percentages do not add up to 100% because of rounding
Source: Harris Poll of 2,455 adults surveyed online Nov. 7-13.

By Michelle Healy and Karl Gelles, USA TODAY 2007

If your reasons for refusing to rent to someone are, in fact, based on information in a credit report or tenant-screening report, you can't just say "Sorry, I found a more qualified tenant." In that case, you must give the applicant the name and address of the agency that reported the negative information or furnished the report. You must tell the applicant that he or she has a right to a copy of the file from the agency, by requesting it within the next 60 days, or by asking within one year of having asked for their last free report.

You must also tell the rejected applicant that the credit reporting agency didn't make the decision to reject the person and can't explain the reason for your rejection. Finally, you must tell applicants that they can dispute the accuracy of their credit report and add their own consumer statement to their report. These notices are known as "adverse action reports" and are a requirement of the federal Fair Credit Reporting Act (FCRA). (15 U.S.C. §§ 1681 and following.)

Tenant Screening Checklist

Did you:

❑ Deal with current tenants fairly and respectfully?

❑ Know and comply with fair housing laws, and act consistently?

❑ Give every applicant over age 18 a rental application to fill out?

❑ Thoroughly check out the information on the applications of your top-most likely tenants (check references, get credit reports, and so forth)?

❑ Keep good records documenting your decision to choose (or reject) a particular tenant?

Preparing a Lease and Getting the Tenant Moved In

Many landlords believe that if they've checked a tenant's credit and references, any additional paperwork isn't all that important. So they spend a few bucks to buy a one-size-fits-all lease from a stationery store and feel they're covered. Or worse, they simply shake hands with a cheerful, "See you on the first!"

Their casual approach couldn't be riskier. "Getting it in writing" may seem formal and unfriendly, but it's the only way to really run a profitable business and avoid problems on both sides. Many of the disputes that landlords face with tenants—over rent, deposits, repairs, roommates, pets, or rights to entry—have little to do with whether the tenant is a decent person and everything to do with whether the basic rules of the tenancy were covered in a lease or rental agreement.

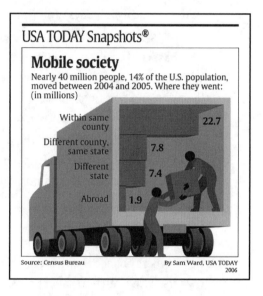

USA TODAY Snapshots®

Mobile society

Nearly 40 million people, 14% of the U.S. population, moved between 2004 and 2005. Where they went: (in millions)

Within same county — 22.7
Different county, same state — 7.8
Different state — 7.4
Abroad — 1.9

Source: Census Bureau   By Sam Ward, USA TODAY 2006

"If the lease spells out what can and can't happen, most people are responsible," says Dennis, a long-time landlord from Petaluma, California. And because state law (and in a few instances, federal and local law) dictates many aspects of the landlord-tenant relationship, it's crucial that your rental document include them, so that both you and the tenant understand the rules of the game.

This chapter will get you started by explaining the key provisions to include in your lease or rental agreement, including the state laws that come into play, and other aspects of preparing this crucial document. And we'll guide you through handling other paperwork and records, such as a move-in checklist inventorying the condition of the rental house, and payment and repair records (to form a paper trail should disputes surface later).

Is the Property Already Rented?

If you've recently bought or inherited rental property, you may also inherit tenants who have existing rental agreements or leases. If they have a lease, you'll need to wait until it expires before changing any of its terms, such as the rent. If they have a rental agreement, you can make changes (such as increasing the rent) with appropriate notice (typically 30 days), following your state rules and any rent control restrictions.

Purchasers. If you're a purchaser, be sure the last owner gives you copies of the lease or rental agreement, plus details on deposits (location and amount), house rules, maintenance and repair records, and all other relevant paperwork.

Inheritors. If you've inherited the property, work with the former owner's executor or trustee (the person in charge of winding up the owner's affairs) to see if the information and documents can be found.

Also take special care that the security deposit is accounted for. Some states require sellers to either refund the deposit, letting the new owners collect them anew, or transfer the deposits to the new owners, with notice to the tenants.

Even if your state doesn't specifically set forth the procedure for handling deposits, it makes sense to do one of the two things described above, even in an inheritance situation. If the deposit isn't properly transferred or returned when you take over, and the tenant later looks to you, the current owner, for its return, you'll probably be stuck returning it, even if you never got it in the first place.

RESOURCE

Where to find a solid lease or rental agreement. *Every Landlord's Legal Guide*, published by Nolo, walks you through the creation of a lease or rental agreement that's valid in your state. For details on this and other Nolo landlord titles, see the introduction to this book.

Which Is Better, a Lease or a Rental Agreement?

Here's a key question to ask when making your first decisions about renting out your property: For what length of time will you and your tenants be mutually committed to your rental arrangement? Do you want to lock both of you in for a year (or more), or do you want to give both sides the ability to call it quits after giving approximately a month's notice?

Leases and rental agreements have a lot in common: Both cover basic issues such as the amount of rent, security deposits, and who can live in the rental unit. The primary difference between them is the length of the tenancy—leases typically last for a year, while rental agreements normally go month to month. Often, but by no means always, your choice will depend on how long you want a tenant to stay. But, since other factors can also come into play, carefully read what follows before deciding.

CAUTION
Watch out for mass-produced, preprinted leases and rental documents. Many ignore state-by-state differences, use illegal or enforceable clauses, or are poorly written and full of hard-to-understand legal language.

How a rental agreement works

A written rental agreement commits you and your tenant to a short rental period, typically a month. It automatically renews each month, unless you give the tenant the proper amount of written notice. State laws usually require 30 days to increase the rent or change another term or to terminate a rental agreement (subject to notice requirements and any restrictions imposed by local rent control ordinances and anti-retaliation and discrimination laws). The tenant can also terminate the agreement on short notice (typically 30 days, although this varies).

TIP

Use a written agreement, even if you're friends. When Amy first moved to California and began renting out her Austin, Texas home, she thought she had the perfect tenant: the roommate she'd been living with all along, plus a friend of his. She says, "We agreed orally that the two would pay a certain rent each month, and give 30 days' notice before moving. So I was pretty surprised when I got an email saying he'd be moving in ten days, and then discovered they expected me to go without half the rent until the other tenant's girlfriend moved in two months later. I eventually got most of the rent covered, but the friendship hasn't fared so well."

How a lease works

A lease obligates both you and the tenant for a set rental period—usually a year, but sometimes longer. With a fixed-term lease, you can't raise the rent or change other terms of the tenancy until the lease runs out. The only exception is when the lease itself allows future, specific changes (such as, "The rent will increase by $100 on October 1, 20xx"), or if the tenant agrees in writing to the changes.

Although a lease offers the security of a long-term tenancy, it can be frustrating to landlords who discover they'd be happier if the tenant departed early. Under ordinary circumstances, landlords can't ask a tenant to move out or convince a court to order an eviction before the lease term expires. There are exceptions here too, however, such as when the tenant fails to pay the rent or violates

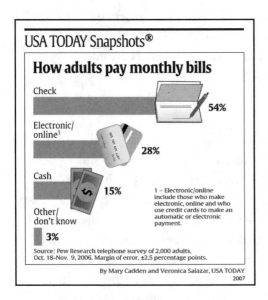

USA TODAY Snapshots®

How adults pay monthly bills

Check — 54%

Electronic/online[1] — 28%

Cash — 15%

1 – Electronic/online include those who make electronic, online and who use credit cards to make an automatic or electronic payment.

Other/don't know — 3%

Source: Pew Research telephone survey of 2,000 adults, Oct. 18–Nov. 9, 2006. Margin of error, ±2.5 percentage points.

By Mary Cadden and Veronica Salazar, USA TODAY 2007

another significant term of the lease, or breaks the law, such as by repeatedly making too much noise, damaging the rental unit, or selling drugs on your property. (We'll explain how to deal with such situations in Chapter 9.)

Which is better for you?

If you're balancing landlording with a full-time job, you're probably best off looking for high-quality, long-term renters who will sign a lease for a year or more. While leases restrict your flexibility, they offer big pluses. For one, tenants are likely to think hard and make a serious personal commitment before entering into a long-term lease, in part because they think they'll be liable for several months' rent if they leave early. (They're not entirely correct in that fear, but we'll get to that later.) And people who plan to live in the property for a long time have an incentive to treat it well.

Many landlords also prefer long-term leases in order to avoid the hassles and expenses of regular turnover, such as cleaning, advertising, showing the unit, checking out applicants, and possibly spending months with no rental income. As Sergio, with rental property in Burlingame, California puts it, "We look for long-term strong tenants who will pay the rent on time and take care of the place. We're not aggressive at raising rents at the end of the year's lease term."

If your area has a high vacancy rate or local landlords have trouble finding tenants for during certain seasons of the year, a lease can be especially good protection. For example, if you're renting near a college that's in session for only nine months a year, or in a vacation area that empties out during summer or winter months, you're far better off with a year's lease. This is especially true if you have the market clout to charge a large deposit, so that a tenant who wants to leave early has an incentive to find someone to take over the tenancy.

Other landlords prefer month-to-month rental agreements, precisely because they offer flexibility, allowing the landlord to increase the rent or end the tenancy on relatively short notice and without giving a specific reason. Kathy, with property in Florida, says, "We don't use a lease, since tenants often need to break it anyway." And Catherine, a Berkeley landlord, explains her preference, "I'm using a month-to-month rental agreement because I used a tenant-matching service and wasn't sure they'd found me someone I'd like to keep over the long term. I've been burned before, by tenants whose life circumstances took a turn for the disastrous."

Also, you may prefer to rent month to month if you're hoping to sell the property within the coming months. Prospective buyers may be put off by the presence of long-term tenants, especially if they hadn't been planning on renting out the property, or if the tenants are paying less than market rental rates. (The new owner takes on the obligations of the previous owner, including leases.) You may also prefer a rental agreement if your house is in a tight rental market where new tenants are easily found and rents are trending upwards.

 CAUTION

A lease guarantees less income security than you'd think. As experienced landlords know, it's usually not hard for a determined tenant to break a lease and avoid paying the remaining rent. A few states allow this without penalty in specific circumstances, such as moving to a health care facility. And nationwide, tenants who enter military service are entitled to break a lease. Most states also require landlords to "mitigate" (minimize) their losses—meaning that if a tenant moves out early, you must use reasonable efforts to find another suitable tenant at the same or a greater rent. If you re-rent the place immediately (or if a judge believes you could have done so with a reasonable effort), the lease-breaking tenant is off the hook—except, perhaps, for having to pay for the few days or weeks the unit was vacant plus your costs of re-renting it.

Why a Verbal Agreement Isn't Really Enough

Legally speaking, oral leases or rental agreements are perfectly valid for both month-to-month tenancies and for leases of a year or less in most states. You and your tenant could, in theory, sit down over coffee and say, "A one-year lease at $1,000 a month, okay?" "Okay." And if you got into a legal spat about the rent, a judge could rule for one of you based on oral evidence alone.

But while oral agreements are easy and informal, using one is never wise. As time passes, people's memories (even yours) have a funny habit of becoming unreliable. You can almost count on tenants claiming that you made, but didn't keep, certain oral promises—for example, to repaint their kitchen or to not increase the rent. Tenants may also forget their own key agreements, such as no subletting. And you probably won't even think to cover certain other issues, such as how deposits may be used. Oral leases are especially dangerous, because they require both of you to accurately remember one important term—the length of the lease—for a considerable length of time.

If something goes wrong with an oral rental agreement or lease, you and your tenants are all too likely to end up in court, arguing over who said what to whom, when, and in what context. This doesn't mean your written agreement needs to be multiple pages long, especially if you know and trust your tenant. But at least get the basic terms written down, including the rent, the length (or term) of the rental, when and where rent is due, and other important matters you've agreed on, such as whether pets will be allowed.

Typical Provisions in Leases and Rental Agreements

Most leases and rental agreements contain a standard set of rental provisions or clauses, often set out as numbered paragraphs. This section explains common terms you should include in your lease or rental agreement, and notes where state laws come into play. Except for the term of the tenancy, leases and rental agreements will usually include the same basic clauses.

RESOURCE

Where to find your state's law. Nolo books and software include complete details on state laws landlords need to know when preparing a lease and running a rental business—from security deposit limits to notice required to end a tenancy. Conscientious landlords include this information in their lease or rental agreement (as recommended below). See the introduction to this book for a list of these resources. You'll also find charts of some of the key landlord-tenant laws in the Property & Money section of www.nolo.com.

Names and addresses of landlord and tenants

Every lease or rental agreement should identify the tenant and the landlord or property owner—called the "parties" to the "agreement." (Agreement is a synonym for contract and may refer to either a lease or a rental agreement.) The tenant is usually called the "lessee" and the landlord is the "lessor." If a property manager or company is authorized to receive notices and legal papers for you, your lease or rental agreement should also include their name and address.

All adults who will live in the rental house, including both members of a couple, should sign the lease or rental agreement. This underscores your expectation that each tenant is legally responsible for the rent (the whole rent, even if roommates have left), for the use or misuse of the property, and all terms of the agreement (a concept known as "joint and several liability").

> **TIP**
> **Gathering signatures is extra important when renting to unrelated roommates.** As Laura, who owns properties in three states, explains: "It can be a hassle when people want to switch roommates—inevitably, one of them takes a job somewhere else, while the other wants to stay. I make sure the lease says I need to preapprove the new person. I also make clear that the remaining tenants need to keep paying the entire rent, and that I'm not going to refund the security deposit if one roommate leaves early. If you're renting to college students, be ready for a lot of this."

If you're signing the lease together with your spouse or other co-owners, you may want to put both names on the lease, particularly if both of you plan to actively participate in managing the property.

Number of occupants

Most leases and rental agreements will specify that the rental property will be the residence of only the tenants and their minor children, and lets the tenants know that they may not move anyone else in as a permanent resident without your consent. Rental documents usually set a limit to the number of people who can live in the rental property.

However, you are not free to set unreasonably low figures (for example, permitting no more than three people for a three-bedroom house) in order to maintain a "quiet atmosphere" or to reduce wear and tear. Federal law requires landlords to allow two persons per bedroom unless you can point to legitimate business reasons justifying a lower number. (Some states are more generous: California, for example, allows two per bedroom plus one more, and Texas and Oklahoma make special allowances for small children.)

Also check your state and local health and safety codes, which probably set a maximum number of tenants based on the size of the property and the number of bedrooms and bathrooms.

CAUTION

You can't discriminate against families with children. Legally establishing reasonable space-to-people ratios is okay, but you can't use overcrowding as an excuse for refusing to rent to tenants with children, especially if you'd rent to the same number of adults. Discrimination against families with children is illegal, except in housing reserved for senior citizens only.

Rental home address and furnishings

The property address is often called "the premises," and this section of the lease should include details on any furnishings, parking space, storage areas, or other extras that come with the property.

If a particular part of the rental property that a tenant might reasonably assume to be included is not, such as a garage you wish to use yourself, be sure you explicitly exclude it from your description of the premises.

Term of the tenancy

The term is the length of the rental. Your agreement should include the beginning date (when the tenant has the right to move in) and whether it's a month-to-month tenancy or a lease. If it's a lease, the ending date should also be specified.

Rent

Your lease or rental agreement should provide specific details on the rent, including:

- **Amount due each month.** Unless you're in a rent-controlled area, you can legally charge as much rent as you want (or, more practically speaking, as much as the market will support). Chapter 1 includes a discussion of how to set rent.

TIP

Raising the rent. If you sign a lease, you won't be able to raise the rent until it expires. You'll have more flexibility with a month-to-month rental agreement.

- **When and where rent is due.** This is your choice, but traditionally rent is due by the first of the month and is mailed to you. If the first falls on a weekend or legal holiday, then rent is usually due the first weekday after that.

- **Acceptable forms of payment.** Specify personal or cashier's check. Accepting cash is a bad idea, because it's risky to regularly handle large amounts of cash.

- **Late fees when rent isn't paid on time.** Late fees can motivate your tenant to make on-time payments. The amount must closely approximate the actual losses you suffer when your tenant pays late, not act as a penalty for late rent. These losses can include the value of your time (or your employee's time) in dealing with the late rent, such as preparing and delivering the notice, plus the interest you're losing because the rent isn't in your bank account (probably minimal). But they can't include indirect consequences, such as late fees on your car payment because you couldn't pay it without receiving the rent check. Also check into (and follow) your state's laws, which might place a legal maximum on the amount of the late fee, and dictate when you can impose it. If your state hasn't set rules, you'll be on solid ground if you: (1) don't apply the late fee until at least three to five days after the due date; (2) charge no more than 4%–5% of the rent; and (3) if you want the late fee to increase each day the rent is late, keep the increases moderate and cap them with an upper limit. An acceptable late charge on rent of $1,000 per month would be $10 for the first day rent is late, plus $5 for each additional day, up to a maximum of 5% of the rental amount.

Rent Control

Laws in only five states—California, the District of Columbia, Maryland, New Jersey, and New York—limit the amount of rent landlords may charge and how and when rent may be increased. Typically, only a few cities or counties in each of these states have enacted local rent control ordinances (also called rent stabilization, rent regulation, or a similar term), but often these are some of the state's largest cities—for example, San Francisco, Los Angeles, New York City, and Newark.

Rent control laws commonly regulate much more than rent. For example, owners of rent-controlled properties must often follow specific "just cause" eviction procedures. And local rent control ordinances may require that your lease or rental agreement include certain information—for example, the address of the local rent control board. In some rent control cities, properties with rents over a specified amount are not subject to rent control (known as "luxury decontrol"), nor are single-family homes.

If you own rental property in a city that has rent control, get your hands on a current copy of the ordinance and any regulations interpreting it. You can count on tenants knowing the rules, and you'll be at a severe disadvantage if you're not up to speed. Check with your local rent control board or city manager's or mayor's office for information.

CAUTION

Don't try to disguise excessive late charges by giving a "discount" for early payment. When the "discount" is substantial, it's simply a roundabout way of charging an excessive late fee, which will make it illegal if challenged.

- **Grace period (if any) before you charge a late fee.** Many landlords don't charge a late fee until two or three days after rent is due, but in most states, you can legally impose the late fee on the due date (that is, you don't need to give a grace period).

- **Bounced check charges.** If your state's law doesn't say how much you can charge, plan on charging what your bank charges you, probably $10–$20 per returned check, plus a few dollars for your trouble.

See Chapter 9 for advice on dealing with tenants who pay rent late or violate another lease term such as moving in extra roommates.

Security deposit

All states allow you to collect a security deposit when a tenant moves in, and hold it until the tenant leaves. The general purpose is to assure that the tenant pays rent on time and keeps the rental unit in good condition. Rent you collect in advance for the first month is not considered part of the security deposit.

It's easy to get into legal trouble over deposits, because they're strictly regulated by state law, and sometimes also by city ordinance. In some states, single-family rentals are exempt from certain aspects of the security deposit rule, such as a requirement to pay interest on the deposit, or to hold it in an account separate from the landlord's personal funds. To avoid disputes, your lease or rental agreement should include details on deposits, including:

- **Dollar amount.** Many states limit the amount you can collect as a deposit to a maximum of one or two months' rent, with the limit sometimes higher for a furnished rental.

- **Restrictions on tenant use of deposit for last month's rent.** Some statutes forbid the tenant from using the deposit as last month's rent. This way, a tenant won't leave you with insufficient funds to cover necessary cleaning and repairs at the end of the tenancy.

- **Where you must keep the deposit and whether you must pay interest.** Several states and cities (particularly those with rent control) require you to put deposits in a separate account and pay the tenant any interest on them. Some states require you to put deposits in a separate "trust" account, rather than mix the funds with your personal or business accounts. Even if you aren't required to keep separate accounts, it's a good idea, as we discuss in Chapter 6.

- **When you must return the deposit.** When a tenant moves out, you'll usually have a set amount of time (in most states, 14 to 30 days) to either return the tenant's entire deposit or provide an itemized statement of deductions and refund any deposit balance.

- **The deductions you may impose.** You can generally withhold all or part of the deposit to cover unpaid rent, damage to the rental property and cleaning costs (outside of "ordinary wear and tear"), or other tenant financial obligations (such as payment of utilities).

CAUTION
Be careful about charging nonrefundable fees. While some states allow landlords to collect a fee that's not refundable (such as for pets or cleaning), most state laws are muddled on the subject. And a few states, such as California, specifically prohibit landlords from charging any nonrefundable fee or deposit. To avoid the legal uncertainties, just factor in the expenses you're worried about when setting the rent, or charge a higher security deposit.

- **How deposit deductions must be itemized when the tenant moves out.** Some states set specific rules and procedures for move-out inspections and preparing itemized statements of security deposit deductions for the tenant.

CAUTION
Watch out for liquidated damages clauses. This item (often found in fixed-term leases) means that if the tenant moves out before the lease expires, he or she is supposed to pay the landlord a predetermined amount of money (perhaps the whole security deposit) to replace whatever amount of rent will be going unpaid. In some states, liquidated damages clauses are unenforceable—which doesn't mean that the tenant can take off scot-free, just that he or she will be liable only for the landlord's actual damages, which the landlord must prove in court.

How High a Deposit Should You Charge?

Normally, the best advice is to charge as much as the market will bear, within any legal limits. The more the tenant has at stake, the better the chance your property will be respected—a particular concern in high-risk situations, like a tenant who has shaky credit or comes with a large pet. And, the larger the deposit, the more financial protection you'll have if a tenant leaves owing you rent. When renting a single-family home, where damage can be more expensive to remedy than similar damage in an apartment, it makes sense to set the deposit as high as you can.

But a high deposit means that prospects need to come up with a large amount of cash that's tied up throughout the tenancy, which may be unattractive to otherwise qualified renters. Here are some alternatives to a high deposit:

Higher rent. Many acceptable, solvent tenants have a hard time coming up with several months' rent, especially if they're still awaiting the return of a previous security deposit from their last rental. These tenants might rather pay a slightly higher rent than an enormous deposit.

Installment payments. You might gain a marketing advantage by allowing a deposit to be paid in installments, rather than as one lump sum.

Renter's insurance. As a term of the lease, in most states you can require the tenant to buy renter's insurance to cover certain damage by the tenant or guests.

Utilities

Your agreement should state who pays for what utilities. Normally, landlords pay for garbage and sometimes for water, if there's a yard. Tenants usually pay for other services, such as gas, electricity, cable TV, and Internet. In single-family rentals, tenants may pay for everything.

Tenant's repair and maintenance rights and responsibilities

A carefully written lease or rental agreement will include a statement that makes tenants responsible for:

- keeping the rental premises clean and in good condition (but not for major maintenance—that should remain part of your responsibility as a landlord)
- reporting defective or dangerous conditions to you, and
- reimbursing you for the cost of repairing damage caused by their abuse or neglect.

Many leases and rental agreements also tell tenants what they can't do in the way of repairs or alterations—such as painting walls, rekeying locks, or adding built-in bookshelves without your permission. Chapter 7 covers landlords' and tenants' rights and responsibilities regarding repairs and maintenance.

You Can't Take Away Tenants' Rights in Your Lease or Rental Agreement

Most states have passed tenant-friendly laws covering subjects such as landlords' access to rental property, the amount and use of security deposits, and tenant rights to a livable home. Tenants also have important legal rights under federal law (particularly in the area of discrimination).

You can't get around these rights by asking tenants to waive them—for example, by including a lease clause saying that the premises are acceptable "as is," or not warranted as fit, safe, secure, or in good repair. Most states will not uphold a clause that diminishes tenant rights to habitable property. (Texas is a notable exception; and in Maine, landlords of single-family homes may shift the duty to maintain a fit home to the tenant.)

Step Aside: Tenants May be Allowed to Make These Repairs or Alterations

In certain narrow situations, tenants can alter or repair the premises regardless of what your lease or rental agreement says. Examples include:

- **Alterations by a disabled person.** Under the federal Fair Housing Act, a disabled person may, with your prior approval, modify living space if needed to make it safe and comfortable. For example, the tenant might need to have the countertops lowered to wheelchair height. Landlords with certain federally financed properties, and those in Massachusetts, must shoulder the modification expense. However, if the modifications will make the unit unacceptable to the next tenant, the disabled tenant must agree to undo them before leaving. Ask for a reasonable description of the proposed modifications, proof that they'll be done in a workmanlike manner, and evidence that the tenant is obtaining any necessary building permits. If you'll need to undo the modifications when the tenant leaves, you can insist that the tenant place enough money to cover the estimated restoration costs in an interest-bearing escrow account (the interest belongs to the tenant).

- **Use of the "repair and deduct" procedure when landlords fail to act.** As explained in Chapter 7, tenants in most states may repair defects or damage that makes the premises uninhabitable or substantially interferes with its safe use or enjoyment.

- **Installation of satellite dishes and antennas.** Federal law gives tenants limited rights to install wireless antennas and small satellite dishes.

- **Specific alterations allowed by state statutes.** Some states allow tenants to install energy conservation measures (like removable interior storm windows) or burglary prevention devices without the landlord's prior consent.

When and how landlords may enter rental property

Nearly every state clearly recognizes the right of a landlord to enter the premises while a tenant is living there, under certain broad circumstances, for example, such as to deal with an emergency (flooding) or when the tenant gives permission. Your agreement should set forth and explain this right.

USA TODAY Snapshots®

Baltimore residents have highest utility bills

Cities with the highest average monthly utility bills[1]:

$371.65 $369.56 $352.52 $348.21 $338.62

Baltimore Phoenix Philadelphia Boston Charlotte

1 – Utility bills include home phone, Internet, television, electricity and natural gas
Source: WhiteFence Index

By Jae Yang and Adrienne Lewis, USA TODAY 2008

Many states have access laws specifying other circumstances under which landlords may legally enter rented premises, such as to make repairs (for example, fix a broken oven), inspect the property, and show the property to prospective tenants and purchasers.

State access laws typically specify the amount of notice required for such entry—usually 24 hours (unless impractical—for example, in an emergency). A few states simply require the landlord to provide "reasonable" notice, often presumed to be 24 hours.

Extended absences by tenant

Some leases and rental agreements require tenants to notify the landlord in advance if they'll be away for a certain number of consecutive days (often seven or more). Such clauses may give you the right to enter the property while the tenants are gone for needed maintenance and to inspect for damage. This type of clause is usually most appropriate for rentals in cold-weather places where landlords want to drain the pipes to guard against bursting.

Limits on tenant behavior and illegal activity

A good lease or rental agreement will contain a clause forbidding tenants from using the rental property or adjacent areas, such as the sidewalk in front of the house, in a way that violates any law or ordinance, including laws prohibiting the use, possession, or sale of illegal drugs. These clauses also prohibit tenants from intentionally damaging the property (called "committing waste," such as by punching holes in the wall), or creating a "nuisance" by annoying or disturbing other tenants or nearby residents—for example, by continuously making loud noise or allowing garbage to pile up.

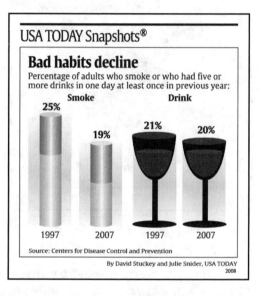

USA TODAY Snapshots®

Bad habits decline

Percentage of adults who smoke or who had five or more drinks in one day at least once in previous year:

Source: Centers for Disease Control and Prevention

By David Stuckey and Julie Snider, USA TODAY 2008

Basically, you can set any kind of restriction you want—as long as it's not discriminatory, retaliatory, or otherwise violates your state law. For example, you may prohibit smoking in the rental property as well as on the deck or in common areas.

We'll discuss some common restrictions involving pets, home businesses, sublets, and guests in the following sections.

Pets

You have the right to prohibit all pets, or to restrict the types allowed—for example, forbidding dogs or cats, but allowing birds. However, you must allow "service" or "comfort" animals used by physically or mentally disabled people (protected by the fair housing laws).

Not every landlord wants to prohibit pets. Allowing them can attract a wider range of tenants. And it offers benefits if you're sharing the property, as Catherine, in Berkeley explains: "I had one great renter who had a dog—we took care of each other's dog when we traveled, shared poop patrol, and more."

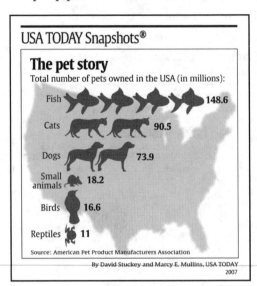

USA TODAY Snapshots®

The pet story

Total number of pets owned in the USA (in millions):

Fish — 148.6
Cats — 90.5
Dogs — 73.9
Small animals — 18.2
Birds — 16.6
Reptiles — 11

Source: American Pet Product Manufacturers Association

By David Stuckey and Marcy E. Mullins, USA TODAY
2007

No matter what you decide, spell out your pet rules—for example, the type and number of pets allowed (such as one cat or one dog under 20 pounds). Also state that the tenants will keep the yard free of all animal waste and keep the dogs on leash and under control (no excessive barking that bothers the neighbors).

See Chapter 8 for a discussion of landlord liability for dog bites and other animal attacks.

> **TIP**
>
> **You may want to waive your no pets policy.** That's what Sarah, a San Francisco landlord of a single-family home, has done in many instances. She explains, "We've said 'No Pets,' but if we find a good tenant, we'll meet the pet and take it case by case. Dog owners in particular seem to be very responsible, maybe because they already have to walk their animals every day. One dog we let move in chewed some stuff up, but the owner was completely willing to pay for it without question." But be careful about waiving your rules when you own a multi-family property. The last thing you want is for a tenant to observe that you're waiving the rules only for some people, and claim that you're refusing to waive the rules for him or her not because the dog appears to be out of control, but because of race, nationality, or another protected characteristic.

Renting to Pet Owners

Open Door, an ambitious program of the San Francisco Society for the Prevention of Cruelty to Animals (SPCA), seeks to show landlords how to make renting to pet-owning tenants a satisfying and profitable experience. The SPCA offers landlords:

- checklists to help screen pet-owning tenants
- pet policies to add to standard leases and rental agreements, and
- free mediation if landlords and tenants have pet-related problems after moving in.

For more information, contact the San Francisco SPCA at 415-554-3000 or via www.sfspca.org/opendoor. Also see *Every Dog's Legal Guide*, by Mary Randolph (Nolo), for more information on renting to pet owners.

Restrictions on home businesses

Are you at all worried that your tenant might run a business from your rental property—potentially burdening neighbors by increasing local traffic, and exposing you to liability if a customer or business associate gets hurt? If so, you may prohibit this with a clause in your lease or rental agreement specifying that the premises are "for residential purposes only." For more on the subject, see "Home Businesses on Rental Property," below.

CAUTION
What if a tenant wants to run a day-care operation in your rental? You may not be able to stop it. Many states give day-care owners the right to conduct business in a rental. However, landlords in California and New York, for example, may limit the number of children. Also, any business a tenant runs must comply with state fire and health regulations regarding minimum facility size and fire exits.

Home Businesses on Rental Property

If a tenant wants to run a business from your rental home, be sure to spell out all the details in your lease or rental agreement. First, you'll need to check local zoning laws for restrictions on home-based businesses, including the type of businesses allowed (if any), the amount of car and truck traffic the business can generate, and other rules about outside signs, on-street parking, number of employees, and percentage of floor space devoted to the business. And if your rental is in a planned unit or a condominium development, check the CC&Rs of the homeowners' association.

Also consult your insurance company as to whether you'll need a different policy to cover the potential liability of tenants' employees or guests. In many situations, a home office for occasional use won't be a problem. But if the business will involve people and deliveries coming and going, such as a therapy practice, jewelry importer, or small consulting firm, seriously consider whether to expand or add coverage. It's not unreasonable to condition your consent on having the tenant pay for the needed additional protection.

You may also want to insist that the tenant buy certain types of liability insurance, so that you won't wind up paying if someone gets hurt on the rental property—for example, if a customer trips and falls on the front steps.

Finally, be aware that a residence used as a commercial site may need to meet the accessibility requirements of the federal Americans with Disabilities Act (ADA). For more information on the ADA, see www.ada.gov.

Restrictions on assignments or sublets

Most leases and rental agreements prohibit "assignments," which happen when your tenant moves out permanently and brings in a replacement tenant for the remainder of the lease. Your rule on prohibiting assignments should state that you won't unreasonably refuse to rent to a proposed newcomer. (That simply reflects your obligation, in most states, to use reasonable efforts to find a replacement once the original tenant leaves.) When you think about it, it's actually to your advantage to have a lease-breaking tenant do the work of finding a suitable replacement.

Your agreement should also prohibit tenants from temporarily renting their (and your) space to someone else while they're away (called a sublet), without your written consent.

Limits on guest stays

It's common for leases to limit overnight guests. For example, you might allow a guest for no more than ten days in any six-month period, with written approval required for longer stays. The idea is to keep long-term guests from gaining the status of full-fledged tenants, who haven't been screened or approved, or signed the lease or rental agreement.

Attorney fees and court costs in a lawsuit

In case of a dispute over the meaning or implementation of a part of your rental agreement or lease, the agreement should specify who will pay the costs of a lawsuit. For example, disputes about rent or security deposits are common. This clause can act as a nice deterrent—even with several properties, Laura says, "I have something in the lease saying the prevailing party will have their legal costs covered, and I've never had a tenant threaten to sue." Attorney fee clauses don't, however, apply to disputes that don't stem from the lease or rental agreement—for example, lawsuits over alleged discrimination.

Grounds for termination of tenancy

Here's an important clause: It states that any violation of the lease or rental agreement by the tenant, or by his or her guests, is grounds for terminating the tenancy according to the procedures established by state or local laws. Chapter 9 provides an overview of how tenancies can be ended.

Lead-based paint and other disclosures

Federal, state, or local laws may require you to disclose certain things about the property before a new tenant signs a lease or rental agreement or moves in, notably the presence of lead-based paint (discussed in Chapter 8). State laws may require other disclosures, too, such as the presence of mold, shared utility arrangements, or recent flooding. And local rent control ordinances often require disclosures, such as the name and address of the government agency or elected board that administers the ordinance.

Some states require landlords to inform tenants of the name and address of the bank where their security deposit is being held, and the name and contact information of the person authorized by the owner to receive legal papers. Check your state and local laws for details on these and other disclosure requirements.

If your property contains a hidden (not obvious) problem that could cause injury or substantially interfere with your tenant's safe enjoyment and use, and the problem is impossible to fix, you're better off legally if you disclose the defective or dangerous condition before the tenant signs the lease. Examples include naturally occurring dangers, such as loose soil, and man-made dangers, such as steep stairs.

USA TODAY Snapshots®

What's in the recycling bin

A little more than three-quarters of adults, or 77%, recycle at home. What adults separate and recycle:

Aluminum or metal cans
67%

Paper
59%

Plastic
57%

Glass bottles
54%

Nothing
23%

Cardboard
3%

Note: Multiple responses allowed.
Source: Harris Interactive online poll of 2,372 adults 18 and older conducted online June 5–11, with figures weighted to reflect the adult population.

By Tracey Wong Briggs and Bob Laird, USA TODAY 2007

Tenant rules and regulations

If your property has more than one unit—even if it's a duplex you share—think about what you might want to require of tenants concerning shared areas like the yard, garage, driveway, or even pool. Also give details on what's considered excessive noise.

There's no need to cover every detail of daily living, however. Landlords of single-family rental houses often find it easier to discuss things like recycling or maintenance tips in a move-in letter, discussed below. To make sure you have some clout, include a clause in the lease or rental agreement giving you the right to terminate the rental arrangement if the tenant repeatedly and seriously violates house rules.

> **CAUTION**
> **Watch out for conflicts with community association rules.** If you're renting out a condo or other property governed by a community association, check to make sure that none of the terms of your lease contradict the CC&Rs or association rules. If, for example, your lease says pets are allowed but the CC&Rs say they're not, your tenant will not be allowed to keep a pet.

Signing a Lease or Rental Agreement

With your lease or rental agreement completely drafted, make an appointment with your new tenants to review and sign this important document. Bring two copies to your meeting (one for you and one for the tenant(s)). Of course, this assumes that you're not interested in negotiating any of the terms. In a soft market, or when you're dealing with prospects whom you really want and might be willing to bend the terms for, you may want instead to negotiate selected issues before your signing meeting.

Before you even think about signing the lease, start with this very important step: Ask for the money, and to be extra careful, don't accept a check. Until you have the tenant's cash, certified check, or money order for the first month's rent and security deposit in hand, signing a rental commitment is a recipe for trouble. Starting with the second rent payment, of course, you may prefer to accept checks (in fact, insisting on cash is inadvisable), and you'll have to trust that your careful tenant screening process weeded out those tenants who would have given you checks that bounce.

Next, encourage tenants to ask questions about anything that's unclear on your lease or rental agreement. "Make sure you sit down with each tenant before they move in and go over the lease, so you both have a good understanding from the beginning about what you expect from each other," says Dennis from Petaluma.

CAUTION

Don't sign until all terms are final and mutually understood.
All of your expectations should be written into the lease or rental agreement before you and the tenant sign. Never sign an incomplete document assuming last-minute changes can be made later. If you've altered a preprinted form by writing or typing in changes, you and the tenant should initial and date each change when you sign the document.

Be sure all adults (18 years of age and older) who will live in the rental unit, including both members of a couple, sign the lease or rental agreement. Doing this makes everyone who signs responsible for all terms, including the full amount of the rent. As Gordon, a landlord in San Jose, California, says, "If you have to evict your tenants, you can evict the guy who signed the lease, but the others may not move out. A smart attorney can get around that, but you can avoid the problem from the get-go if they all sign the lease."

After everyone signs, give one copy of the signed lease or rental agreement to the tenant and keep the other one for your files.

USA TODAY Snapshots®

Dreaming of a dutiful disposal

Most wanted household invention:

Garbage can that cleans and empties itself
60%

Stovetop that cleans itself daily
59%

Dryer that folds clothes
47%

Never-ending roll of toilet paper
39%

Dishwasher that puts dishes away
37%

Automatic desk cleaner/organizer
24%

None
13%

Respondents could choose more than one.
Source: Harris Interactive online survey of 3,588 adults (July 12-16) for S.C. Johnson & Son Inc. Margin of error, ±3 percentage points.

By Mary Cadden and Bob Laird, USA TODAY 2007

Should You Ask for or Accept Cosigners?

Some landlords require cosigners on rental agreements and leases, especially when renting to students who depend on parents for much of their income. The cosigner signs the rental agreement or lease or a separate document, agreeing to cover any rent or damage-repair costs the tenant fails to pay.

In practice, a cosigner's promise may have less legal value than you'd think. Suppose your tenant doesn't pay the rent, and the cosigner doesn't step up. Most landlords will simply evict the tenant, because the alternative (suing in small claims court to force the guarantor to honor the promise) is too much trouble (and is practically impossible if the cosigner lives in another state).

Still, a tenant who thinks you can (and will) notify and sue a cosigning relative or friend may be less likely to default on the rent. Similarly, a cosigner asked to pay the tenant's debts may persuade the tenant to pay, or may (as many parents will) come to the tenant's rescue.

Because of the practical difficulties associated with cosigners, many landlords refuse to consider them, which is legal in every situation but one: If a disabled tenant who has insufficient income (but is otherwise suitable) asks you to accept a cosigner, you must at least investigate the proposed cosigner's suitability. If that person is solvent and stable, federal law requires you to accept the cosigner, in spite of your general policy.

If you decide to accept a cosigner, you may want to have that person fill out a separate rental application and agree to a credit check—after all, a cosigner who has no resources or connection to the tenant will be completely useless. Should the tenant and prospective cosigner object, you may wonder how serious they are about the arrangement. Once you're satisfied that the cosigner can genuinely back up the tenant, add a line at the end of the lease or rental agreement for the dated signature, phone, and address of the cosigner.

Getting the Tenant Moved In

A clearly written and easy-to-understand lease or rental agreement is critical to starting a tenancy. But there's more that can be done to help establish a positive relationship. On or before the tenant's move-in day, set up a time to go over your house rules and important information about the rental, walk through the house, and hand over the keys. Bring a welcome gift such as a bottle of wine or a gift certificate for a local restaurant. Be cordial and allow enough time to answer all the tenant's questions.

Give new tenants a move-in letter and house rules

A good move-in letter will provide all kinds of valuable information for the new tenants, such as:

- your phone numbers (during the day and after hours) and emergency contacts
- how and where to report maintenance and repair problems
- location of garbage cans, trash pickup days, and available recycling programs
- maintenance dos and don'ts, such as how to avoid overloading circuits and use the garbage disposal properly
- where to find appliance manuals, water shut-off valves, smoke detectors, and other important information
- homeowners' association rules (if any), and
- any other useful information about the property and neighborhood.

Many landlords highlight important lease terms in their move-in letter, such as their policy regarding late fees and adding a roommate or pets.

> **TIP**
>
> **Renting out a condo or house in a common-interest development (CID)?** Remember to give the tenant a copy of the community association rules (often called CC&Rs), and emphasize that failing to comply with them may give you no choice but to evict.

Inspect and photograph the rental property

To ward off future arguments, it's absolutely essential that you and your tenant (ideally, together) check the place over for damage and obvious wear and tear before the move-in (but after your own prepping of the property, discussed in Chapter 3). You and the tenant should document what you find with an inventory describing the general condition of each room (and any furnishings), backed up with photos or video, and signed by both (or all) of you.

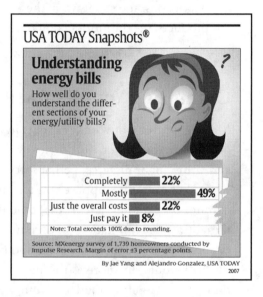

USA TODAY Snapshots®

Understanding energy bills

How well do you understand the different sections of your energy/utility bills?

Completely	22%
Mostly	49%
Just the overall costs	22%
Just pay it	8%

Note: Total exceeds 100% due to rounding.

Source: MXenergy survey of 1,739 homeowners conducted by Impulse Research. Margin of error ±3 percentage points.

By Jae Yang and Alejandro Gonzalez, USA TODAY 2007

Write down, in as much detail as is practical, both serious problems, such as a broken heater, and minor flaws such as a stained kitchen counter, dirty drapes, or faded paint. Ideally, you'll have fixed all major problems before the tenant moves in, but if not, now's the time to do so (especially any habitability or security problems).

This inventory will protect both you and your tenant when the tenant moves out and questions why you withheld all or part of a security deposit. Coupled with a system to keep track of the rental property's condition (as discussed in Chapter 7), your inventory will also be extremely useful if a tenant withholds rent, breaks the lease and moves out, or sues you outright, claiming the unit needs substantial repairs.

Besides just being useful, many states require landlords to give new tenants a written statement on the condition of the rental premises at move-in, including a comprehensive list of existing damages, and give tenants the right to inspect the premises to verify the accuracy of the list and note any problems.

RESOURCE

Where to find a room-by-room inventory and relevant state laws. Nolo publishes several books, such as *Every Landlord's Legal Guide,* that include detailed forms for inspecting and inventorying the rental property at move-in and move-out and making security deposit deductions, and state laws in these areas. For a complete list of Nolo products, see the introduction to this book.

Organizing Your Rental Records

Making written notes of key events in a tenant's rental history, and organizing your rental documents, will come in very handy if you and your tenant disagree, perhaps in court, about what happened and when. For example, suppose you terminate the tenancy of a tenant who chronically paid rent late. If that tenant claims that your real reason was illegal (say, discrimination on account of race), your records, including late fee notices, requests for rent, and bank records will help you establish your true motive. You never want to be in a position where the only evidence before a judge is your word against the tenant's.

Start by setting up a file folder for the following documents (it's also a good idea to keep electronic copies where possible):

- tenants' contact information, including phone numbers (home and work, plus emergency contacts), plus vehicle make, model, color, year, and license plate number
- a copy of your tenant's rental application, references, and credit report
- your copy of the signed lease or rental agreement
- deposit information, including the location and interest-rate terms of your deposit, and
- inventory and photos or video of the condition of rental unit at move-in time.

After your tenant moves in, add these documents to your file:

- your written requests for entry
- rent increase notices and late fee notices
- records of tenant repair requests and how and when they were handled, and
- any other correspondence with your tenant.

Chapter 6 provides advice on keeping important financial and tax records.

CAUTION

Don't keep copies of tenant credit reports. Under the "Disposal Rule" of the Fair and Accurate Credit Transactions Act of 2003, you must destroy the report when you no longer need it. Use a shredder or burn the credit report.

Manage Your Rental Income to Maximize Tax Deductions

D o you know how to give an accountant a supersize migraine? Put the rental payments from your tenants right into your family bank account, dip into the same account when you need to buy things for the property, don't bother saving receipts or keeping records, and let your kids use the maintenance and office supplies you originally bought in connection with the rental property.

This will guarantee that, at the end of the year, you and your accountant tear your hair out trying to figure out whether your rental property business made or lost money, which expenses will be tax-deductible (important if you did make a profit), and whether you were even active enough as a landlord to claim business-owner deductions. In the worst-case scenario, you could end up in an IRS audit, perhaps having to pay back taxes and penalties for disallowed deductions.

But wait, there's a better way: Treat your rental property as a business from the beginning, even if it's only half of your duplex or a spare room in your house. That includes:

- drawing a clear line between your business and personal finances

- taking steps to shield you and your family from personal liability for business debts

- learning what tax deductions you're allowed, how to conduct business so you can claim them, and how to prove you deserve them

- keeping your income and expense records in good order

- making sure you're actually earning a profit, and

- getting professional help when needed.

We'll show you how to do all these things in this chapter. You should read it even if you don't expect to turn a profit—that picture may change, and it's worth developing good habits, and keeping good records, from the start.

TIP

Good financial management translates into a good credit record. Because you're probably operating as a sole proprietor, your ability to pay business bills on time and repay loans is as important to your credit record as how you handle your personal credit card. A good credit record will make it easier to take out loans—which you may need for property improvements or to weather a rough patch. Conversely, a poor credit record will hurt your ability to not only take out loans at reasonable interest rates but accomplish other life goals, like getting a new job. For more on the hows and whys of keeping up a good credit score, see the credit and debt portion of the Nolopedia (www.nolo.com).

Keeping Your Business Finances Separate

It's not hard to keep your personal finances separate from your rental property finances—but it gets harder the longer you wait to create an appropriate system. Start by setting up a separate bank account, which you'll draw on for business expenses.

Opening and using a separate bank account

One of your first steps in becoming a landlord should be to choose your favorite local or online bank and open a separate checking account. If you incorporate your business activities or form an LLC (as discussed below), open the account in the name of that business. If not, just use your own name. (In theory, you could register a separate business name with your state or county government—often called a "DBA," for "doing business as"—but there's little point, because the laws will probably require to include your last name in your DBA anyway.)

> **CAUTION**
> **Shop around for bank rates.** Look for a low-cost or even free checking account, and read the fine print regarding extra fees for things like going below the minimum balance or bouncing a check. Avoid using the word "business" when asking about accounts—some banks immediately raise their checking account rates for businesses, no doubt imagining the massive profits you'll bring in.

Because you'll probably have to spend money on your property before it earns a dime, it's good to seed your checking account with some start-up cash ("capital contributions") from your personal account. Once you start earning rental income, deposit it into your business account and pay all expenses out of that account (after charging expenses to your business credit card, if you have one). Repay yourself for those capital contributions by writing a check to your personal account. When writing checks, always use the memo line to write what the money is being spent on.

> **CAUTION**
> **Landlords in certain states must put tenants' security deposits into a separate bank account.** Adding them to a separate, business account won't do it in these states. (However, your property manager, if you hire one, may take care of this for you.) Check your state's laws, available at www.nolo.com and in *Every Landlord's Legal Guide*, by Marcia Stewart, Ralph Warner, and Janet Portman (Nolo).

Opening and using a separate credit card account

For convenience, you may want to open a separate credit card account for your business. Credit cards are convenient, may offer benefits like cash back, and avoid keeping all of your money in your checking account, which is relatively easy prey for identity thieves.

> **TIP**
> **Already have more than one personal credit card account?**
> You could simply pay one down to a zero balance and start using it
> exclusively for your business.

Be scrupulous by making business purchases on your business credit
card only, even if you find the perfect plants on sale and forgot to bring
the right card. If you must make an exception, save the receipt and write
a memo for your files as soon as you're home, then repay your personal
account out of your business account.

Do your best to pay off the entire credit card debt month by
month—mounting interest can quickly undercut your profits. Credit
card interest rates are typically the highest of any type of loan.

> **TIP**
> **What if you buy something for mixed use?** For example,
> suppose you pick up a tray of ground cover that you'll use partly for
> business and partly for your home. One option is to ask the cashier to
> divide the bill between two credit cards. Another is to pull out both
> your business and personal checkbooks and use separate checks to pay.
> If you must use only one credit card, go with your personal one, then
> make a note for your files and repay the proportional share from the
> business checking account. (After-the-fact conversions of property from
> personal to business raises eyebrows at the IRS.)

Sharing property between your home and business

There's no need to rush out and buy two sets of everything—a new
lawn mower, power saw, or computer, for example. If you already have
or need to buy something at home, you can use it for your business,
too. The catch is that, if you want a tax deduction, you'll need to keep
track of what percentage of the property's use is dedicated toward your
business.

With computers and other "listed property" (described below), that percentage must be greater than 50% for the IRS to recognize the business use. The same is true for property you want to deduct under Section 179 (described below). Telephones are a separate case—the first line into a home is always considered personal, so you can't deduct its cost no matter how much you use it for work (though you can deduct long-distance calls). With other property, however, you can simply take a proportional amount of the applicable tax deduction based on your percentage of business use.

USA TODAY Snapshots®

Top challenges for sole proprietors
What is your primary challenge in running a small business by yourself? Top responses:

Inability to focus on generating new business	35%
Spreading time across multiple projects/roles	27%
Limited resources	23%
Running business more efficiently	23%
Not having enough time to focus on own passions	23%

Lemonade 10¢

Note: Multiple responses allowed.

Source: Visa/Score Sole Proprietor survey of 1,000 sole proprietors 18 and older. Margin of error ±3 percentage points.

By Jae Yang and Alejandro Gonzalez, USA TODAY 2006

A related issue is whether you'll actually decide to create a separate office within your home in order to qualify for the home office deduction. We'll discuss that below under "Deducting for use of a home office."

Shielding Yourself From Liability for Business Debts

We're assuming you're currently operating as a sole proprietorship, meaning you haven't done anything special or filed any papers with your state. You create a sole proprietorship simply by going into business by yourself. The same goes for partnerships: Two people going into business together create a partnership. There's no need to register with the state or sign a partnership agreement.

Starting out as a sole proprietorship or partnership is certainly convenient, but there's a catch: As a sole proprietor or partner, you and your business are legally one and the same when it comes to debts and liability. It won't matter how hard you've worked to keep your books and finances separate. If someone claims you owe them money—perhaps a contractor whom you've refused to pay for shoddy work, or your tenant who sues you for medical costs after slipping on the badly lit back porch—your own assets could be on the line.

That's why some businesses that start out as sole proprietorships or partnerships eventually decide to convert to a separate legal entity, usually a limited liability company (LLC) or a corporation.

> CAUTION
> **No business structure can completely shield you from all liability.** Even if you operate as a corporation or LLC, a creditor can go after your personal assets if, for example, you personally guarantee a loan or lease (which many banks require of landlords); your business owes federal or state income, payroll, or other taxes; or you fail to abide by corporate rules (for example, you mix corporate and personal funds and don't keep records of meetings and shareholders).

Pluses and minuses to forming a corporation

Incorporating means that you formally declare that your business is a separate legal entity from you, its owner. Once you incorporate, the corporate entity becomes responsible for your business's debts and liabilities instead of you (with certain limitations).

The process of incorporating can be a bit worky, however. It involves choosing a name, filing articles of incorporation with your state, paying filing and other fees (often hefty), adopting bylaws, appointing a board of directors (most states allow just one director, who can be you), and issuing shares (probably to yourself).

Running a corporation is also more complicated than running a sole proprietorship or partnership. You'll need to comply with federal and state securities laws concerning record keeping, corporate taxation, and more.

The upshot is that forming a corporation may require more time and expense than you want to invest. For many landlords, the personal liability issue can be dealt with in other ways. See "Alternative ways to minimize your risk," below.

Pluses and minuses to forming an LLC

Limited liability companies, or LLCs, are a relatively new type of business entity, and less complex to form and run than a corporation. Yet, just like corporations, the owners of an LLC are not personally liable for business debts (with similar exceptions).

To form an LLC, you need to file articles of organization with your state, pay filing and other fees, and draft an internal operating agreement. Although you'll have to pay annual fees, you won't have to deal with many of the other ongoing requirements that corporations face, such as holding regular board meetings and keeping minutes. And your taxes will be much simpler, because you can choose to simply pay them through your individual tax return. Again, however, you may want to look for simpler alternatives.

Alternative ways to minimize your risk

Forming a separate legal entity isn't the only way to deal with unexpected events that require you to dip deeper into your own pockets than you can handle. Another important measure is buying adequate insurance to protect yourself (see our discussion of insurance in Chapter 8).

Also, simply behaving in a responsible manner will help forestall problems before they arise—for example, by signing written agreements with contractors to help head off disputes, following health and safety codes, and making repairs and taking other preventative safety measures on your property before a tenant gets injured (as discussed in Chapter 7). See Chapter 2 for more on the pros and cons of LLCs.

Spent a Lot of Money? Take More Tax Deductions!

A surprising number of your landlording expenses can be turned into tax deductions. When Lisa first began renting out the Berkeley, California house she formerly lived in, she says, "I had no idea how much I'd save in taxes—enough that, once I ran the numbers, I went straight to my HR director's office and changed my wage withholding so I could start enjoying the benefits with my very next paycheck. The reason wasn't just the deductions for mortgage interest, property tax payments, and expenses, but the surprisingly large depreciation deduction."

Apart from your day job, you'll hopefully have some new income from the property as well, so you've got every interest in offsetting it with some deductions.

USA TODAY Snapshots®

Two lengthy codes
Number of pages in:

King James Bible **1,472**

U.S. tax code **20,000**

Sources: Amazon.com and Internal Revenue Service

By David Stuckey and Adrienne Lewis, USA TODAY 2005

The basic formula works like this:

- Add up your gross income (mostly rent received over the year).
- Deduct your start-up expenses.
- Deduct your operating expenses (mortgage interest and property tax included).
- Deduct your depreciation and amortization expenses.
- Deduct any Section 179 expenses. (This deduction is much more limited for landlords than other business owners.)
- The result is your taxable income, or the amount the IRS will ask for a bite of.

Let's take a closer look at the various federal tax deductions available to landlords, and how you can make the most of them. Most states also impose income taxes, which you'll have to research on your own—but state income tax laws tend to mimic the federal system. Our goal here is not to provide every legal detail or prepare you to fill out a tax form, but to raise your awareness of likely tax-reducing strategies—and dead-end tax traps.

 TIP

We're assuming you'll really be acting like a business owner. If you're merely a property "investor," you won't have access to as many tax deductions. For example, if you're lax about placing ads, and the property sits vacant for months at a time, the IRS could classify you as an investor (and make you pay penalties and back taxes if you claimed business-owner deductions). The key is to earn a profit by actively running a business by working at it regularly, systematically, and continuously. Hiring a property manager to take over much of the activity still counts, for IRS purposes.

Who Gets the Deductions If You Co-Own?

If you share ownership of your property with someone other than your spouse, you can share the tax deductions, as well. For example, if you take title to the property as tenants in common, you'll have to list each of your percentage ownership interests (60%/40%, for example), on your property deed, and the IRS will expect you to share the expenses and tax deductions in equal proportions.

If you've placed ownership of the property into a partnership or LLC, the deductions will pass through to the partners or members. The deductions can then be allocated among you as you wish, subject to IRS "substantial economic effect" rules (which let the IRS disregard allocations of losses done only to avoid taxes).

This is a complicated area of tax law, so see a tax expert to work out the details.

It's entirely possible—especially if you recently bought the property—that you'll be able to wipe out all your taxable rental income with your expenses, and not have to pay any tax at all on the rental income. Of course, you'll need to keep good records of every penny spent in order to do this. And unfortunately, one of the most valuable contributions you'll be making to your rental property is your own time—and that's not tax deductible.

If you actually show a tax loss on the property, you may be able to deduct the loss from other income, but this gets more complicated. It's governed by what are called the passive-loss and at-risk rules, which we don't cover in this book.

RESOURCE

For in-depth information on all the topics in this section, see *Every Landlord's Tax Deduction Guide*, by Stephen Fishman (Nolo). It also covers some topics not discussed here, such as the tax implications of employing your children, and how to deduct business losses. For personalized advice, consult an accounting or tax professional—you can deduct that expense, too.

Deducting start-up expenses below $5,000

You can deduct up to $5,000 of your start-up expenses the first year you're in business. Start-up expenses are any expenses you incur before offering your property for rent, so long as they're related to getting your business up and running. Once you're in business (that is, after you've placed an ad or otherwise started offering the property for rent), all your expenses are considered operating expenses, which we'll discuss below.

TIP

You may need a business license. Some cities or localities require that all landlords—or at least those whose properties have more than a minimum number of units—pay an annual license fee and possibly undergo a property inspection. Check with your city for details.

Examples of possible start-up expenses include:

- costs of researching and investigating the rental market
- educational information, including how-to books (like this one), classes, or seminars
- attorney and accounting fees (except legal and other fees paid to complete the purchase of the rental property)
- licenses
- insurance premiums
- meals, food, and lodging if you have to travel overnight to get the property ready to rent
- repairs to get the property ready to rent
- office supplies, such as telephone, paper, and notebooks (but not equipment and other long-term assets)
- printing bank checks
- advertising your property for rent (such as ads and signs), and
- any other operating expenses that you paid before offering the property for rent, such as landscaping and gardening costs, property maintenance, and utilities (excluding utility connection fees).

What's absent from the above list? Some pretty big-ticket items, actually. Not only is the cost of the property itself excluded, but all equipment, furniture, appliances, and other property that's expected to last more than one year. These items are considered long-term assets, and are deductible only in limited amounts per year, via depreciation. Also absent from the list are any expenses directly related to the purchase of the property, such as closing costs, escrow fees, attorney fees, travel expenses related to the purchase, title insurance, and transfer taxes. These costs are added to the property's basis and depreciated over time, as described below.

Deducting start-up expenses over $5,000

What if your start-up expenses add up to more than $5,000? You can deduct start-up expenses over $5,000 in equal amounts over the first 15 years you're in business. However, this is a long time to wait to get the full deduction value of your expenditures. One useful strategy is to put the property on the rental market as soon as possible, so that you never run through the $5,000. That automatically triggers the switch into the realm of operating expenses (upon which there's no set limit).

Putting the property on the market doesn't mean you have to do an advertising blitz. Starting with a simple "For Rent" sign on the property will do. Keep proof of your first ad in case of an IRS audit—a date-stamped picture of the "For Rent" sign is all you need.

Another problem with spending more than $5,000 during your start-up period is that, if your expenditures end up exceeding $50,000, you won't get to use the full $5,000 start-up deduction. Your allowable deduction is reduced by any amount you spend over $50,000 on start-up expenses. For example, if you spend $54,000

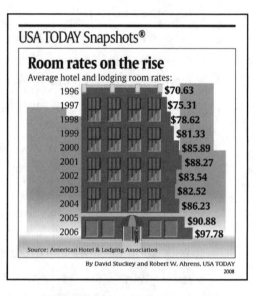

in startup expenses, you'll lose $4,000 of your first-year deduction. That means you'll get a $1,000 first-year deduction and you'll have to spread out (amortize) the remaining $53,000 worth of deductions over the next 15 years.

Deducting operating expenses

The operating-expense deduction is sort of a catchall for the many day-to-day costs you'll face as a landlord. But it doesn't cover everything you might think of. For one, it excludes long-term, capital expenses (such as equipment purchases), which we'll discuss below. For another, it excludes expenses that might be considered excessive or personal. In IRS-speak, you can claim a tax deduction only if an operating expense is ordinary and necessary, current (likely to be used, or used up, within a year), directly related to your rental activity (not for your personal benefit), and reasonable in amount (sorry, no lavish meals, luxury hotel stays, or paying your ten-year old $100 an hour to sweep the deck).

Here are examples of expenses the IRS recognizes as ordinary and necessary to a rental business.

- **Interest payments on mortgage loans, other loans, credit cards** (discussed below).
- **Property and other taxes** (discussed below).
- **Professional fees.** For example, attorney, accounting, property management, and rental broker fees.
- **License renewals.** If you must register your rental with local government, these fees are deductible.
- **Ongoing insurance premiums.** This includes not only homeowners' insurance, but a portion of your car insurance if you regularly use it for your landlord business.
- **Homeowners' association dues.** If your property is a condo, townhouse, or in a community development, you'll be paying association dues, which cover repairs and maintenance.
- **Local transportation expenses.** For example, you might travel from your home office or other office to make regular property visits, shop for supplies, or transfer garbage to the dump. You can deduct either an IRS amount based on mileage, or actual costs of owning and operating your car. Note that if you don't work from home, trips from your home to your landlord-business office or place of business are considered nondeductible commutes.

> **CAUTION**
>
> **Got a traffic or parking ticket while on landlord business?** Don't try to deduct it. For public policy reasons, taxpayers can never deduct government fines or penalties.

- **Out-of-town travel costs.** You may have to travel overnight and outside your city limits to spend time at the property or attend to related business matters (for example, to attend a seminar or visit an attorney). Transportation, hotel, and related expenses like Internet access, phones, and laundry are fully deductible. Meals and beverages are deductible at 50% of their cost. As an alternative to actual meal expenses, you can deduct a standard daily meal allowance, or "per diem" (which varies depending on your destination). If you plan to mix vacation time into your trip, the value of your deduction may be reduced depending on the percentage of time you spent on rental activities—spending at least four hours a day on rental activities will protect you.

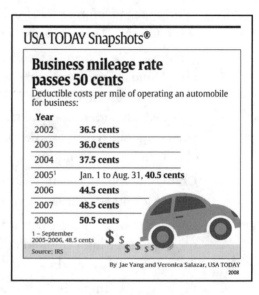

USA TODAY Snapshots®

Business mileage rate passes 50 cents

Deductible costs per mile of operating an automobile for business:

Year	
2002	**36.5 cents**
2003	**36.0 cents**
2004	**37.5 cents**
2005[1]	Jan. 1 to Aug. 31, **40.5 cents**
2006	**44.5 cents**
2007	**48.5 cents**
2008	**50.5 cents**

1 – September 2005-2006, 48.5 cents

Source: IRS

By Jae Yang and Veronica Salazar, USA TODAY 2008

- **Keeping up the property.** Upkeep costs include property repairs, maintenance, cleaning, environmental remediation of problems that arose after you bought the property and in the ordinary course of business operations, and gardening. It doesn't include improvements, or work that makes the property better than it was before —these must be deducted via depreciation, as discussed below.

- **Disability access.** You can deduct the costs of making your property accessible to the elderly or disabled according to the federal Americans with Disabilities Act (ADA) standards (limited to $15,000). This is a special deduction, because such changes would normally be considered "improvements," and subject to depreciation.

- **Office supplies.** You can deduct the cost of supplies you use in your office, including software, paper, postage, and notebooks (but you can't deduct equipment and other long-term assets).

- **Education and information.** Books, magazine or newsletter subscriptions, classes, or seminars are deductible.

- **Advertising and tenant screening.** Unless you rent via word of mouth and skip any screening of potential tenants (a risky step), you'll need at least a "For Rent" sign, and will probably pay for classified ads and prospective-tenant credit checks (of course, if you charge the tenant for the cost of pulling a report, you cannot also deduct this expenditure).

- **Utilities.** If you (not your tenant) pay the gas, water, garbage, electric, or other utility bills, you can deduct them.

- **Business meals and entertainment.** For example, you might take the head of the local landlord association to lunch, to get some free advice. However, these costs are only 50% deductible.

- **Business gifts.** These are limited to $25 per gift recipient per year (however, if you give a gift to all the employees of a business, such as a holiday fruit basket delivered to your gardening service, you may deduct the entire cost, as long as it's reasonable).

- **Membership fees.** Joining a landlords' association would be considered reasonable. But don't try deducting fees for country, social, or athletic clubs.

- **Home office expenses.** You may deduct these expenses, but it's tricky—see the discussion below before deciding to take the home office deduction.

TIP

Renting a unit that's attached to your home? If, for example, you live in half of a duplex, or have a cottage on your property, you'll need to figure out what portion of the property expenses are personal, and what portion can be called rental operating costs. The easiest way to do this is to calculate the percentage of square footage occupied by the rental unit, then apply that percentage against your overall costs for household operating expenses like insurance, utilities, mortgage interest, landscaping, and repairs and maintenance. Of course, some items can be separately calculated. For example, if you have separate yards with a fence in between and the gardener charges separately for each, or separate utility meters, use these figures.

Deducting mortgage and other loan interest

In most cases, interest you pay on loans taken out to pay expenses on your rental property are tax deductible. By contrast, if you took out a loan using your rental property as security, but spent the money on personal things, the interest wouldn't be deductible.

Unless you've inherited a paid-off property, or converted a house you lived in for many years, the mortgage interest on your rental property may be among your biggest expenses. Your monthly mortgage payment is composed of principal (a direct repayment of what was borrowed) and interest, or the amount you pay the lender for the privilege of using its money. You can't, unfortunately, deduct your principal payments as an operating expense.

However, your interest payments are tax deductible in the year you pay them. This includes any private mortgage insurance (PMI) premiums that your lender requires (which is likely if you made a low down

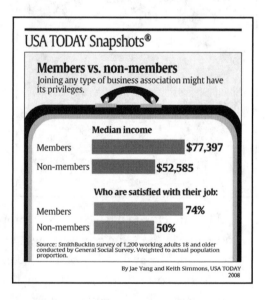

payment, because this insurance protects the lender against your default). You may not deduct, at least for the current year, the points you paid to get your mortgage (unlike the rules for primary homes); these must ordinarily be spread out over the term of the loan before deducting them.

Will you be taking out a loan to improve the property (for example, add a room or remodel)? Your interest payments on this loan are also deductible.

Loans you take out to repair the property, such as a home equity loan, are treated slightly differently. In these cases, you may deduct not only the interest paid, but the principal amount during the years that you repay it.

Finally, interest paid on your business credit card can be deducted (but remember, you should be paying your card off monthly, except in emergencies). You can also deduct interest on a car loan, even if you use your personal car for business—just figure out what percentage of the time you use the car for business, and then deduct that percentage of the loan interest.

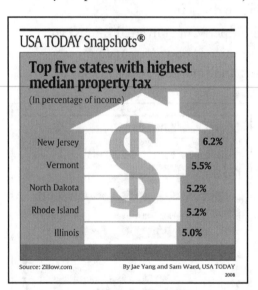

USA TODAY Snapshots®

Top five states with highest median property tax

(In percentage of income)

New Jersey	6.2%
Vermont	5.5%
North Dakota	5.2%
Rhode Island	5.2%
Illinois	5.0%

Source: Zillow.com   By Jae Yang and Sam Ward, USA TODAY 2008

Deducting property-tax payments

Although the United States has no federal property tax, your state, local, and municipal governments may all be poised to extract property taxes from you. Fortunately, you can deduct these as an operating expense.

How much you'll have to pay in property tax each year usually depends on the value of your house, but thousands of dollars a year is common. The availability of a tax deduction will offset only a fraction of the full cost, so always check whether you're being overcharged. Your state will allow you to appeal the assessment within a certain time period, which is worth following up on if the assessment is demonstrably off base. Unfortunately, you can't count on your assessment going down when house values do, as described in "Why Property Taxes May Go Up Even When Home Values Drop," below.

Why Property Taxes May Go Up Even When Home Values Drop

Reporting in 2007, USA TODAY's Dennis Cauchon found that property taxes were rising nearly everywhere for homeowners even as house prices were falling in many parts of the country.

A key reason: Despite the downturn, the market value of millions of homes still exceeds their assessed value used for tax purposes.

"Some people are irritated to learn the news," says Jim Todora, a property tax assessor in Sarasota County, Florida. "Their home's value may have gone down, but their property tax is still going up."

Property tax limits were passed to prevent big increases during times of soaring home values. Those laws let assessments rise, slowly but steadily, until they reach market value.

Property taxes from homeowners and businesses go mostly to local governments, paying for schools, roads, police and other services. Collections rose 7% last year to a record $377 billion, although the median home price climbed just 1% nationwide and fell in many places. The disconnect is likely to continue.

All but five states limit how quickly property taxes can rise. After a decade of soaring housing prices, it can take years for a home's tax value to catch up to its market value, even with the current dip.

In the long run, property tax limits save homeowners money. Clark County, Nevada, Treasurer Laura Fitzpatrick would owe $4,781 in taxes on her Las Vegas house if it were assessed at market value. Instead, she'll pay $3,036. "Those are big savings, even if this year my taxes went up more than the value of my house," she says.

Other reasons few tax bills will shrink:

- **Higher tax rates.** Many local governments where home values have softened—including the Washington, DC suburbs of Northern Virginia—are increasing tax rates to offset lower assessments. The city of Fairfax, Virginia, for example, plans to raise its tax rate by 4.5% to offset a 3% decline in house values.

Why Property Taxes May Go Up Even When Home Values Drop, cont'd

- **Delayed assessments.** Property taxes often are based on market values that are several years old. New Hampshire revalues property once every five years, most recently in 2006 when prices peaked.

"People read about how the market has crashed," says Polk County Assessor Jim Maloney in Des Moines. "But that change doesn't show up for a long time."

 "Property taxes up as house prices fall; Most values higher than assessments," by Dennis Cauchon, April 25, 2007.

RESOURCE

Interested in your state's assessment rules? Go to the tax assessor's page on your local government's website (www.netronline.com is a useful portal for individual counties) or view summaries on websites like www.retirementliving.com.

Deducting for use of a home office

If you use part of your own home regularly and exclusively for your rental property business, you may be able to deduct a portion of the related home expenses—such as your mortgage interest, utility bills, cleaning, and home repair costs. And the home office deduction would let you deduct the full amount of any expenses that are solely and directly connected to your home office, such as painting the room and adding a rug or lamp.

But there's a major catch to this deduction. Unless you can really set aside space and equipment in your house for exclusive business use, you'll have trouble qualifying for the deduction. It doesn't have to be a whole room. If you can at least set off part of a room for exclusive use, you may yet qualify—but you'll get less of a deduction, due to the small size of the area identified as your home office. And even in a small section of a room, you may need the same desk area and computer to manage your landlord business as to handle personal bills, not to mention surf the Web and send personal emails—so you couldn't meet the exclusive use test.

If you sell your house, you'll have to pay capital gains tax on the profit earned from the area used as a home office within the last two years. Normally, without your home office, the capital gains tax exclusion of $500,000 for married couples filing joint returns and $250,000 for singles would shield a nice chunk of your profits. But if, for example, you claimed one-fifth of your home as a home office, you'd lose the benefit of that exclusion for one-fifth of your sale profits, which would become fully taxable.

Deducting for depreciation

Depreciation deductions can be complicated—but lucrative enough to be worth spending time learning about. In any case, depreciation is not an optional deduction. Even if you choose to ignore it, the IRS will dock you when you sell the property (in effect, by adding the depreciation you should have claimed to your sales profits, upping your capital gains tax bill).

The basic concept of depreciation is that the cost of certain assets are not everyday operating costs—yet deserve some sort of tax deduction—because the asset will:

- last for over a year
- get worn out or used up over time
- remain in your hands as owner for more than one year, and
- be used in your rental business.

Examples of common depreciable assets for landlords include the rental building and its structural components, personal property bought for the rental property (such as appliances, furniture, and carpets), and personal property bought for use on the rental property, such as tools and equipment.

CAUTION

Receipts aren't always enough. For certain types of depreciable property, called "listed" property, the IRS will want to see documentation showing that you actually used it for your business, not for your personal life. Listed property includes cars and other vehicles, motorcycles, boats, airplanes, computers, cell phones, and property used for entertainment, recreation, or amusement, such as cameras and stereos. You'll need to keep a log book showing when and how the property is used. (One exception to the record-keeping requirement is for computers used 100% for business—you don't need to keep records.)

You can either combine the depreciation of your rental property (all buildings, components, and improvements) with the personal property assets inside it (such as appliances), or depreciate them separately. Separating them is harder, but although it won't increase your total deductions, it can give you higher deductions in the early years of ownership.

How long the depreciation period lasts. Instead of deducting your asset costs in the year you pay them (as with a regular deduction), you spread out your deductions over a certain number of years (the "recovery period"). The IRS provides preset recovery periods, based in part on how much time it thinks will pass before the asset wears out or gets used up.

The IRS also offers more than one possible method for divvying up the total depreciation amount for each year. These methods go by names like "straight-line" (the same amount every year) and "accelerated" depreciation. We're not going get into their details here; you can find more information in *Every Landlord's Tax Deduction Guide*, by Stephen Fishman (Nolo), and in IRS Publication 946, *How to Depreciate Property*.

In the case of real estate and structural components, the deduction is spread over 27.5 years—by which time the buildings are assumed to have "worn out." Of course, the land itself won't wear out, which is why land can't be depreciated—you have to subtract its value from your purchase price before taking the depreciation deduction. (This is true even for condo owners, despite the fact that you don't personally have title to any land. But you still own an interest in commonly held land, the size of which should be listed on your deed.)

Other assets have a much shorter recovery period, in most cases five or seven years, and only three years for software. The shorter the recovery period, the sooner you get the full value of your deduction. For that reason, you'll probably need to do some research before deciding how to claim your deduction. You'll soon realize there's a history of arguments between taxpayers and the IRS about issues like whether carpeting is personal property (with a five-year recovery period) or a structural component (with a 27.5-year recovery period). (The current view is that carpeting is a structural component if it's glued down, while it's personal property if it's tacked down. But the conclusions aren't that consistent on other property, like tiles.)

When the recovery period ends prematurely. If you sell your property before the recovery period is up, you can't continue to take the deduction. In fact, you must stop taking depreciation for any asset that you either sell, destroy, dispose of, or stop using for your rental business before the recovery period ends.

CAUTION

Buying art, collectibles, or antique furniture for your rental? Don't expect to depreciate it. Although such items might eventually wear out, the fact that they're increasing in value in the meantime make them ineligible for depreciation.

How to calculate each depreciable asset's true cost. As mentioned earlier, the cost of buying a house is more than its purchase price. You can add in attorney fees, closing costs, transfer taxes, and the cost of making later improvements to the property. Added together, these are called the property's "basis." The full basis of a piece of property can be depreciated.

What if you inherited the property, and so didn't pay a dime for it? You're still expected to claim depreciation deductions for it. Since you obviously can't use its purchase price as your starting point, your "basis" is instead its fair market value at the time of the previous owner's death. Of course, you still need to subtract out the value of the land.

Rather than buying or inheriting property that they decide to rent out, some owners convert a property that they previously lived in to rental use. In this case, your basis for depreciation purposes is either the property's fair market value on the date of the change, or your own adjusted cost basis in the property on that date, whichever is less.

> **RESOURCE**
> See IRS Publication 551, *Basis of Assets*, for more detail on calculating cost basis.

How to depreciate additions and improvements. When you add to or improve your rental property, you must separately depreciate the new structures or components. Examples of additions or improvements might include adding a new room, replacing the roof, remodeling, replacing appliances, adding fences or other structures, or installing new plumbing or wiring. The recovery period for these is 27.5 years. A simple repair (which returns the property to the condition it was in before the problem arose that required fixing) is not an improvement.

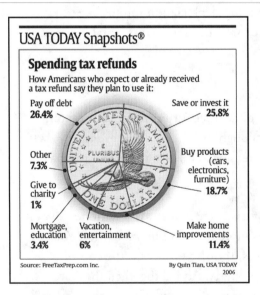

USA TODAY Snapshots®

Spending tax refunds

How Americans who expect or already received a tax refund say they plan to use it:

Pay off debt **26.4%**

Save or invest it **25.8%**

Other **7.3%**

Buy products (cars, electronics, furniture) **18.7%**

Give to charity **1%**

Mortgage, education **3.4%**

Vacation, entertainment **6%**

Make home improvements **11.4%**

Source: FreeTaxPrep.com Inc.

By Quin Tian, USA TODAY 2006

Interestingly enough, certain changes to the land itself can be depreciated, including grading, clearing, excavations, and landscaping. However, the recovery period for these is 15 years.

Figuring out which work constitutes an improvement and which constitutes a repair can be tricky—and it's in your interest to classify as much as possible of the work as repairs, so that you can immediately deduct their costs. You can plausibly claim that some parts of a project are repairs and some are improvements. For example, you might have your kitchen floors redone after the dishwasher floods (a repair) and also install a new dishwasher (an improvement). See the list of examples of improvements below.

IRS List of Examples of Home Improvements	
Additions	Walkway
Bedroom	Fence
Bathroom	Retaining wall
Deck	Sprinkler system
Garage	Swimming pool
Porch	**Interior Improvements**
Patio	Built-in appliances
Heating & Air Conditioning	Kitchen modernization
	Flooring
Heating system	Wall-to-wall carpeting
Central air conditioning	**Insulation**
Furnace	Attic
Duct work	Walls
Central humidifier	Floors
Filtration system	Pipes and duct work
Plumbing	**Miscellaneous**
Septic system	Storm windows, doors
Water heater	New roof
Soft water system	Central vacuum
Filtration system	Wiring upgrades
Lawn & Grounds	Satellite dish
Landscaping	Security system
Driveway	

Depreciation exception: Section 179

A piece of the tax code called Section 179 lets business owners deduct the entire cost of certain long-term personal property in one year, rather than having to depreciate it. This allowance is subject to a maximum annual deduction of $250,000 in 2008. It changes annually, with the limit scheduled to go back down to $128,000 in 2009 and 2010 (plus inflation adjustments), then to $25,000 in 2011. It's also limited to the total of your profit from all your businesses and your salary (if you have one).

Unfortunately, because of its various rules and exceptions, this section is nearly useless for landlords. You can use it only for personal property not contained in your rental property, such as computers, office equipment, office furniture, and business vehicles. On top of that, Section 179 property must be used for your business more than half the time, and you must have purchased the property in the year you claim the Section 179 deduction.

Proving What You've Spent: Record Keeping

To save yourself from stress next April, track your income and expenses as they arise. That will give you a clear picture of your rental property's profitability, and help you claim the maximum in tax deductions. For example, without a paper trail, you won't be able to easily convince the IRS that the cleaning supplies you bought on a certain date were not for use in your home, but were used to prepare your vacant rental for an open house (and are therefore deductible).

> **TIP**
>
> **How long should you keep financial records?** The IRS expects you to keep any receipts and other records concerning the property's purchase and capital improvements for as long as you own the property. (And because repairs and improvements can be hard to distinguish, it's worth keeping repair records around, too.) The rest should be kept for three to five years, depending on local law. But if a child is ever injured on your property, keep those records permanently, since the claim could arise years later.

According to Kathy, who rents out a duplex in Seffner, Florida, "At first, when we bought our duplex, the mortgage payments wiped out all our rental income, so I didn't bother much with keeping track of expenses for tax purposes. But now, 28 years later, with the place paid off, you can bet I record everything—like my mileage when I go to the property, or my mileage to the bank when I make a deposit. It all goes into a ledger I keep."

Here's how to begin; and if at some point you own more than one rental property, follow the same system to separately track your expenses for each:

- **Buy a receipt book.** Some states require you to give tenants a receipt, but it's a good practice in any case, especially if they sometimes pay with cash. The receipts should list the tenant's name, amount paid, date paid, and mode of payment (including check number).

- **Create files for expense receipts.** Each file should be labeled with one expense category, for example "Start-up Expenses," "Operating Expenses," and "Depreciable Property Expenses." Also keep separate files for your bank and credit card statements, filed in chronological order.

- **Make sure your expense receipts make it into the files.** Receipts are important—the IRS won't necessarily accept, for example, a canceled check alone as proof of what you purchased, because it contains no independent verification of what you spent the money on. But you won't always be near your filing cabinet when making a purchase. Some landlords like to keep a separate envelope in their purse or glove department, making it easy to slip the receipt in right after buying something. Write on the receipt what the item was, why you bought it, and, if you paid by check, the check number. Transfer these regularly to your file.

- **Track your cash spending.** A handful of quarters into the parking meter, a couple bucks for highway tolls, a few more dollars for cleaning fluid—it adds up. Your purse or glove compartment makes a handy place to keep a little notebook, in which you record every cash purchase, including the amount, date, and business purpose. If the cash came out of your personal account, repay yourself from your business account using a check, to create an automatic record. Like any normal human, you may sometimes forget to follow all these practices, so try to avoid using cash whenever possible.

- **Ask servicepeople for detailed, and in some cases split-up invoices.** An invoice that states what was done, and preferably describes it in terms of "repairing, patching, replacing," and so forth, will help show whether the expense was for a repair or an improvement. Or if an electrician both repairs the wiring in your rental property and adds new wiring to a new porch on that property (an improvement), asking for separate invoices will allow you to deduct for the repair this year while depreciating the improvement cost. Invoices help in mixed-use situations, too. For example, if you're renting out one unit of the duplex you live in and a roofer redoes the shared roof, asking for separate invoices will allow you to pay one from your business account and one from your personal account.

- **Keep a log showing use of listed property.** As mentioned earlier, cars and other modes of transport, cell phones, and various entertainment devices can be claimed as tax deductions only if you can show you used them for your business, not personal use. Whether you create a computer document or make notes in a folder, keep track of the dates and uses of these items.

- **Track long-distance phone calls on your personal phone.** If your property is far away, long-distance calls become part of your tax-deductible operating costs, in which case another notebook is in order. Keep track of the date, time, and purpose of your calls. (Or, you could just get a separate phone.)

- **Track use of your personal car on rental business.** As a first-time landlord, you're probably not going to invest in a new business car. That will probably mean logging a lot of miles in the family car. That expense notebook in the glove compartment? You can also use it to log the date, destination, before-and-after odometer readings, and purpose of your car trips (for example, to the rental property, the hardware store, or the bank). If you wish, you can stop doing this after 90 days (or after one week each month), call that your "sampling period," and use the results to extrapolate your rental mileage for the entire year. If a trip is for mixed purposes—for example, you drive from your home office to the dump with garbage from both your home and rental property, you can call it a business trip.

- **Keep business property separate or identifiable after you've bought it.** Whenever you buy things with your business account—perhaps new paint, a screwdriver, or office supplies like postage stamps and a printer and paper—keep them in a separate place, label them as business property, or do whatever else will remind you not to convert them to personal use.

- **Keep notes on tenant complaints.** If a tenant raises an issue that leads to a repair, having a record will help establish that the work was indeed a regular operating expense, not part of a larger improvement.

- **Make calendar notations about your business activities.** Both when you're at home and if and when traveling for rental reasons, having notes in your calendar regarding what you did and who you met with will help support your expense-deduction claims.

- **Save paperwork.** Don't throw away correspondence (including email) related to your rental property. Hang onto relevant business cards. Agendas from seminars or conventions you attend are also valuable pieces of your paper trail if you're ever audited.

Are You Rich Yet? Tracking Income and Expenses

Take another look at the projections you made regarding annual income and expenses in Chapter 1. You'll want to run the same type of numbers once you're in business, on a monthly basis—and using real, not projected numbers. The idea is to pull information from your bank and credit card statements and files of invoices and receipts, keep tabs on whether your income and expenses are balancing out as expected, and find out what's actually left in the till. If you're using a property management company, it should send you monthly financial reports—and you should review them carefully and raise any relevant questions.

You can do a bare-bones analysis the old-fashioned way, using the Monthly Income/Expense Worksheet below, a pencil, and a calculator. Of course, some months will be odd ones, for example if you paid your taxes or bought a large piece of equipment. The purpose is not to create an average, but to get regular snapshots of your expenses and your cash on hand. As you look back over these worksheets, you'll be able to spot which months you need to plan ahead for.

Unfortunately, a simple analysis like this one leaves out many factors, like the impact of tax deductions. And handmade worksheets are hard to work with at tax time. (We put more categories above than you'll find on Schedule E, to make sure you didn't forget anything.) That's why many landlords find it worthwhile to invest in an accounting software package. Co-author Michael Molinski, for example, finds *QuickBooks* (for general small-business use) easy to adapt and use. Quicken also gets high customer ratings on its *Rental Property Manager*, which not only allows you to track your expenses, income, and tax deductions, but also converts the information into a Schedule E at tax time and provides helpful tips for managing your property. Another well-regarded software package is *TenantPro* (http://tenantpro.com/), whose customers appreciate its level of technical support.

You can also hire an accountant to put all your rental data together and produce financial reports. You'll have to decide whether the cost is worth the reduced effort on your part.

Monthly Income/Expense Worksheet	
Month: _____ Year: 20_____	
EXPENSES	
Advertising and tenant screening	$
Local transportation	$
Out-of-city travel, meals, lodging	$
Cleaning and maintenance	$
Homeowners' insurance (if not included in mortgage payment)	$
Legal and other professional fees (accountant, property manager)	$
Mortgage payment (principal and interest, plus property taxes and insurance, if included)	$
Other loan payments	$
Repairs	$
Supplies (for office and rental property)	$
Income tax	$
Property tax (if not included in mortgage payment)	$
Utilities (if not covered by tenant)	$
Gifts and entertainment	$
Licenses	$
Homeowners' association dues (in condos and some developments)	$
Educational publications, subscriptions, and memberships	$
Tools and equipment	$
Construction and improvements	$
Other, miscellaneous expenses	$
TOTAL EXPENSES	**$**
INCOME	
Rental income	$
Other income (such as late fees, interest on security deposit, or damage reimbursements; landlords of multi-unit properties may also charge for items like laundry or parking)	$
TOTAL INCOME	**$**
RESULTS	
Net income this month (total income − total expenses)	$
Cash remaining from last month (get from last month's worksheet)	$
Total cash on hand this month	$

At the other end of the spectrum is the minimalist approach espoused by Phil, a landlord in Berkeley, California, who says, "We're somewhat accidental landlords, with only two units, and I just put all my records and receipts into one folder and use *Turbo Tax* at the end of the year. We don't even have an accountant—*Turbo Tax* has a premier version that addresses rental real estate." If you take Phil's approach, at least be scrupulous about running all expenses through your business checking account, and reviewing your monthly statements to make sure your balance is as expected.

How Much Cash to Keep in Reserve

As soon as you start turning a profit (which may take months or years), think about setting some of it aside for a rainy day. (We're assuming you're already setting aside enough to cover irregular expenses like property taxes and insurance.) It's simply bad business practice to spend everything in your business account and leave nothing to fall back on. That means resisting the temptation to either churn your profits back into property improvements or make them your weekend play fund.

Instead, take a portion of your business profits and transfer them to an interest-earning savings account. (This is comparable to the "emergency fund" that financial advisers suggest you keep for your family, with three to six months of living expenses, just in case of a job loss or other emergency.)

How much should you keep in your reserve fund? As with your main property, it's best to set aside enough to pay for unexpected events like the roof starting to leak or a flood in the basement. Experts recommend saving the equivalent of 5% of a home's purchase price (or current value) each year to cover maintenance and repairs. Also keep enough to pay the mortgage and other monthly costs if the tenant unexpectedly moves out. This should cover as many months as are appropriate given the local average vacancy rate.

What to Do When Expenses Exceed Income

What if you're still not making any business profits, and are perhaps struggling to cover the rental property's expenses? This can be both a short-term problem, in terms of how you pay the bills, and a long-term concern if your goal is to hold onto the property for a certain length of time. Here are the first steps toward dealing with the situation:

- **Figure out whether the problem is short or long term.** It's not uncommon to get into a temporary cash crunch—for example, because a tenant moves out unexpectedly and the place needs repainting before you rent it again. Your approach to that can involve temporary, stopgap measures—unlike situations where the monthly rent never covers monthly expenses. Also, if the tenant has simply stopped paying rent, see Chapter 9 for a discussion of how to restart the flow.

- **For short-term problems, look for sources of financing.** Can you loan cash to the business from your personal funds? That's a rational approach, as long as you can spare the money and you keep records of the transfer. However, it may mean shifting money that's currently held in stocks, bonds, or other investments. Talk to your financial adviser about whether, given the comparative rates of return between your real estate investment and others, this shift would be wise. If not, or if you don't have any personal sources of cash to draw upon, consider a home equity loan or line of credit from a bank; you'll be able to deduct the

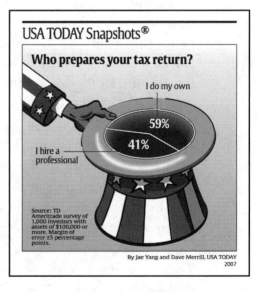

USA TODAY Snapshots®

Who prepares your tax return?

I do my own 59%

I hire a professional 41%

Source: TD Ameritrade survey of 1,000 investors with assets of $100,000 or more. Margin of error ±5 percentage points.

By Jae Yang and Dave Merrill, USA TODAY 2007

interest at tax time. Use credit cards only for minor expenses or as a last resort, due to their high interest rates.

- **Look at your largest outflows for areas to cut.** For example, can you cut expenses by refinancing your mortgage, shopping around for cheaper homeowners' insurance, or (if you're paying utilities) performing energy-saving repairs like sealing cracks?

 TIP

Make sure you're in good communication with your tenant. Some cash crunches come about because the tenant isn't in the habit of calling you about minor maintenance issues before they turn into expensive emergencies. Such a situation often develops when landlords aren't responsive to tenants' early calls. And you need to stay on top of things like collecting late rents or terminating a tenancy for nonpayment.

- **Look into raising the rent.** Unfortunately, you can't do this every time cash is tight. If your tenant has a lease, you'll have to abide by its terms until the expiration date (though you could offer to buy the tenant out). And you'll have to comply with state and local laws governing rent increases, not to mention take into account local market conditions. See Chapter 1 for a full discussion of when and by how much you can raise the rent.

- **Prioritize your debts.** Put off paying your bills until close to their expiration date, and talk to creditors about accepting even later payments where possible. But whatever you do, don't miss a mortgage payment. If the problem is serious enough that you'll have trouble paying the mortgage, talk to your lender about workout options. For details, see the foreclosure section of the free Nolopedia at www.nolo.com.

- **For long-term problems, reexamine the numbers.** Go back to the analysis you did in Chapter 1 and reconsider whether the property is likely to sufficiently appreciate in value to make your current losses worthwhile. Also talk to your tax or financial adviser about whether the losses will help you shelter other income (a complex area requiring individual advice). If keeping the property no longer looks worthwhile, see Chapter 11 for advice on selling.

Finding Professionals to Help You

Plenty of first-time landlords get by without professional advice, relying instead on software programs for bookkeeping and tax preparation. But hiring a professional can make your life easier, and potentially help you save money in the long run. Below are the most likely categories of pros to help you. Notice that the list doesn't include so-called "tax preparers," of the sort you'll see in storefront offices during tax time. In most states, no licensing is required to be a tax preparer, so we don't advise taking your chances on them.

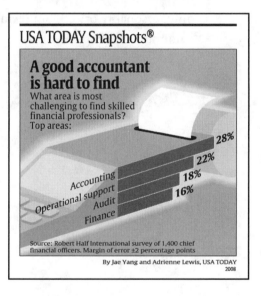

USA TODAY Snapshots®

A good accountant is hard to find

What area is most challenging to find skilled financial professionals? Top areas:

Accounting 28%
Operational support 22%
Audit 18%
Finance 16%

Source: Robert Half International survey of 1,400 chief financial officers. Margin of error ±2 percentage points

By Jae Yang and Adrienne Lewis, USA TODAY 2008

- **Enrolled agents (EAs).** With at least five years of experience and licensing from the IRS, these are a reliable choice for tax advice and tax return preparation.
- **Certified public accountants (CPAs).** These provide sophisticated accounting and tax work, and are licensed and regulated in each state.
- **Licensed public accountants.** These are also reliable, though not as highly regarded as CPAs.

- **Tax attorneys.** If you get into serious trouble with the IRS or other tax agency, an attorney can provide legal representation. But for most tax advice, consulting a CPA will be more cost effective.

Here are some tips for choosing a qualified professional:

- **Get recommendations.** Ask friends, business associates, or your local landlord association.

- **Look for experience in assisting landlords.** You're dealing with sometimes unique issues and tax considerations, so it helps to have an accountant or tax pro who's familiar with them.

- **Interview two or three prospects.** Choose the one who is not only reasonably priced, but seems knowledgeable and easy to communicate with. ●

Keeping Things Shipshape: Repairs and Maintenance

Everyone wants a nice place to call home, including your tenant. And while you're not required to turn the place into a palatial estate, you are responsible for keeping it in good repair and in a habitable condition. Besides, if someday you want to move back into this home, or retire in it, undoing years of poor maintenance will be a major bother.

To show you what your responsibilities entail, this chapter will cover:

- your responsibilities, and the tenant's responsibilities, for keeping the property livable

- how to prevent and respond to problems, and

- whether to hire the tenant or someone else to help you meet some of your repair and maintenance obligations.

Keeping your property in good repair requires some upfront work, but it will help keep your tenants happy—and a happy tenant will likely complain less and stay longer, reducing turnover and interruptions to your income stream. If you end up with a tenant whose repair demands are unreasonable (asking for cosmetic upgrades, not genuine repairs), having a fundamentally safe and sound rental will also let you confidently decline such requests.

Finally, regular attention to upkeep may prevent more major (and expensive!) problems later, because you'll catch the small repairs early. In the long run, that will save you money, reduce the chance of injuries, and ultimately translate into lower insurance premiums.

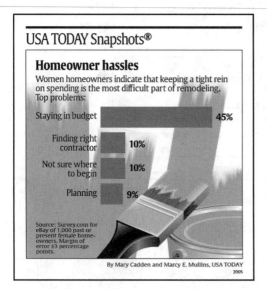

USA TODAY Snapshots®

Homeowner hassles

Women homeowners indicate that keeping a tight rein on spending is the most difficult part of remodeling. Top problems:

Staying in budget 45%
Finding right contractor 10%
Not sure where to begin 10%
Planning 9%

Source: Survey.com for eBay of 1,000 past or present female home-owners. Margin of error ±3 percentage points.

By Mary Cadden and Marcy E. Mullins, USA TODAY 2005

CAUTION
Don't invade the tenant's privacy just to make repairs.
Landlords in many states must give notice of entry when making repairs or doing inspections. You'll need to research and comply with your state's rules. Then make sure your lease or rental agreement mentions these rules and your own policies, to minimize disputes with those tenants who feel landlords never have the right to enter their property.

Dealing With the Legalities: Your Repair and Maintenance Obligations

Your obligation to keep the property in good shape is imposed by law. But how do you know what's expected of you? And what does the tenant have to do? Here are some guidelines.

What are you responsible for?

Your responsibility to repair and maintain the property is based on several different legal principles. If you're worried about meeting all your obligations, start by learning and complying with the basics. First, figure out any repair and maintenance requirements imposed by your local housing codes. For example, many cities require landlords to install smoke detectors in residential units, or security items such as viewing devices in doors that open onto a hallway. Your local building or housing authority, and health or fire department, can provide this information.

Also get a copy of and carefully read your state's housing laws, which should lay out rules for repair, maintenance, and many other landlording responsibilities. Again, your local building or housing authority should be able to point you to the appropriate code sections, usually available online. To find a direct link to your state's statutes, visit www.nolo.com/statute and select "State Laws."

Keeping your property habitable

According to a legal concept called the "implied warranty of habitability," you're required to offer and maintain livable premises. This means you must make sure the property meets minimum requirements (sometimes spelled out in local building codes), generally including:

- maintaining electrical, plumbing, sanitary, heating, ventilating, air-conditioning, and other facilities and systems
- supplying water, hot water, and heat in reasonable amounts at reasonable times
- providing trash receptacles and arranging for their removal, and
- maintaining any common areas in a safe and clean condition.

Every state but Arkansas has, by judicial decision or statute, adopted the implied warranty of habitability (and even in Arkansas, local laws may require that rental housing be habitable). Your state may specify additional requirements for making the place habitable, especially when features or services that might be essential in some places, like storm doors or shutters, might be virtually useless in other parts of the state.

The requirements won't always be listed somewhere obvious like in building codes, however. Often, it's the courts that decide what makes a place "habitable." But you can assume that if an aspect of a dwelling (such as a weatherproof roof) makes it a fit place to live, you're probably responsible for maintaining it.

> **CAUTION**
>
> **Don't try to evade your responsibility to keep the place habitable.** Some landlords have tried advancing one of these two theories:
>
> - The tenants saw the place when they moved in, so it's no fair for them to complain now. In other words, by moving into an unfit rental, the tenant effectively agreed to accept those conditions, and waived the protections of the implied warranty.
> - The tenant signed a lease saying the landlord won't provide habitable housing, and is bound by that signature.
>
> Nice try, but courts almost always reject these theories. You're better off making sure your property is in good shape.

Common Myths About Repairs and Maintenance

Many landlords (and tenants) are under the mistaken impression that every time a rental property turns over, certain cosmetic changes, such as a new paint job, are required. But ugliness isn't a habitability problem—it's the actual condition of the rental property that determines what's needed in terms of repair and maintenance. Some changes may be called for during the tenancy, rather than at the end.

Paint. No state law requires you to repaint the interior every so often (local ordinances may, however), as long as the paint isn't creating a habitability problem—for example, it's so thick it seals a window shut. Lead-based paint, however, may create legal problems.

Drapes and carpets. So long as drapes and carpets aren't so damp or mildewed as to constitute a health hazard, and carpets don't have dangerous holes that could cause someone to trip, you aren't legally required to replace them.

Windows. A tenant is responsible for a broken window only if the tenant or a guest intentionally or carelessly broke it. If a burglar, vandal, or neighborhood child broke a window, however, you're responsible for fixing it.

Keys. You may need to change the locks and rekey the property for each new tenant. Even if it's not legally required, it's a good idea.

Keeping the property useable

Landlords have another legal responsibility with an obscure name: the covenant of quiet enjoyment. As courts define it, this amounts to an implied promise that you won't act (or fail to act) in a way that interferes with or destroys the ability of the tenant to use the rental property. And if the tenant can't live in your place, you have for all practical purposes evicted him or her (called "constructive eviction").

For example, if failing to fix a leaky roof means the tenant can't use the bedroom, you've failed to meet your obligations under the covenant. That lets the tenant wave goodbye to your property, without having to pay any rent as of the time you should have fixed the problem.

USA TODAY Snapshots®

Safety precautions at home

Percentage of adults in the USA who have:

Smoke alarms
96%

Fire extinguishers
80%

Carbon monoxide detectors
46%

Source: 2006 Fire Safety Census, a telephone survey of 1,005 adults 25 and older conducted in August 2006 by KRC Research for Liberty Mutual and International Association of Fire Fighters. Margin of error ±3.1 percentage points.

By Tracey Wong Briggs and Veronica Salazar, USA TODAY 2008

Keeping your promises

Beyond the basics, your property may have features like drapes, a washing machine, a swimming pool, or a dishwasher. Although keeping these things in working order may not affect the habitability of the place, you may still be legally required to repair and maintain them. Usually that's either because your lease or rental agreement says so expressly, or because it's implied, for example because you've repaired it in the past or advertised it as part of the property. After all, if you advertise a "hot tub in the backyard," the tenant can reasonably expect that the hot tub works under normal use, and that you'll keep it that way.

Minor repairs

Your most frequent tenant calls are likely to be about minor complaints —leaky faucets, temperamental appliances, worn carpets, or noisy heaters —not about major problems that make the house unlivable. Most of the time, these minor repairs are your responsibility.

But you can make an exception if the tenant or one of the tenant's guests caused a minor repair problem. In that case, the tenant either needs to take care of the repairs, or if your lease or rental agreement prohibits the tenant from doing so, pay you to do deal with them.

Relocating Your Tenants During Renovations or Repairs

Most repairs to your rental property will be quick and won't inconvenience your tenants much. For example, fixing the clogged toilet, replacing a fixture, or even laying new carpets mostly require your tenants to stay out of the way and perhaps move belongings aside so workmen can do their jobs. In these situations, you need not compensate tenants for the very temporary loss of the use of their home, and you certainly don't have to move them out (and pay for alternate lodging) while the work is being done.

Tenants may need to move out, however, if repairs are lengthy or involve chemicals that no one should be exposed to. Whether you or your tenants pay for the nights away depends on why the work is being done. If it's to maintain the rental in a fit and habitable condition, or you simply want to spiff the place up, you pay. But if you're doing cosmetic upgrades at the tenant's request, or the work is needed as a result of the tenant's negligence, the tenant can fairly be expected to cover the expense of temporarily moving out.

For instance, tenting and fumigating a termite infestation means that your tenants obviously cannot live there. Because maintaining a fit home is your responsibility, and tenants can't be blamed for the presence of termites, you'll need to pay for the cost of their temporary living quarters.

What if you decide to refinish the hardwood floors? Most contractors will advise occupants to remain away from the home for at least three days, both to allow the finish to dry and to avoid the very toxic odors. Whether you have to pay for alternate lodging depends on the reason for the work: If it's because a pipe burst and flooded the room, chances are it's not the tenant's fault, and you should pay for the hotel stay. But if the refinishing job is really a cosmetic upgrade requested by the tenant, or the flood was the result of the tenant forgetting to turn off the bathtub faucet, the tenant should bear the expense of living elsewhere.

You can also draw the line at fixing up ordinary wear and tear. It's not your job to keep the rental premises looking just like new, just to stop deterioration. Nevertheless, if a tenant that you're happy with asks for a basic spruce up—replacing some shabby-looking but still functional blinds, for example—it may be worth doing. You'll probably have to make the changes if the tenant moves out, anyway.

> **TIP**
>
> **Best thing I ever did: Establish good communications with our tenants.** Phil, who owns a triplex, explains, "I work fulltime, and I probably could be more proactive about things like checking whether the rental units' roof needs fixing, or improving the landscaping. But we at least make sure to keep good dialogue going with our tenants, so that we know if something needs immediate attention, and they know we'll see to it quickly."

What is the tenant responsible for?

You aren't the only one with responsibilities—the tenant has some too. These include:

- **Keeping the rental unit in a reasonably clean and safe condition.** If the tenant doesn't do things like mop the tile floor in the kitchen every once in awhile, in which case you'd have to replace the caked grout before the next tenant moves in, you may legitimately deduct the costs from the security deposit. Before the end of the tenancy, if you discover that poor housekeeping has resulted in the need for repairs or property replacements, you may either cover the cost from the security deposit (and demand that the deposit be replenished to its original level), or simply bill the tenant for the cost.

- **Disposing of waste cleanly and safely.** Tenants are responsible for the consequences of unsanitary habits. For instance, if mice or ants invade the kitchen because your tenant forgot to wash the dishes before leaving on a two-week vacation, the tenant is responsible for paying the extermination and clean-up costs.

- **Keeping plumbing fixtures clean.** For example, bathtub caulking that has sprouted mold and mildew will render the tub unusable (or at least disgusting). Since it could have been prevented by proper cleaning, the tenant is responsible. On the other hand, if the bathroom has no fan and the window has been painted shut, the bathroom will be hard to air out, so the resulting mildew might be your responsibility.

- **Using electrical, plumbing, sanitary, heating, ventilating, air-conditioning, and other facilities and systems properly.** Examples of abuse by tenants include overloading electrical outlets and flushing large objects down the toilet. Catherine, who rents out a cottage behind her house, says: "After I had to call Roto Rooter out for the third time in six months, I had them put what they pulled out into a baggie, and told my tenant, 'If you put this stuff down one more time, you're paying the plumbing bill.' It was Clorox wipes, which say they're flushable, but not with our old Berkeley pipes. And I'd already warned the tenant about flushing anything other than toilet paper."

- **Fixing things the tenant breaks or damages.** If a tenant causes a serious habitability problem on your property—for example, carelessly breaking the heater—the tenant is responsible. You must make sure the repair happens, but you can bill the tenant for it. (The tenant can't just choose to forego heat, either.)

- **Reporting problems in the rental.** Some states require tenants to inform the landlord, as soon as practicable, of defective conditions on the premises that the tenant believes to be unknown to the landlord and believes are the landlord's duty to repair. As we'll explain further below, your best bet is to ask the tenant to notify you of problems immediately, even if the law doesn't require it.

To protect yourself (and to notify your tenant of what's required), make sure your lease or rental agreement spells out these basic tenant obligations. And use common sense in dealing with tenant psychology.

For example, many tenants will ignore their maintenance obligations if they have to pay extra to comply. Gordon, a landlord with property in San Jose, California, says, "If the tenants have to pay for the water, they're not going to water the lawn. One way around this is to have an irrigation system on a timer. Another way is to keep the water in your name, and just raise the rent a bit."

> **TIP**
>
> **Best thing I ever did: Learn to regularly remind tenants of key maintenance obligations.** As Kathy explains, "I've found that the one thing my tenants are worst at remembering is to replace the filter on the air conditioner. Here in Florida, if you don't change the filter at least once a month, it starts freezing up, gets a drainage problem, and the pipes get moldy. By impressing upon my tenants that they must change the filter every time they pay their electric bill, and reminding them about it when we talk, I at least reduce the amount of money I'm spending repairing the AC."

If you don't meet your obligations: What the tenant can do

If you don't maintain your property in a fit and habitable condition, in compliance with legal requirements, your tenant may take action. The tenants' rightful responses may include one or more of the following:

- **Withholding rent.** In some states or cities, if you don't keep the property livable, your tenant may be able to stop paying rent until necessary repairs are made. This is called rent withholding or rent "escrowing," because tenants often have to deposit the withheld rent in an escrow account until the repairs are done, at which point the money will be released to make the rent payment (maybe after some negotiations between you and the tenant on how you'll compensate the tenant for the inconvenience).

- **Repairing and deducting.** In states that allow this, a tenant can simply repair the problem and subtract the cost from the next month's rent. In most states there's a maximum dollar limit or a specific percentage of the month's rent the tenant can spend—for example, $300 or less than one half the monthly rent, whichever is greater. Also, states usually limit this to essential services, such as heat or water. And many states limit how often tenants may pursue this option, such as no more than twice in any 12-month period.

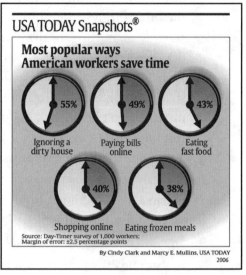

USA TODAY Snapshots®

Most popular ways American workers save time

55% Ignoring a dirty house

49% Paying bills online

43% Eating fast food

40% Shopping online

38% Eating frozen meals

Source: Day-Timer survey of 1,000 workers; Margin of error: ±2.5 percentage points

By Cindy Clark and Marcy E. Mullins, USA TODAY 2006

CAUTION

Don't drive tenants to repair and deduct. Though it will mean the repair gets done with little effort on your part, a repair that isn't done well could cost you in the long run. Moreover, when tenants use repair and deduct, you have no receipt (with your name on it) to prove the expense for tax purposes.

- **Reporting code violations to housing inspectors.** A tenant may complain to a local building, health, or fire department about problems such as inoperable plumbing, a leaky roof, or bad wiring. If an inspector comes out, you may be ordered to correct the problem—and subjected to a fine or penalty if you don't do so within a certain amount of time (often five to 30 business days).

- **Filing a lawsuit.** The tenant may sue and ask the court to order a rent refund for the period that housing conditions were substandard; payment of repair costs of property lost or damaged as a result of the problem (for example, furniture ruined by water leaking through the roof); compensation for personal injuries caused by the problem, and attorney fees. In some states, tenants may also get the court to order you to repair the defects, with rent reduced until you show the court proof that you've remedied the defects.

- **Moving out.** If you fail to make the rental property habitable, the tenant ultimately has the right to move out—either temporarily or permanently. These drastic measures are justified only in the case of truly serious problems; for example, where essential services are missing, or the place has been partly or totally destroyed. Tenants may move out if environmental health hazards such as lead paint dust make the place uninhabitable. Your state statute may have specific details, such as the type of notice tenants must give you before making their exit. You may have anywhere from five to 21 days to fix the problem, depending on the state and, sometimes, the seriousness of the situation.

Tenants can't use the first two options—withholding rent or repairing the problem and deducting it from the rent—just because they feel like it. Three conditions must be met:

- **The problem is serious, not just annoying, and imperils the tenant's health or safety.** Not every building code violation or annoying defect in a rental home is serious enough to justify such heavy action.

- **The tenant told you about and gave you a reasonable opportunity to fix the problem.** In some states, the law will tell you exactly how much time you have to make the repairs (ten days to three weeks is common); in others, you must respond within a reasonable time under the circumstances.

- **The tenant (or a guest) didn't cause the problem.** If they did, then you can't be expected or required to pay for it.

Adopting a Good Maintenance and Repair System

Early attention to repair and maintenance issues will forestall many problems—but not all of them. And most unexpected problems are your responsibility. You'll need a system that helps you prevent problems when you can and deal with them quickly when you can't. (At least maintenance and repair costs are tax deductible, as discussed in Chapter 6.)

Creating a maintenance and repair strategy

We suggest creating a systematic approach to maintenance and repairs, as follows:

When you have a new tenant:

- **Get everything in shipshape before the tenant moves in.** Do a thorough evaluation and fix any problems. You'll want to repeat this every time there's tenant turnover, before the move-in. You may want to create a checklist, tailored to your property, to make sure you don't miss anything.

- **Clue the tenant in.** Set out the tenant's responsibilities for repair and maintenance in your lease or rental agreement, and point them out before the tenant signs.

- **Show new tenants how to handle routine maintenance.** Explain the basics, such as how to avoid overloading circuits, properly use the garbage disposal, and locate and use the fire extinguisher. Identify problems the tenant should definitely not try to handle, such as electrical repairs. Include a brief list of all these maintenance dos and don'ts as part of your move-in materials (discussed in Chapter 5).

Throughout the tenancy:

- **Be accessible.** Make sure the tenant can reach you to report any problems immediately. Have an answering machine, voicemail, or other service available at all times, and check your messages frequently. Also consider creating a form to take repair requests, then give the tenant a few copies at move-in and explain how to use the form.

- **Keep a written log of all complaints (including those made orally).** This should include a box to write your immediate and any follow-up responses (and subsequent tenant communications), as well as a space to enter the date and brief details of when the problem was fixed. Try to respond in writing to every tenant repair request (even if you also do so orally).

- **Respond quickly.** Handle repairs (especially urgent ones) as soon as possible, but definitely within the time your state law (if any) requires. Notify the tenant by phone and follow up in writing if repairs will take more than 48 hours, excluding weekends. Keep the tenant informed—for example, if you have problems scheduling a plumber, let your tenant know with a phone call or a note. We'll discuss responding to complaints further below.

On a regular basis:

- **Have biannual tenant reviews.** Twice a year, give your tenants a checklist on which to report any potential safety hazards or maintenance problems, such as an entryway rug showing signs of fraying (replace it now, before it gets worse and someone trips). You might also want to create a form for this purpose, and give it to the tenant to fill out and return within a specified time period, such as a couple weeks. Respond promptly and in writing to all requests, keeping copies in your file.

RESOURCE

Looking for checklists, move-in letters, and more? Go to *Every Landlord's Legal Guide,* by Marcia Stewart, Ralph Warner, and Janet Portman (Nolo). The attached CD-ROM is full of helpful landlord forms and standard documents, which you can customize to your needs.

- **Use written reminders.** Remind your tenant of your policies and procedures to keep the property in good repair in every written communication, by printing it at the bottom of all routine notices, rent increases, and other communications. Tenants will be more likely to tell you about maintenance and repair problems if you remind them that you're truly interested.
- **Conduct an annual safety inspection.** Once a year, make time for a "safety and maintenance inspection," where you check that items such as smoke detectors, heating and plumbing systems, and major appliances are safe and in working order. These inspections are not required by law, but they're a good idea. Be sure not to overdo it—once a year is sufficient.

Your Right to Conduct a Safety Inspection

In many states, you have the right to enter a tenant's home to conduct a safety inspection, but you usually need to notify the tenant first. Some states specify 24 hours' notice, others simply state that it must be "reasonable notice." To be on the safe side, check your state's statutes and, if all that is required is "reasonable notice," allow 24 hours at least.

If a tenant objects and your state allows you to enter for this purpose (and if you've given adequate notice), the tenant's refusal is grounds for eviction. If your state doesn't allow the landlord to enter and inspect against the tenant's will, point out to the tenant that you take your responsibility to maintain the property very seriously. Remind the tenant that you'll be checking for problems that the tenant might not notice, which could develop into bigger problems later. If you still get a refusal, write a confirming letter to the tenant—it may protect you later, if the tenant claims a safety hazard or that there's damage to the property (and the damage could have been prevented had you known about it).

Responding to tenant complaints

You should respond almost immediately to all complaints about defective conditions, by talking to the tenant and following up (preferably in writing). Explain when repairs can be made or, if you don't know yet, tell the tenant that you'll be back in touch promptly. Different problems require different levels of action:

- **Personal security and safety problems.** Respond and get work done immediately to fix problems that could result in tenant injury or property damage.

- **Major inconveniences to the tenant.** Respond and attempt to get work done as soon as possible, or within 24 hours if the problem is a major inconvenience to the tenant, such as a plumbing or heating problem. Otherwise, you risk a tenant using one of the self-help remedies above, or simply feeling dissatisfied and moving out.

- **Minor problems.** Respond within 48 hours (on business days) if the problem is not too serious. You'll avoid a tenant's major dissatisfaction, and you won't have to worry that your inaction will trigger the tenant's inappropriate but highly annoying use of remedies such as withholding rent or making repairs and deducting their cost from the rent.

If you can't take care of a repair right away, let the tenant know your timeline. For the sake of speed, do this orally (a message on the tenant's answering machine should serve), and then follow up in writing. If there's a delay maybe because the part you need to fix the oven has to be specially ordered, explain this.

As important as these repairs are, you can't just march onto the property to make them until you've taken steps to protect the tenant's rights. You can enter the rental premises only with the tenant's consent, or after having given the amount of notice required by state law, usually 24 hours. Try to pick a reasonable time of day, to keep the peace (and potentially follow the law), except in cases of emergency, or where it's impractical to do so.

Responding to problems at a distance

If your property is in another state and you haven't hired a property manager, you face additional challenges in getting repairs done. Laura, who lives in Washington state, describes how she handles this for her Nevada and Florida properties: "My tenants know enough not to call me at 3:00 in the morning. Of course, their timing can still be horrible—just before my son's wedding, I got about 50 phone calls concerning the water heater in one of my houses. Still, I've found that I can accomplish a lot by phone. I view dealing with repair issues as a partnership with my tenants. Sometimes I'll have them call the repair person to make an appointment, which makes more sense given that they're going to have to be the one to let the person in. I tell them to

Can Tenants Alter the Property?

Your tenant may want to personalize the place—paint the living room, install a closet system, or put in a dishwasher, for example. If it's a tenant whom you like and would hate to lose, think about allowing it, after considering:

- **Is the improvement or alteration easily undone?** Repainting is easy to redo, while knocking out a wall to install a wine closet is more permanent.

- **Does the improvement or alteration enhance your property?** For example, a nice paint job or a wine closet might actually add value.

- **Does the law allow the tenants to make the particular improvement or alteration?** For example, in some cases the law might protect a tenant's rights to install a satellite dish, and you'll need to comply with such laws. See Chapter 5, "Step Aside: Tenants May Be Allowed to Make These Repairs or Alterations," for more on the subject.

If you and the tenant reach an understanding, put it in writing, carefully describing the project and materials, including whether the improvement or alteration is permanent or portable, the terms of the reimbursement, if any, and how and when you'll pay the tenant, if at all, for labor and materials.

Anything your tenant attaches to a building, fence, deck, or the ground itself (called "fixtures") belongs to you, unless you agree that it's the tenant's. Either way, it's wise to spell out in your lease or rental agreement who will own the improvement. And make it clear that if the tenant later fails to properly restore the premises, or removes an alteration that was meant to be permanent, you'll deduct the resulting costs from the security deposit or take further legal action if necessary.

have the repair person call me after arriving at the house. Then we'll plan the job and I'll usually pay for it over the phone, and ask the repair person to send me the receipt. This system tends to go smoothly."

It's also smart to line up a list of potential repairpeople while you're in town visiting the property, rather than waiting until an urgent situation arises. We'll discuss how to find good people later in this chapter.

No Thanks! Hiring Someone Else to do the Work

If you live far from your rental property, don't have time to deal with the hassle of repairs or maintenance, or are simply too busy or not very handy, you may want to hire someone to take care of maintenance and repairs for you. Your primary options are to hire a property manager, a handyperson, or the tenant.

 TIP

Learning some maintenance and repair skills may be smart. "I do a lot of my own maintenance," says John, who has owned multiple properties since 1975. "It gets me on the property and shows a presence; it shows that I care. Besides, you have to learn to do some repairs yourself, because you can't afford to hire someone for every little thing."

Hiring a property manager

If you hire a property manager, that person's package of services will probably include overseeing maintenance. This can have its advantages, especially since many property management companies have a professional on staff to deal with maintenance problems, and have vetted a host of other specialized professionals like plumbers, electricians, and general contractors.

But watch out for a few potential bumpy spots, too. For example:

- **Make sure the property manager will respond immediately.** Ask for a commitment to a specific turnaround time. You don't want your property damaged, or your tenant injured, because the property manager didn't get around to acting promptly.

- **Confirm that the property manager is available 24 hours a day, 365 days a year.** That will avoid issues like a desperate call from a tenant on Christmas morning, complaining that the heater is broken and the manager is nowhere to be found.

- **Find out whether you'll be charged extra for maintenance calls.** Some property management companies make money by tacking on administrative fees when hiring outside contractors or vendors.

- **Know whether the property manager is authorized to conduct repairs without your prior approval.** Your contract should specify what level of repairs may be done without getting an okay from you first. You want your property manager to be able to act quickly if there's an emergency, especially if you're on vacation or otherwise unavailable. On the other hand, you don't want to give a manager authority to undertake a major or expensive repair or replacement, such as replacing the stove without consulting you first.

Also, keep in mind that the property manager will probably not conduct annual inspections or periodically ask the tenant whether any repairs are needed. This is something you'll either have to do yourself, negotiate with the property management firm to include in your agreement, or pay extra for.

For more information on hiring a property manager, see Chapter 10.

Hiring a handyperson

As a middle-ground option between doing the work yourself and paying for the deluxe services of a property manager, you can hire others. Your best bet is to find a reliable handyperson for basic repairs, and hire a contractor (discussed below) for more specific or skill-intensive tasks.

A good handyperson will have an extensive background in home repair. Many are even trained and licensed contractors. You'll want someone who is available 24 hours, in case of emergencies. Choose someone who's been in business for awhile, and thus will be likely to stick around and become familiar with your property.

USA TODAY Snapshots®

Clicking on home improvement
Online retail spending on home improvement products: (in billions)

2001 $1.8

2006

$13.6

Source: Jupiter Research

By David Stuckey and Robert W. Ahrens, USA TODAY
2008

To find a competent handyperson, ask other rental property owners or real estate professionals for recommendations. It's best to find one who carries primary health insurance and liability insurance, which will protect you if the handyperson is injured on the job, causes any property damage, or injures others. A reputable worker will be willing to provide this proof.

An insured handyperson will probably charge more than an uninsured one might—but it's worth it, for the extra security of knowing you or your insurance company won't end up paying for the consequences of any accidents.

Also, for the sake of both your project and your financial risk, make sure the person you hire has complied with any state rules and licensing requirements. In some states, for example, it's illegal to hire unlicensed contractors for certain kinds of work.

Hiring a contractor

In some cases, you, your handyperson, or your property manager may not have the skills needed for the task at hand. In that case, you'll probably hire a contractor, such as a plumber or electrician. Again, you're looking for someone who's available quickly when you're in a jam—especially if you're not nearby.

Don't Become an Accidental Employer

When you hire someone to fix a leaky faucet, mow the lawn, or retile the bathroom, you probably don't think of that person as your "employee." But the IRS or other governmental agencies may feel differently if that person becomes a regular worker who takes orders from you—unlikely in a single-family rental, but something to bear in mind if you expand into multi-unit properties.

Once the government considers you an employer, and not simply someone who hires an independent contractor for a specific job, your obligations to the worker (and the government) will change dramatically. For example, you'd need to secure proof of the worker's authorization to work in the United States, to withhold and pay Social Security and Medicare taxes, and maybe also pay workers' compensation insurance and state unemployment taxes.

For IRS purposes, the more control you exercise over the tasks a worker does and how he or she does them, the more likely the IRS is to consider the person an employee. Workers are more likely independent contractors if they:

- can earn a profit or suffer a loss from the work
- furnish the tools and materials needed to do the work
- are paid by the job, not by the hour
- work for more than one place at a time
- invest in equipment and facilities
- pay their own business and traveling expenses
- hire and pay any assistants, and
- set their own working hours.

For more information, see IRS Publication 15-A, *Employer's Supplemental Tax Guide*, and *Working With Independent Contractors*, by Stephen Fishman (Nolo).

Ask other rental property owners or real estate professionals for recommendations. Look for someone who is properly licensed and insured. You can often find this information on your state's contractor licensing board website, but get confirmation from the contractor in case anything has changed.

Hiring the tenant

You may want to delegate some of the responsibility of managing the property to your tenant. It's not always a bad idea. After all, the tenant is aware of the problems, and is highly motivated to fix them. On the other hand, because tenants aren't normally interested in the long-term condition of the property, many won't attend to repairs with the same concern that owners bring to the job.

USA TODAY Snapshots®

Convenient return policy important

If a retailer's return policy is not convenient, would you continue to shop there?

No 82% — Yes 16%

Don't know 2%

Source: Newgistics survey of 1,061 adults 18 and older. Margin of error ±3 percentage points.

By Jae Yang and Steve Conley, USA TODAY 2006

But first, make sure the tenant has the necessary expertise, which will probably depend both on the task and the tenant. Second, make sure hiring the tenant is cost effective. While it's certainly convenient—you don't have to find a professional to handle it—it isn't necessarily cheaper. If you credit or pay the tenant hourly, but it takes twice as long (or causes further damage), you won't save money.

Compensating the tenant for repairs

If you decide to allow the tenant to make repairs from time to time, you have two options for how to pay the tenant. You can:

- **Reduce the rent.** This will probably be your tenant's preference. Of course, you'll want to agree to this practice ahead of time, agree to the payment terms, and lay out your agreement in writing, within the rental agreement.

- **Pay directly for the work.** Paying an on-site tenant to do repair and maintenance is preferable to giving the tenant a reduction in rent for work performed, because if the job isn't done right, you can simply cancel the work arrangement rather than amend the lease or rental agreement. Plus, there will be no question that the tenant is still obligated to pay the full rent as usual. If you choose this route, be sure to write down what you expect your tenant to do, and for how much money.

> **TIP**
>
> **In a multifamily property, beware of turning a tenant into an employee.** No matter which method of compensation you choose, if your tenant will be performing regular maintenance duties in a multi-family rental situation (such as dealing with minor plumbing repairs and sweeping the lobby and front steps), your tenant will be your employee. As an employer, you'll need to comply with the requirements described in "Don't Become an Accidental Employer," above. (In a single-family situation, it's unlikely that making a tenant responsible for yard upkeep, and including that provision in your lease, would carry the same risk.)

Types of repairs a tenant can't do

Even though it may be cheapest to buy a book at a local hardware store, throw some parts into your cart, and hire the tenant to replace the water heater or repair faulty wiring, it's not a good idea for such major repairs, because:

- **The quality of the repair may be low.** Unless your tenant just happens to be a skilled contractor, you risk the repairs being inadequate, so that you end up redoing them (or worse).

Let Your College Kid Be the Landlord? Maybe

St. Cloud State University sophomore Parker Lahti is majoring in real estate. At 19, he's also a homeowner.

Other students, too—with a little help from Mom and Dad—are combining academics with the real-world responsibilities of mortgage payments and home repair. The houses—sometimes called "kiddie condos"—are turning college students into landlords who collect rent rather than pay it.

Lahti's house has four bedrooms, two bathrooms, a laundry room, a two-car garage, and a basement he'll use for entertaining. And with his roommates sharing the $1,200 monthly note, Lahti says, they're getting a pretty good deal. Each will pay $300 a month, once he finds someone to fill the fourth bedroom. On-campus apartments in St. Cloud rent for about $319 a month.

Full-time students without a job or credit history can, with their parents' support, get a condo loan from the Federal Housing Authority. Many expenses, such as repairs, may be tax-deductible.

Lahti's father agreed to buy the house but told Lahti the payments would be his responsibility. "It teaches him a little bit about working with tenants and paying utility bills," Tom Lahti says.

Students may find being a homeowner harder than it sounds, Jan Baldry, a real estate broker in Waukesha, Wisconsin, says. For one, they have to be careful about whom they accept as renters. Students "have a reputation for being wild and messy and moving out without giving any notice," she says.

The situation also could cause headaches for parents. "When your child calls at midnight and says the bathroom shower doesn't work, you're the one who has to fix that," Baldry says.

 "Homeownership 101; College kids are landlords, Thanks to Mom and Dad," by Scott Brooks, September 8, 2003.

- **You're legally responsible if the tenant gets injured or injures someone else.** A tenant who doesn't know what he or she is doing can easily cause injuries, especially if dealing with sensitive systems like electricity, heating, or wiring. Hiring the tenant means you'll be responsible for these injuries—even if they occur later (for example, when the newly installed light fixture comes crashing down during a dinner party). Of course, you could always try to recoup your losses by suing that tenant (called "seeking indemnity" in legalese), but your chances of recovery will be slim unless your tenant has significant assets. On the other hand, a maintenance or repair service will generally carry its own insurance (confirm this before you engage their services).

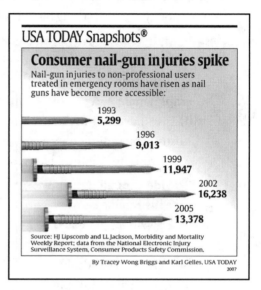

USA TODAY Snapshots®

Consumer nail-gun injuries spike

Nail-gun injuries to non-professional users treated in emergency rooms have risen as nail guns have become more accessible:

1993 **5,299**
1996 **9,013**
1999 **11,947**
2002 **16,238**
2005 **13,378**

Source: HJ Lipscomb and LL Jackson, Morbidity and Mortality Weekly Report; data from the National Electronic Injury Surveillance System, Consumer Products Safety Commission.

By Tracey Wong Briggs and Karl Gelles, USA TODAY 2007

- **The law may not permit you to delegate major repairs to the tenant.** Judges and legislators fear that the tenant will rarely be in the position, either practically or financially, to do the kinds of repairs that are often needed to bring a structure up to par—and it's still your duty to make the place habitable. A few states allow the landlord and tenant of a single-family dwelling to agree in writing that the tenant is to perform some of the landlord's statutory duties, but generally landlords retain the duties imposed by health and safety codes and the implied warranty of habitability.

Avoiding problems

Repair and maintenance arrangements between landlords and tenants often lead to dissatisfaction—the landlord feels that the tenant has neglected certain tasks, or the tenant feels that there's too much work for the money. To keep things flowing smoothly:

- **Put it in writing.** Any agreement as to repairs or maintenance should be written and signed, either as part of the lease or rental agreement or as a separate employment agreement. This will avoid mutual misunderstandings about who's responsible for what.

- **Provide enough detail so that the tenant knows exactly what's expected.** Whether it's repairing a broken window, dealing with a routine plumbing problem, or landscaping, give specific descriptions and limits to the tasks.

USA TODAY Snapshots®

Yard care
Outdoor maintenance equipment owned by consumers:

79% — Mower (non-riding)
60% — String trimmer
55% — Chain saw
52% — Leaf blower
48% — Hedge trimmer

Source: *Consumer Reports* National Research Center

By David Stuckey and Robert W. Ahrens, USA TODAY
2008

- **Pay fairly.** If you don't, you'll increase the tenant's resentment, while decreasing motivation to get the job done. If you ever have a dispute with the tenant, a judge won't look kindly on an unreasonably low payment for the tenant's hard work, especially if it doesn't even add up to minimum wage.

- **Treat the delegation of duties as separate from your other duties as landlord.** Your agreement with your tenant has nothing to do with your other responsibilities. For example, if you and your tenant agree that the tenant will do gardening work in exchange for a reduction in rent, and you're watching the shrubs die or take over the sidewalk, you may not respond by shutting off the water or retaliating in other ways. The proper recourse is to discuss the problem with the tenant and, if it persists, to cancel the arrangement. ●

CHAPTER

8

Landlord Liability for Injuries, Crimes, and More

As a landlord, you have some level of legal responsibility for your tenant's safety. In addition to providing a well-maintained place to live, you're legally required to create an environment that protects your tenant from certain dangers. In this chapter, we'll cover those dangers and how to avoid them, including:

- your responsibility for tenant injuries
- dealing with environmental problems like mold and lead
- protecting tenants from crime, and
- buying insurance to protect yourself.

Fortunately, the likelihood of having problems that will result in serious legal or financial liability is low, especially if you follow the preventative measures we recommend throughout this book. And with a good insurance policy, even if you're confronted with some surprises, you'll be covered.

Ouch, That Smarts: Liability for Tenant Injuries

It's probably no surprise that you must keep your property safe for your tenant and any guests—and it's a responsibility to take seriously.

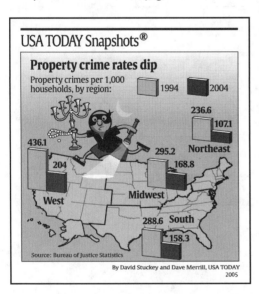

USA TODAY Snapshots®

Property crime rates dip

Property crimes per 1,000 households, by region: ☐ 1994 ☐ 2004

West: 436.1, 204
Midwest: 295.2, 168.8
Northeast: 236.6, 107.1
South: 288.6, 158.3

Source: Bureau of Justice Statistics

By David Stuckey and Dave Merrill, USA TODAY 2005

After all, an injured tenant can seek financial recovery for medical bills, lost earnings, pain and other physical suffering, permanent physical disability and disfigurement, and emotional distress. Tenants can also look to you for the costs of property damage that resulted from faulty or unsafe conditions. As Jason, a landlord in Texas, remembers, "The tree in front of our rental house was overgrown and overdue for a trimming, but I put it off. Last winter, a storm broke a major branch, crushing my tenant's car, which was parked in the driveway. My insurance carrier paid for it, because I'd been remiss in not taking care of the tree, but my premiums went up."

Consistently practicing good maintenance serves a double purpose: It will not only help prevent tenants from getting injured (or having their property damaged) in the first place, but will help you defend yourself if a tenant claims you're responsible for an injury or damage.

You're not responsible for everything

It isn't always easy to determine whether you're legally responsible for a tenant's injury. Basically, you may be liable for injuries resulting from:

- **Negligence.** An injured tenant may claim you acted negligently— that is, carelessly, in a way that wasn't reasonable under the circumstances—and thus caused the injury. Landlords have been found negligent after a tenant fell down a staircase due to a defective handrail, a tenant's child was scalded by water from a water heater with a broken thermostat, and a tenant received electrical burns when attempting to insert a stove's damaged plug into the wall outlet.

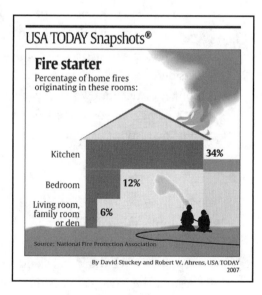

USA TODAY Snapshots®

Fire starter
Percentage of home fires originating in these rooms:

Kitchen 34%

Bedroom 12%

Living room, family room or den 6%

Source: National Fire Protection Association

By David Stuckey and Robert W. Ahrens, USA TODAY
2007

- **Violation of a health or safety law.** Many state and local laws require smoke detectors, sprinklers, inside-release security bars on windows, childproof fences around swimming pools, and so on. Some states say that a landlord who doesn't take reasonable steps to follow the laws will be considered negligent, and responsible for any resulting tenant injuries. Additionally, your violation of a health or safety law may indirectly cause an injury and lead to liability. For example, if you let the furnace deteriorate in violation of local law and a tenant is injured trying to repair it, you may be liable, unless the tenant's repair efforts were extremely careless themselves.

Dog Bites and Other Animal Attacks

Hard to believe, but you may be liable for injuries caused by your tenants' animals, be they common household pets or more exotic, wild animals.

Dangerous domestic pets. If a person injured by a vicious animal can prove to an insurance adjuster (or a jury) that the landlord knew (or should have known) that the animal had dangerous tendencies, and failed to take reasonable steps to prevent the injury (such as demanding that the animal leave the property or evicting the tenant), the landlord may be held liable.

Dangerous exotic pets. Keeping wild animals is generally considered an "ultrahazardous activity." So if your tenant keeps a monkey or tiger and you know about it (or should have), a court will assume that you understood the dangers presented, and may hold you responsible if the animal injures someone.

- **Failure to make certain repairs.** If your lease or rental agreement prohibits the tenant from making repairs or alterations without your consent, you can get into trouble if you're told about such a problem but don't fix it, and then the tenant gets injured as a result. The legal reason is that you breached the contract (the lease) by not making the repairs. (You may be found negligent, as well.)

- **Failure to keep the premises habitable.** If a problem is so serious that the rental unit becomes unfit for human habitation—and you knew of the problem and had a reasonable amount of time to fix it—you could get into trouble for any resulting tenant injuries. What type of problem makes a house uninhabitable may vary by circumstance, however. For example, a large, jagged broken window would make the premises unfit for habitation in North Dakota in winter, but a torn screen door during summertime in southern California would not.

- **Reckless or intentional acts.** If you harm a tenant on purpose or "recklessly," you may be in hot water. In the legal sense, "recklessness" usually means extreme carelessness regarding an obvious defect or problem (like ignoring a fire hazard for months). Acting recklessly can be very expensive, making you potentially liable for "punitive" damages: extra damages, beyond the cost of the injury, to punish you for bad behavior.

Me? I'd Never Hurt a Fly!

If you hit a tenant during an argument, that's an intentional act. But so are emotional or psychological injuries inflicted intentionally, such as:

- **Sexual harassment,** or repeated, disturbing attentions of a sexual nature (or a single outrageous act) that leave a tenant fearful, humiliated, and upset.

- **Assault,** even if it's nonphysical—for example, threatening or menacing someone.

- **Repeated invasions of privacy,** such as by unauthorized entries into the tenant's living space.

- **Other duties imposed by law.** In rare instances, courts or state legislatures have decided that landlords are automatically liable for certain kinds of injuries. This legal principle is called "strict liability," or liability without fault. It's usually imposed only when a hidden defect poses an unreasonably great risk of harm to people who can't detect or avoid the danger. For example, Massachusetts landlords are strictly liable if their tenants are poisoned by lead-based paint.

Liability for injuries to guests and trespassers

If you act negligently and a tenant's guest or even a trespasser (who wasn't invited by you or the tenant onto the property) is injured, will you be responsible? In a few states, you're liable without regard to why the injured person was there in the first place. As a general rule, however, you don't owe the same "duty of care" to a nontenant as you do to your tenant, especially if it's a trespasser. For example, a tenant who gets hurt by falling from an unfenced porch can make a fairly strong argument that you were negligent; but a trespasser, even an innocent one who has come to the wrong address, and falls off the same porch, might have a harder time recovering from you.

If a tenant is at fault, too

If the tenant is partially to blame for getting injured, your picture isn't so grim. For example, a drunk tenant who, while stumbling around, tripped on a loose brick on the front steps may not be able to collect as much, or at all, from the landlord.

If a tenant knows of a danger and takes a chance anyway, thus causing or worsening the injury, the law will say that the tenant has "assumed the risk" of injury. In some states, such a tenant may not be entitled to recover anything, regardless of any negligence by the landlord. In other states, a tenant's recovery will be lowered based on how much the tenant appreciated (but ignored) the danger involved.

While a tenant's own carelessness may decrease the hit to your wallet (or your insurance policy), it won't decrease the time you'll spend dealing with the incident. For example, Walt, with a single-family rental in Miami explains, "My tenant, Dorothy, definitely knew that the bedroom casement window had become hard to lift and secure, but she didn't say a word about it. The first I heard was one night when she called from the hospital, after the window had come crashing down on her arm and hurt her wrist, real bad. She sued me. At least the jury got the picture that Dorothy was partly at fault, so she got only a portion of the damages she'd asked for. (My insurance company paid.) Still, I had to spend days going to the lawyers' offices and preparing for and attending the trial."

How to prevent liability problems

Here are some great ways to protect yourself from lawsuits and hefty insurance settlements and at the same time make your tenants' lives safer and happier.

- **Follow the maintenance plan in the last chapter.** Look for dangerous conditions and fix them promptly; comply with all health, safety, and building codes; conduct regular safety inspections; ask tenants to report problems; and document problems and resolutions.

- **Warn of dangers you can't fix.** You won't always be able to do much about some dangers like a steep driveway or winding stairs. But if you know, or should know, about such defects, you have a duty to tell the tenant about them. The best way is to mention them in your lease, rental agreement, or move-in letter. If appropriate, also post warning signs near the hazard.

USA TODAY Snapshots®

Breaking in

Most common places that burglars enter homes:

Front door **34%**

First-floor window **23%**

Back door **22%**

Basement **4%**

Unlocked entrance **4%**

Garage **9%**

Storage area **2%**

Second floor **2%**

Source: The National Burglar & Fire Alarm Association

By David Stuckey and Alejandro Gonzalez, USA TODAY 2008

- **Look for tenant security issues.** Install and maintain basic security features such as deadbolt locks, smoke detectors, fire extinguishers, window locks, outside lighting, and any other features appropriate for your property.

- **Be vigilant about dangers to children.** If children are drawn onto your property by an irresistibly interesting (to children) but dangerous feature, such as a stack of building materials or an abandoned refrigerator (known in legal jargon as an "attractive nuisance"), you must exercise special care. Because young children can't read, or tend to ignore warnings, you should place physical barriers between the children and the attractive feature. And if the danger is of the type that can be cleaned up or removed (like the refrigerator), you should do so.

Never Jump on a Trampoline While Blindfolded

When Kimberly Ingram and her family bought their trampoline from Sam's Club in Sunnyvale, Texas, four years ago, she never thought she'd have to post a sign warning: "Do not jump on trampoline blindfolded."

But on May 10, Ingram's ten-year-old daughter, Katie, became one of the thousands of victims of trampoline-related injuries when she fell and broke the radius bone in her wrist during a game of blindfolded tag.

In 2004, the Consumer Product Safety Commission found that more than 89,000 people were sent to emergency rooms with trampoline-related injuries. And another study, this one by the Hasbro Children's Hospital in Rhode Island, found that spring and summer are the time when trampoline injuries hit their peak, and 91% of them happen at home.

 "It's the peak season for trampoline injuries," by Arienne Thompson; June 16, 2005.

⚠ **CAUTION**
Tenants can't sign away rights to be compensated for injuries.
Landlords used to protect themselves from most tenant lawsuits with
an "exculpatory clause"—lease language absolving the landlord in
advance of responsibility for tenant injuries, even those caused by the
landlord's negligence. There may be unusual situations when a narrowly
worded exculpatory clause would be appropriate—for example, if
you've delegated appropriate repair and maintenance duties to a tenant
(described in Chapter 8)—but in general, they're rarely enforced by
courts, so our advice is not to use them.

- **Supervise contractors.** If construction is being done on your
  property, make sure the person in charge secures the site and
  removes or locks up dangerous tools or equipment when the site
  is left unattended. Consider sending your tenant written notice
  of the intended project, suggesting extra precautions during the
  construction period.

Liability for Environmental Health Hazards

If your property poses any environmental health hazards to tenants
and you know about them, you've got to tell tenants, and most of the
time, you must remedy the problem—even if you didn't cause it. (This
is a relatively new duty, imposed in the last few decades.) This liability
is based on many of the same legal theories described above, such as
negligence and negligence *per se* (negligence that's automatic when a
statute is broken).

Asbestos

Exposure to asbestos is linked to an increased risk of cancer. Homes
built before the mid-1970s often contain asbestos insulation around
heating systems, in ceilings, and in other areas. Until 1981, asbestos was
also widely used in many other building materials, such as vinyl flooring

and tiles. Asbestos that breaks down and enters the air—for example, when it's disturbed during maintenance or renovation work—can give rise to significant health problems.

OSHA Regulations and Asbestos

The U.S. Occupational Safety and Health Administration (OSHA) requires rental property owners of homes built before 1981 who employ maintenance employees (including outside contractors for repair and maintenance jobs) to notify these people that a property may contain asbestos, and in some cases, test for it. You can avoid the responsibility only by having a licensed inspector test and confirm no asbestos is present in the home.

OSHA regulations also require custodial workers (such as the handyman who installs smoke detectors in the acoustic tile ceilings) to have gone through specialized training and use particular work procedures. The procedural rules get extra strict after any intentional disturbance of asbestos or asbestos-containing materials.

If you hire a contractor to perform major renovations or repairs that involve asbestos, the contractor must comply with OSHA's education and prevention rules. But if your own employees do the work, the burden falls on you to learn and implement the rules (see our resource suggestions in this chapter).

If you learn there's asbestos on your property (perhaps when complying with OSHA's testing and maintenance requirements, above), you can't pretend not to know about it. It becomes an undisclosed and dangerous defect that you must tell tenants about and take steps to remedy. Some states may also say you've breached the implied warranty of habitability, potentially giving the tenant the right to break the lease and move out without notice, pay less rent, withhold the entire rent, or sue to force you to make the place habitable.

Unless the asbestos material has begun to break down and enter the air, it's usually best to leave it alone and monitor it. You can do this as part of your regular safety inspection, discussed in Chapter 7, and you can also require your tenant to report any deterioration to you. If you must disturb asbestos, warn the tenants first, giving them an opportunity to avoid the area. You might even consider temporarily relocating your tenant. The costs of a few days or weeks in alternate housing will pale compared to the expense of a personal injury lawsuit.

If you learn that asbestos material is airborne (or is about to be), seek an expert's advice on remedies. When removal is necessary, hire trained asbestos removal specialists, and check to make sure the debris is legally disposed of in approved hazardous waste disposal sites. Don't allow tenants to make repairs to or otherwise invade any spaces containing asbestos, for example by drilling holes in the ceiling to hang plants.

> **RESOURCE**
> **Asbestos resources.** For more on asbestos rules, inspections, and control, see OSHA's website at www.osha.gov or call 800-321-OSHA. Also check into OSHA's interactive computer software, called "Asbestos Advisor" (available free at www.osha.gov), which will help identify asbestos on your property and suggest the most sensible solution.

Lead

As we all know, exposure to lead-based paint and lead water pipes may lead to serious health problems, particularly in children. Buildings constructed pre-1978 are likely to contain some lead, whether it's in the paint, pipes, or solder used on copper pipes.

You must, under federal law, inform the tenant, even before signing or renewing a lease or rental agreement, of any information you have on lead paint hazards on the property. If you've had your property tested, that includes showing tenants a copy of the report, or a summary written by the inspector. It also includes giving the tenant the lead hazard information booklet *Protect Your Family From Lead in Your*

Home, by the Environmental Protection Agency (EPA) and available at www.epa.gov/lead/pubs/leadprot.htm. Agencies in many states have developed their own pamphlets, which you can use instead of the EPA version if the EPA has approved them.

With a few limited exceptions, every lease and rental agreement must include a disclosure page, even if you haven't tested for lead. You can use the one developed by the EPA, "Disclosure of Information on Lead-Based Paint and/or Lead-Based Paint Hazards," available at www.epa. gov. The form has a place for tenants to initial, indicating that they've received it. Note the date they received it, and if you and the tenant are also signing the lease or rental agreement on the same day, enter the time you signed it, too. If you're ever challenged, or investigated by a government agency, you'll be able to prove that the tenant received the disclosure form before signing the rental documents.

> **CAUTION**
>
> **You have additional obligations if you renovate the property.** When you renovate a building constructed before 1978, EPA regulations require that current tenants receive lead hazard information before any renovation work begins. A copy of the EPA pamphlet *Protect Your Family From Lead in Your Home* will do.

Most states also require landlords to carefully maintain any existing lead paint and lead-based building materials, and they mandate who may work on lead paint abatement. If you're subject to a state statute, you must comply with it as well as the federal law.

There's no federal legal requirement that you be proactive and test for the presence of lead. But you may want to anyway, for these reasons:

- **Controlling lead is much easier than going through a lawsuit.** Besides, do you really want to live with the knowledge that a child's health has been damaged?

- **Ignorance may not shield you from liability.** At some point, a court will no doubt rule that the danger of lead paint in older housing is so well known that owners of older housing can be presumed to know of the danger.

- **You can't simply refuse to rent to tenants with children.** Though you may feel this protects them, this is illegal discrimination in all states.

- **You can't shift responsibility with a clause in your lease or rental agreement.** An exculpatory clause, which attempts to absolve you from any responsibility for lead-based injuries, won't protect you. In fact, it may work against you, showing that you knew of the lead problem.

- **Any refinance or sale will probably bring the problem to light.** Your lender may require lead testing before approving a loan.

- **Your insurance company may soon require lead testing as a condition of issuing a policy.** Claims based on lead-based injuries are very expensive—expect the insurance company to require testing before issuing a homeowners' policy, or to exclude claims based on lead. Review your coverage with your insurance broker.

> **RESOURCE**
> **Lead hazard resources.** Information on the evaluation and control of lead dust, disclosure forms, copies of the *Protect Your Family From Lead in Your Home* pamphlet, lists of EPA-certified lead paint professionals, and more may be obtained from the National Lead Information Center at 800-424-LEAD or www.epa.gov/lead.

Lead is relatively easy to detect—you can buy home-use kits that contain a simple swab, which turns color when drawn over a lead-based surface. Knowing how much lead is present, and how to best clean it up, however, are subjects for a certified lead abatement specialist. Plan on speaking with one if a lead test, done professionally or with an at-home kit, comes up positive.

Radon

Radon is a naturally occurring radioactive gas associated with lung cancer. It can enter and contaminate a house built on soil and rock containing uranium deposits or through water from private wells drilled in uranium-rich soil. Radon can become lethal when trapped in tightly sealed homes (well insulated or with poor ventilation), when escaping from building materials that have incorporated uranium-filled rocks and soils, or when released from aerated, contaminated household water. Problems occur most frequently in areas where rocky soil is relatively rich in uranium and in climates where occupants keep their windows tightly shut.

You're not legally required to test for radon, but you should do so if levels are known to be high in your area (ask your city planning department or insurance broker). For the best results, hire an EPA-certified inspector. Testing takes at least three days, and sometimes months. Do-it-yourself testing kits are also available; make sure the kit says "Meets EPA Requirements."

If testing indicates high radon levels, be sure to warn tenants and correct the problem. Start by giving them the EPA booklet *A Radon Guide for Tenants* (see "Radon resources," below.) Ventilation measures will effectively disperse the gas in most situations. These measures range from the obvious (open the windows and provide cross-ventilation) to the somewhat complex (sealing cracks in the foundation or sucking radon out of the soil before it enters the foundation). According to the EPA, a typical household radon problem can be solved for $500 to $2,500.

RESOURCE

Radon resources. Contact the EPA Radon Information Line at 800-767-7236, or visit the EPA website (www.epa.gov/iaq/radon). The site has links to state agencies that regulate radon and gives information on finding a qualified radon reduction provider. You can also download a copy of *A Radon Guide for Tenants* and other publications.

Carbon monoxide

Carbon monoxide (CO) is a colorless, odorless, lethal gas; a byproduct of fuel combustion produced by nonelectric home appliances such as gas dryers, refrigerators, ranges, water heaters or space heaters, oil furnaces, fireplaces, charcoal grills, and wood stoves. If appliances or fireplaces aren't vented properly, CO can build up within a home and poison the occupants. Unlike radon, whose deadly effects work over time, CO can build up and kill within a matter of hours. And, unlike any of the environmental hazards discussed so far, CO cannot be covered up or managed.

If you have a regular maintenance program, discussed in Chapter 7, you should be able to spot and fix the common malfunctions that cause CO buildup. Here's how to avoid problems:

- Check chimneys and appliance vents for blockages.
- Prohibit tenants from using indoor, portable gas or charcoal grills.
- Warn tenants never to use a gas range, clothes dryer, or oven for heating.
- Prohibit nonelectric space heaters, or specify that they must be inspected annually. Tenants can get recommendations from fuel suppliers.
- Check the pilot lights of gas appliances regularly. They should show a clear blue flame; a yellow or orange flame may indicate a problem.

RESOURCE

Carbon monoxide resources. The EPA website offers useful instructional material, including downloadable educational pamphlets, at www.epa.gov/iaq/co.html. Local natural gas utility companies often offer consumer information. Also contact the American Gas Association for consumer pamphlets on carbon monoxide; it's at 202-824-7000 or www.aga.org.

Mold

Across the country, tenants have won multimillion dollar cases against landlords for significant health problems—such as rashes, chronic fatigue, nausea, cognitive losses, hemorrhaging, and asthma—allegedly caused by exposure to "toxic molds." But not all mold produces toxins, and most mold is not otherwise harmful—for example, the mold that grows on shower tiles isn't dangerous. The trouble is, it takes an expert to know whether a particular mold is harmful or just unsightly and annoying.

Mold often grows on water-soaked materials, such as wall paneling, paint, fabric, ceiling tiles, newspapers, or cardboard boxes. However, all that's really needed is an organic food source, water, and time. Throw in a little warmth, and the organism will grow quickly, sometimes spreading within 24 hours. Humidity sets up prime growing conditions. Floods, leaking pipes, windows, or roofs may lead to mold growth in any structure.

No federal or state laws set permissible mold exposure limits or building tolerance standards for residences. Some local ordinances identify mold as a legal nuisance or a property condition that the landlord must clean up. Check with your city building, health, or environmental health departments to find out whether your city has passed any relevant laws.

Law or no law, your legal duty to provide and maintain habitable premises naturally extends to fixing leaking pipes, windows, and roofs—the causes of most mold. If you're lax, and mold grows as a result, you may be held responsible for a tenant's resulting health problems.

But instead of worrying about unlikely lawsuits, focus on preventing the conditions that lead to mold growth. The following steps are especially important if your rental house is in a humid environment or has had past mold problems:

- **Check for and fix moisture or mold problems before new tenants move in.** This will help prevent problems before they start.

- **Make sure every tenant understands how to help prevent mold growth.** Use your lease or house rules to educate tenants about sensible housekeeping practices and how to fix problems should they arise. Give tenants specific advice, such as how to ventilate the rental unit, avoid creating areas of standing water, and clean vulnerable areas, such as bathrooms, with cleaning solutions that will discourage mold growth.

- **Encourage tenants to immediately report signs of mold.** This includes reporting conditions that may lead to mold, such as plumbing leaks and weatherproofing problems.
- **Do all necessary repairs and maintenance to clean up or reduce mold.** For example, consider installing exhaust fans in rooms with high humidity (bathrooms, kitchens, and service porches) or provide tenants with dehumidifiers in chronically damp climates.

Should You Test For Mold?

Properly testing for mold will cost you more than you want to pay. Although over-the-counter kits can be bought for around $30, their results are questionable. A professional's basic investigation for a single-family home will run you $1,000 or more. To further complicate matters, there are relatively few competent professionals in this new field, and no state or federal certification programs to govern them.

If you have visible signs of mold, you're much better off simply getting rid of it, using the procedures described below. The procedures are the same no matter what kind of mold it is.

Most mold is relatively harmless and easy to deal with. A weak bleach solution (one cup of bleach per gallon of water) will remove mold from nonporous materials. Use gloves and avoid exposing eyes and lungs to airborne mold dust (use a mask). Allow for frequent work breaks with plenty of fresh air.

Clean or remove all infested areas, beginning on a small patch to make sure you don't develop adverse health reactions such as nausea or headaches. (If you do, call in an experienced professional.) Contain the work space with plastic sheeting and enclose debris in plastic bags. Don't try removing mold from fabrics such as towels, linens, drapes, carpets, and clothing—you'll have to dispose of these already ruined items.

If the mold is extensive, consider hiring an experienced mold remediation company with excellent references. For more information, check out the sites noted in "Mold resources," below.

> **CAUTION**
>
> **Check your insurance policy.** You may be dismayed to find that it excludes mold damage from coverage (or will on the next renewal). Even if mold is covered, many insurers try to wiggle out by claiming that it falls within the "pollution exclusion." Most policies won't cover you if you commit or allow pollution, the classic example being deliberately dumping solvents onto the property. Talk to your insurance broker if you're concerned about mold coverage.

> **RESOURCE**
>
> **Mold resources.** For information on mold detection, removal, and prevention, visit the EPA website at www.epa.gov/mold.

Bedbugs

Bedbugs are biting, obnoxious pests that nest in mattresses, bed frames, and beyond. In fact, they can infest an entire room or house, spreading via cracks in the walls, heating ducts, and other openings. They're also excellent stowaways, crawling into luggage, clothing, pillows, boxes, and furniture as these are moved from an infested home or hotel to another location. Secondhand furniture is a common source of infestation.

You'll learn that bedbugs have infested your property when the tenant complains of widespread, annoying bites that appear during the night (fortunately, bedbugs don't carry disease-causing germs). To minimize the outbreak, take the following steps immediately:

- **Confirm the infestation.** Make sure you're not dealing with some other pest, such as fleas. Because several kinds of insects resemble bedbugs, you'll need to capture a critter or two and study them. Go online for pictures, and compare your samples. If it looks like a bedbug, call an experienced pest control operator, pronto.

> **TIP**
> **Bring in the pros.** A can of Raid isn't going to do the job, and will end up costing you more in the long run. Depending on the size of the rental, expect to pay from $100–$750 for the initial service, and $75–$300 for follow-up treatments. If you find a company that offers to control bedbugs for $50 per unit, get another bid.

- **Declutter, move the tenant out, exterminate, vacuum—and do it again.** Bedbugs thrive in clutter, so tenants must remove all items from closets, shelves, and drawers and wash all bedding and clothing in hot water. As University of Kentucky professor of entomology Michael F. Potter told USA TODAY's Donna Freydkin, "As little as five or ten minutes kills everything on high heat. Cold will not kill the eggs and not all the adults." Put washed items in sealed plastic bags, then move the tenant out during treatment. Most of the time, tenants can return the same day. Upon return, the tenant—or you—must thoroughly vacuum. Exterminators may recommend a second and even a third treatment, with exhaustive cleaning and clutter-removing in between.

Your insurance will probably not cover the cost of hiring a pest control company for bedbugs (nor for any other vermin or insect infestation). However, insurance may cover you for the tenant's claims for lost or damaged belongings, medical expenses, and related moving and living expenses, as well as your loss of rent. If your tenant has renters' insurance, suggest referring the matter to the insurance company.

Don't Let the Bedbugs Bite

First come the bites, amazingly itchy, raised red welts that appear literally overnight. Then, you might notice scarlet spots on your sheets from smashed bugs or perhaps clusters of little black dots that you assume are dirt but are in fact constellations of fecal matter.

And one day, you might wake up in the wee hours of the morning, flip on the lights and find red bugs, slightly bigger than ticks, crawling on your sheets, pillows, and legs.

Welcome to the most retro pest of the 21st century, the bedbug. The bugs, which were thought to be wiped out by powerful pesticides such as DDT 30 years ago, are back and infesting major urban areas, suburbia, and the heartland.

Debbie Wunder and her husband, Rusty Pistachio, picked up the insects from a hotel in Curacao in the Netherlands Antilles. They didn't realize until later that they were bringing them home to Manhattan. He was eaten up all over; she didn't get a single bite, which isn't unusual, experts say. Bugs often feast on one person and ignore another.

The bedbug problem, says Michael Raupp, professor of entomology at the University of Maryland, "is across the board. This is a general problem and is on the upswing in all of our states."

Once you pick them up in a hotel, a subway, or a rental car and they invade your living space, it's difficult to get rid of them. They're becoming ever more resistant to the few sprays that are approved to fight them after DDT was banned in 1972.

Wunder, who now lives in Los Angeles with her husband, bought covers for her new mattress and box spring, washed or dry-cleaned all her clothing, and says she's become a bedbug vigilante.

"I will never ever sleep in a hotel bed without doing a thorough check of the mattress and linens," she says.

 "They're ba-a-ack for a snack; It's easy to say 'Don't let the bedbugs bite'—until the paranoia-inducing, bloodsucking parasites shake you awake," by Donna Freydkin, November 7, 2007.

No tenant is going to be happy to hear that you've had a past bedbug problem, and no statute or court decision directs you to reveal a rental's bedbug history. Nevertheless, if a prospect questions you directly about bedbugs, especially if the issue is clearly of critical importance to the person, you must answer truthfully. Otherwise you risk the tenant breaking the lease or suing you for damages. Even if you don't disclose, if you had a problem and it reappears, the tenant may still pursue these options, creating quite a headache for you.

Keeping Tenants Safe: Liability for Crime

Even the safest neighborhoods have occasional incidents of crime, and depending on the circumstances, you may be held at least partially responsible for resulting tenant injuries and losses. Once again, preventive measures are your best response. Thankfully, the most successful prevention techniques—proper lighting and good locks, for example—are inexpensive. And they'll help you avoid the greater costs produced by actual incidents of crime, including increased insurance premiums and lost income due to rapid turnover.

Here are some suggestions to effectively and reasonably protect your tenants:

- **Meet or exceed basic legal requirements for safety devices.** Buy and maintain deadbolt locks, good lighting, and window locks, especially when they're required by state and local housing codes. (Ask your state or local housing agency or rental property owners' association.)

- **Respond to the environment.** Examine and research the vulnerability of your property and neighborhood. If your tenants will pay more rent if you make the building safer, you'd be foolish not to do it.

- **Tighten up management practices.** For example, strictly control who has a key to the property.

- **Educate your tenants about crime problems and prevention strategies.** Make it clear that they—not you—are primarily responsible for their protection. Explain what they can do to minimize the chances of assault or theft (avoid being alone on the street or in outside parking lots late at night). Also warn tenants of the limitations of the security measures you've put in place.

- **Don't hype your security measures.** You don't want to inadvertently promise a higher level of security than you're prepared to provide. Derek, who rents out a house in Atlanta that he inherited from his mother, learned this lesson the hard way: "I'd described the neighborhood as 'safe and secure,' and basically promised my new tenant that the security service hired by the homeowners' association was on duty 24/7. Guess what: The tenant got mugged at about 7 p.m. while walking his dog. Then I found out that the 'security service' consisted of an off-duty policeman making the rounds now and then. The tenant's lawyers argued that my tenant would never have ventured out if he'd known the true state of security, and I lost the case."

- **Deal with common security problems.** At the top of your list should be fixing burned-out exterior floodlights and broken locks (the top way landlords are found liable for tenant injuries caused by criminals) and cutting back overgrown shrubbery that provides a convenient lurking spot for criminals. Also ask tenants for their suggestions, and quickly respond. If an important component of your security systems breaks, be prepared to fix it on an emergency basis and provide appropriate alternative security.

- **Purchase adequate liability insurance.** This will protect you from lawsuits related to crime on your rental property.

These steps will not only limit the likelihood of criminal activity on your property, but will also reduce the risk that you'll be found responsible if an assault or robbery does take place.

Protecting Neighbors From Illegal Tenant Activities

It shouldn't be your fault when tenants break the law. Yet, increasingly over the last decade, stricter laws and court decisions have made landlords liable when they fail to sufficiently respond to tenants' activities, especially ongoing illegal activities such as drug dealing. You might face:

- **Nuisance lawsuits.** A legal "nuisance" is a pervasive, continuing, and serious condition—like a pile of garbage or group of drug dealers—that threatens public health, safety, or morals. Every state has a nuisance abatement law, which allows the government, and sometimes the neighbors, to fight back, often by court order and fines against the landlord. In some states, neighbors can sue in small claims court, seeking monetary compensation (each neighbor may sue for the maximum limit) and an order requiring the landlord to evict the troublemakers, install security, and repair the premises.

- **Forfeiting the property.** Federal and state forfeiture proceedings—where the government takes your property because of the illegal activities of one or more tenants—are the most dramatic and devastating consequence of owning crime-ridden rental property. Forfeitures are relatively rare, but may be accomplished on the basis of a single incident.

If you suspect that a tenant or potential tenant may be up to something illegal—or that you're being paid rent from ill-gotten gains—check out *Every Landlord's Legal Guide*, by Marcia Stewart, Ralph Warner, and Janet Portman (Nolo).

TIP

Protect yourself, too. Take precautions for your own personal safety, by:

- **Promptly depositing rent checks and money orders.** If possible, do not accept cash.
- **When showing your property, bringing someone with you.** If you must show the property alone, at least let someone know, and say when you expect to be done.
- **Going high-tech.** Especially if the property is in a high-crime area, carry a cell phone and small alarm device (such as beeper-sized box that emits a piercing alarm when its pin is removed).

Insurance Coverage for Property and Liability

After scaring you with everything you can be sued or otherwise held responsible for, here's a reason to breathe a sigh of relief: You can protect yourself from many problems by buying adequate insurance. A well-designed insurance program can cover your rental property for both physical losses and people's injuries.

Getting adequate liability coverage

Commercial general liability coverage will reimburse for injuries or losses suffered by others as the result of defective conditions on your property or your carelessness. Equally important, it covers the cost of settling personal injury claims, including lawyers' bills for your defense.

For example, if your tenant gets injured falling down a defective staircase that you knew about, had a chance to fix, but failed to repair, your insurance company would handle any lawsuit or claim brought by the tenant and pay any settlement or award. The same would be true if your tenant's child's playmate, over for the afternoon, drowned in the backyard pool that you'd failed to equip with a legally required anti-suction device.

Liability policies usually state a dollar limit per occurrence and an aggregate dollar limit for the policy year. For example, your policy may say that it will pay $300,000 per occurrence for personal injury or a total of $1 million in any one policy year.

Depending on the value of your property and of your personal assets, buying even more coverage (called an "umbrella policy") is an excellent idea, especially if you're in a large metropolitan area, where personal injury damage awards are likely to be very high. Umbrella policies are not expensive. Don't put your property at risk of being sold to pay a court judgment!

When choosing liability coverage, consider buying a policy that provides protection for not only physical injury claims, but also claims of libel, slander, discrimination, unlawful and retaliatory eviction, and invasion of privacy suffered by tenants and guests.

You can also suggest, and in most states you can require, that your tenant buy liability insurance as part of a renter's policy. Having a renters' policy in place will protect your own insurance. Here's how it works: Suppose the tenant starts a fire on the stove and burns the kitchen. Your own property insurance would cover the damage—but so would the tenants' insurance. If you require that the tenant's policy be "primary," (that is, applied first to any claim), you can insist that the tenant's carrier, not yours, cover the damage. You're always better off when you don't have to go to your carrier with a claim.

Getting adequate property coverage

Your property insurance should cover losses from a whole host of perils, such as damage from fire, storms, burglary, and vandalism. In negotiating coverage, there are four main questions to consider:

- **What features of the rental property are insured?** Be sure your insurance covers all the property you want protected, be it outdoor fixtures, appliances like washing machines, property used to maintain the house (such as gardening equipment and tools), personal property you're leaving in the house (for example, if it will be partially furnished), and personal business property such as computers.

> **TIP**
>
> **Make sure your tenants know that your insurance doesn't cover loss or damage to their personal property.** If a thief steals your tenants' jewelry or a fire damages their clothing and electronics, they're on their own. Your tenants will need to purchase their own renters' insurance to cover personal property losses—it's relatively affordable, at around $150 to $300 per year.

- **What perils will be insured against?** Coverage for damage caused by fire and smoke is common in the most basic policies. Standard policies also cover damage from wind, hail, lightning, explosions, volcanoes, riots and vandalism, theft, water damage (from burst pipes, for example), and similar events.

- **What perils will be excluded from coverage?** Damage from mudslides, windstorms, the weight of snow, police activity, power outages, sewer backups, dry rot, vermin, war, nuclear perils, losses if your house is vacant for 60 days or more, or losses caused by your own—or your tenant's—intentional or criminal actions, poor maintenance, or failure to preserve or protect the property after it's been damaged, may all be excluded from your policy. Earthquake insurance on the house itself and flood insurance are typically separate. (They're typically expensive and have a very high deductible, but are still worthwhile if your building is highly susceptible to earthquake or flood damage.)

> **TIP**
>
> **Check out "loss of rents" insurance.** This will reimburse you for the lost rental income if your property is sidelined—for example, due to a fire or other calamity.

- **How much insurance should you buy?** "Inadequate insurance coverage plagues homeowners across the USA," say USA TODAY's Kathy Chu and Elizabeth Weise. Be sure to carry enough insurance on the building to rebuild it if it's destroyed.

That doesn't usually mean you'll get a blank check—most policies cover "replacement cost," or a preset dollar amount that was calculated when you first got the policy. (That's better than "actual cash value coverage," which pays only the property's replacement cost minus any depreciation or wear and tear since it was built.) The problem with replacement cost coverage, as Chu and Weise found, is that the cost of building materials has climbed "far above overall inflation. Prices of construction materials can rise even more after natural disasters." Increased demand for home contractors after a disaster may also drive up prices. For a reality check, ask a local contractor how much a structure like yours would cost to build today. If it's more than the amount offered by your insurance, work with your insurance rep to raise your replacement cost figure. Another worthwhile option is buying an "inflation guard," which raises the stated value of your house by a set percentage each year. At least there's no need to insure the total value of your real property (the legal term that includes land and buildings), because land doesn't burn or get knocked over.

USA TODAY Snapshots®

In case of emergency...

Slightly more than half (52%) of adults say they have disaster supply kits. Of those who have kits, items they say they definitely have:

Flashlight	94%
Extra batteries	88%
First aid kit	85%
Three-day supply of non-perishable food	76%
Three-day supply of water	72%
Battery or hand-crank radio	71%

Source: Telephone survey of 1,000 adults 18 years and older conducted by ORC International for the American Red Cross, May 4-7, 2006. Margin of error is ±3.1 percentage points overall, 6 percentage points for those who have kits.

By Tracey Wong Briggs and Marcy E. Mullins, USA TODAY
2008

- **Is your house old enough that it will need code upgrades during reconstruction?** Building codes normally require that an older building be rebuilt to modern standards and codes, which is often much pricier than simply replacing it as it was. Ask for "ordinance or law coverage." It's almost never included in standard policies, but is worth paying a little extra for.

TIP
Tell your insurance company about remodels or upgrades.
USA TODAY's Sandra Block discovered (in 2006) that, "Nearly 40%
of Americans who have made significant home improvements since
2003, such as adding a room or deck, said they hadn't updated their
homeowners' insurance, or weren't sure if they had. If your policy is
based on the value of your home before you remodeled, you may
not recoup the money you spent to add a bathroom or update your
kitchen."

Converting your existing homeowners' policy

If you're an accidental landlord converting your own house to a rental,
you may want to continue with your current insurance company.
However, you can't just sit back and expect your homeowners' policy
to remain in effect. Contact the insurer and ask that the policy be
rewritten to fit your new role as a landlord. (In fact, current industry
practice is to actually split rental property insurance into two separate
policies, one for property and one for liability.) If you don't change your
coverage, your insurer could simply deny any of your later claims. Of
course, you don't have to stick with your existing insurer—comparing
prices is a fine idea, too.

TIP
Buying a new home to live in? You can save money, according
to Mike Mansel, certified insurance counselor (www.insuranceadvisor.
pro), by "looking into using the same insurance company for both
your rental property and your new home. That way the insurer can
simply extend the liability portion of your homeowners' policy to the
rental property—which will be less expensive than buying two separate
liability policies. After that, you'll just need to buy a separate fire policy
for the rental, also with the same company."

During the conversion, your insurer will reassess the level of risk regarding the fire portion of the policy. It may say that your property is now at higher risk of damage because of possible vacancies and because tenants tend to be harder on a property than a homeowner. Your rates may go up a bit for this part of the policy. However, your overall rates will probably go down, because you'll no longer need coverage for personal possessions (unless you're leaving a lot behind).

Do a careful comparison between your new and old policies before signing. You may discover that coverage you assumed would still be included is no longer there, but can be added in.

CAUTION

Don't let your house sit empty for 60 to 90 days or more. If you have a typical homeowners' policy, this will result in it being canceled. Check your policy to be sure, and talk to your insurance agent if you think this might become an issue.

Working with your agent to get the best coverage

Not all insurance agents are created equal. Get recommendations from other landlords, or from real estate people with several years' experience. A good agent will listen to your needs and help you find a policy that addresses them, and will:

- **Analyze your business operations.** Steer clear of any agent who, without learning the specifics of your property and business, whips out a package policy and claims it will solve all your problems.

- **Make you feel comfortable discussing your needs.** While some policy buyers try to keep their rates down by downplaying areas of unusual risk, this is a bad idea. If you don't disclose all the facts, you may not get the coverage you need, or the insurance company may later try to deny you coverage because you misrepresented the nature of your operation.

- **Explain what's excluded.** Does the policy exclude damage from a leaking sprinkler system? From dog bites? From an earthquake? If so, and these are risks you face, find out whether they can be covered by paying a small extra premium.

- **Represent only highly rated carriers.** Insurance companies are rated according to their financial condition and size. The most recognized rater is the A.M. Best Company, which assigns letter ratings according to financial stability (A++ is the highest) and Roman numeral ratings reflecting the size of a company's surplus (XV is the best). Since 80% of American companies receive an A rating or higher, there's no reason to choose a company rated anything less. As to surplus, you'll be on solid ground requiring an "X." Your local public library will likely have the *Best's Key Rating Guide*, or you can find it online at www.ambest.com.

Saving money on insurance

Few landlords can afford to adequately insure themselves against every possible risk. Here are some guidelines to help you keep costs down:

- **Set priorities.** Ask yourself: What types of property losses would threaten the viability of my business? What kinds of liability lawsuits might wipe me out? Tailor your coverage to protect against these potentially disastrous losses. Get enough property and liability coverage to protect yourself from the most common claims, adding coverage for serious risks where it's reasonably priced.

- **Select a high deductible.** The deductible is the amount you must pay out of pocket before insurance coverage kicks in. The cost difference between a policy with a $250 deductible and one with a $500 or $1,000 or even higher deductible is significant— particularly if you add up the premium savings for five or ten years. Consider using the money you save to buy coverage you would have otherwise gone without, such as for loss of rents.

- **Reduce your risk.** Good safety and security measures, such as regular property inspections, special fire prevention measures, adding dead-bolt locks, or requiring that tenants buy renters' insurance, may eliminate the need for some types of insurance or lead to lower rates or discounts. Also ask your insurance agent what you can do to get a better rate.

- **Comparison shop.** No two companies charge exactly the same rates. But be wary of an unusually low price, which may be a sign of a shaky company. Or it may be that you're unfairly comparing policies that provide very different types of coverage. Make sure you know what you're buying, and review your coverage and rates periodically.

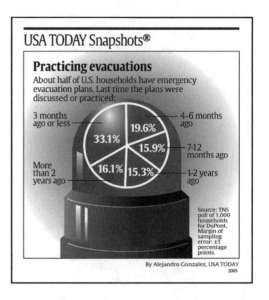

USA TODAY Snapshots®

Practicing evacuations

About half of U.S. households have emergency evacuation plans. Last time the plans were discussed or practiced:

3 months ago or less — 33.1%
4-6 months ago — 19.6%
7-12 months ago — 15.9%
1-2 years ago — 15.3%
More than 2 years ago — 16.1%

Source: TNS poll of 1,000 households for DuPont. Margin of sampling error: ±3 percentage points.

By Alejandro Gonzalez, USA TODAY 2005

RESOURCE

For more information on choosing business insurance: See the Insurance Information Institute's website at www.iii.org. Also check out *Every Landlord's Property Protection Guide,* by Ron Leshnower (Nolo), which gives detailed advice on evaluating insurance and reducing the risk of injury and property damage at your property.

Living in Perfect Harmony? Dealing With Difficult Tenants

Despite your careful screening, you're bound someday to have a less-than-perfect tenant. It may be one who's chronically late with the rent, disturbs the neighbors with loud parties or a constant stream of visitors, or brings in a dog without your permission. Whatever the problem, you'll want to know how to resolve it quickly, with minimum hassle or expense.

In this chapter, we'll help you figure out how to deal with difficult tenants and enforce the terms of your lease or rental agreement. We'll cover:

- common tenant problems and what to do about them
- different methods for resolving disputes, and
- how to evict a tenant, if that becomes necessary.

 TIP

Lesson learned the hard way: It's not my house anymore. Amy, who rents out her former home in Austin, Texas while she attends graduate school out of state, says, "After my first set of tenants left, I discovered that they'd painted all the rooms different colors and that their dogs, which I hadn't known about, had destroyed the backyard and the storm door. That was crushing—I still felt like it was my house."

Common Tenant Problems—And What to Do About Them

While tenants come in all shapes and sizes, most tenant problems boil down to a few common and recurring themes. Here, we'll cover some of the problems you're likely to encounter, and how you may wish to approach them. Later in the chapter, we'll explain specific negotiating strategies, as well as how to legally get the tenant to leave.

Late rent

While being a day or two late every once in awhile shouldn't be a reason to evict—especially if it's an otherwise reliable tenant—you probably do want to enforce on-time payments. This will help show that you're serious about this business relationship, and help avoid reinforcing late-payment habits.

USA TODAY Snapshots®

The check's in the mail

The order in which Americans pay bills when they are late:

Mortgage/rent — **79%**
Car payment **41%**
Auto insurance **39%**
Credit card/cellphone **38%**
Cable/satellite television **32%**

Source: Survey of 1,000 consumers for AmeriCredit for Market Facts

By Darryl Haralson and Frank Pompa, USA TODAY 2004

The first time your tenant is late, simply call and make sure the payment didn't get lost, forgotten, or misplaced. If the tenant apologizes profusely and pays you immediately—especially a tenant with a history of on-time payments—you may have nothing more to worry about.

The next time it happens, however, you should probably invoke the late-fee clause in your lease or rental agreement.

> **TIP**
>
> **Enforce your right to the late fee.** Your tenant may decide to pay the rent, but not the fee. If you're thinking, "I'll take it out of the security deposit," check your state's laws first—many forbid that. Instead, if your lease or rental agreement says that the fee is considered "additional rent," you'll be able to use a "Pay or Quit" notice to demand the late fee, and you can begin eviction proceedings if the tenant doesn't pay the fee (or move). If your rental document doesn't describe the fee as additional rent, you'll have to sue in small claims court to get it—hardly worthwhile for such a small amount.

If the tenant promises to send a check soon but doesn't, fails to respond to your call, or says "Sorry, I can't make the payment," your next step will probably be to send a termination notice (often called a "Pay or Quit") notice. This notice should explain that the tenant must pay rent within a designated time or move out. If the tenant doesn't comply, you can file an eviction lawsuit. (Proper termination notices and evictions are covered later in this chapter.)

Breaking the lease early

A lease obligates you and the tenant for its entire term. But tenants' life circumstances don't always cooperate, and you may well encounter times when a tenant needs or wants to break the lease and move out early. Sometimes, the reason for their leave-taking is legally recognized (as when the landlord refuses to repair a problem that makes the rental unfit). But more often, it's love, a job, school, or the prospect of a better deal somewhere else.

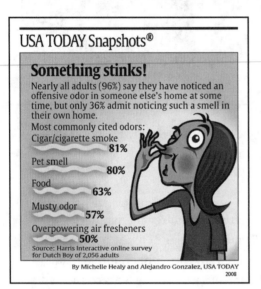

USA TODAY Snapshots®

Something stinks!

Nearly all adults (96%) say they have noticed an offensive odor in someone else's home at some time, but only 36% admit noticing such a smell in their own home.

Most commonly cited odors:

Cigar/cigarette smoke **81%**

Pet smell **80%**

Food **63%**

Musty odor **57%**

Overpowering air fresheners **50%**

Source: Harris Interactive online survey for Dutch Boy of 2,056 adults

By Michelle Healy and Alejandro Gonzalez, USA TODAY 2008

What can you do about it? If you suspect that the tenant is about to split, have a conversation. Together, you may be able to address an underlying issue, such as the tenant's fear that you won't change your no-pets rule to make room for a new puppy. Or maybe the tenant is leaving because you haven't held up your end of a bargain—have failed to repair a leaky roof, for example—in which case you might negotiate a last chance to do your part. (By the way, if that tenant leaves for such a reason, you won't be able to ask for rent on the balance of the lease.)

But suppose the tenant is departing for purely personal reasons, and you can't work something out. Now, you're faced with a vacancy you weren't prepared for. The tenant is still responsible for the balance of the rent left on the lease, but that's not the end of the story. In most states, you must take reasonably prompt steps to re-rent the unit. Once it's re-rented, your former tenant's liability for the balance ends.

Nip Security Deposit Deductions in the Bud

At the end of your tenant's lease, you'll get inside the rental to assess its condition. You can fairly deduct from the security deposit those sums needed to remedy damage beyond normal wear and tear, and necessary cleaning.

But don't wait until then to take a look around. You might want to have a look mid-lease, to make sure minor problems don't develop into big ones, and to educate your tenants as to what to expect when they move out. As Stuart, with property in Davis, California, says, "No matter how clearly we try to explain security deposits in advance, each time the lease is up and I inspect the place, the tenants mouths drop at the deductions. They always seem to think the security deposit is just for rent, not for cleaning."

If you want to do a mid-lease inspection, follow your state's rules regarding landlord entry, giving the required amount of notice and scheduling the visit on an allowable day. When you find a problem—a hole in the wall, stained carpets—decide whether to fix it now or later (maybe it will be just as efficient to clean the carpets in six months, when the tenants leave).

Who pays? As long as the problem is one for which you could legitimately use the security deposit, you can demand that the tenants pay directly, or you may use the deposit. If you use the deposit, be sure to demand, in writing, that the tenants replenish the deposit. Failure to do so would be grounds for terminating the lease.

Other violations of the lease or rental agreement

Even rent-paying tenants are frequently known to violate important terms of the lease or rental agreement. Here are some of the most common violations, and what steps to take before terminating the agreement:

- **Moving in a pet.** If your agreement specifically forbids pets, or limits them to a certain type of pet, but your tenant moves one in anyway, you must decide whether you're willing to allow it. You may decide to ignore your rule if the tenant is reliable, the pet appears well-behaved, and you have not promised other tenants in a multi-family building that the property will be pet-free. Sometimes, it's not worth the bother of forcing the tenant to get rid of the animal or move out. However, if you decide to let the pet stay, you should amend your rental agreement to reflect it, and may want to increase the security deposit or require an additional "pet deposit" (check your state's security deposit law to find out whether you may charge additional sums or separate pet deposits). Also remember that certain types of animals—namely non-domestic pets, such as monkeys—may heighten your legal liability. Talk to your insurance company to find out, and for more information on liability, see Chapter 8.

> TIP
>
> **Best thing I ever did: Build a fence.** Stuart thought his tenant was bringing only one dog—a small, sweet pit bull. But, he says, "Then a friend joined them, who had other pit bulls—which were not so sweet or friendly. The neighbor, who has some small dogs, started complaining, afraid that the tenants' dogs would eat hers. But the pit bulls hadn't actually done anything wrong, and if I kicked out the tenants I wasn't likely to get replacement ones for a few months. So I went up and built a reinforced chain-link fence. That kept the neighbor satisfied."

- **Moving in other occupants.** A new boyfriend or girlfriend, an out-of-town buddy who's job-hunting—any of these people might have the tenant saying, "Sure, stay as long as you like," without remembering your rental terms. But your lease or rental agreement should prohibit tenants from moving in additional occupants without your consent (other than the occasional short-term guest, or a new spouse or child, whom you probably can't legally refuse). If you suspect that someone has moved in, talk with the tenant. If you're inclined to allow the new occupant to stay, you still need to go through the same formal screening steps you took when selecting your original tenant. If you don't want to accept the newcomer, or your screening turns up red flags, you can demand that the person leave. If necessary, give your original tenant a "Cure or Quit" termination notice, which offers two choices: either get rid of the unauthorized occupant or move out.

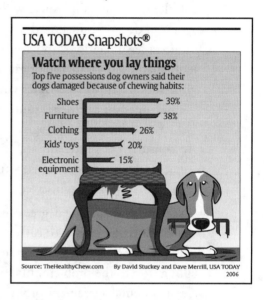

USA TODAY Snapshots®

Watch where you lay things

Top five possessions dog owners said their dogs damaged because of chewing habits:

Shoes	39%
Furniture	38%
Clothing	26%
Kids' toys	20%
Electronic equipment	15%

Source: TheHealthyChew.com   By David Stuckey and Dave Merrill, USA TODAY 2006

> **TIP**
>
> **You can terminate any month-to-month tenancy with proper notice (30 days in most states).** You needn't give a reason, as long as your motives aren't discriminatory or retaliatory. Note, however, that tenants in rent control cities with "just-cause" eviction protection, and all tenants in New Hampshire and New Jersey (which have statewide just-cause protections) may be able to resist a termination where the landlord can't provide a justifiable reason.

- **Illegal subleasing.** Instead of moving others in, the tenant might simply move out, either permanently or temporarily, and have a newcomer (a "subtenant") move in without asking your consent. You might find out what's happening when you see a new name on the rent checks. If you're willing to allow the arrangement, you can do so—but should first do careful screening, and create a direct legal relationship with the subtenant. With a permanent subtenant, terminate the original lease and sign a new one (the subtenant now becomes your tenant). With a temporary subtenant, you can write a sublease signed by all three of you, which will expire on the agreed-upon date. If you prefer not to consider the subtenant at all, or you find the subtenant unacceptable, you can refuse your consent and, if the newcomer moves in anyway, begin eviction procedures.

- **Excessive noise.** Some degree of noise is normal, but a tenant's loud parties, blaring music, or early morning carpentry projects can disturb neighbors and others. You'll want to act immediately to put a stop to the problem, first by pointing out any clauses in your lease or rental agreement prohibiting excessive noise. Even without a written provision, talk to the tenant immediately if you hear a complaint, then follow up with a warning letter if it isn't resolved. Not taking action could lead to legal troubles like code citations or a small claims lawsuit. In fact, if your rental property has other tenants, they have a right to quiet enjoyment of the premises.

RESOURCE
For more information on state and local noise laws, visit the Noise Pollution Clearinghouse's website at www.nonoise.org/lawlib.htm).

Of course, there are plenty of other lease or rental agreement terms that your tenant may violate. Your state's law will most likely insist that you give the tenant a few days (anywhere from three to ten days is common) to correct, or "cure," a lease or rental agreement violation.

You would do this using a "Cure or Quit" notice—that is, telling the tenant to fix the problem or leave. However, there are two important "but ifs" that would allow you to use the less generous "Unconditional Quit" notice:

- **Repeated violations.** In some states, if the tenant has violated the same lease clause two or more times within a certain period of time, the tenant may lose the right to a second chance.

- **A violation that can't be corrected.** Some lease violations have a permanent—and therefore incurable—effect. For instance, if your lease prohibits tenant alterations without your consent, and your tenant nevertheless removes the living room wallpaper, you can hardly demand that the tenant cease violating the lease clause. It's simply too late to save the wallpaper.

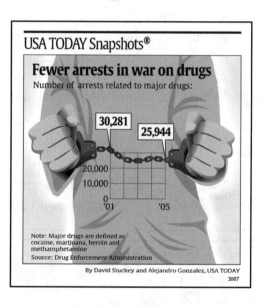

USA TODAY Snapshots®

Fewer arrests in war on drugs

Number of arrests related to major drugs:

30,281

25,944

20,000

10,000

0

'01   '05

Note: Major drugs are defined as cocaine, marijuana, heroin and methamphetamine
Source: Drug Enforcement Administration

By David Stuckey and Alejandro Gonzalez, USA TODAY 2007

Past criminal convictions

Although you're generally free to reject prospective tenants with criminal records, you won't necessarily find out about these convictions until you've already rented the unit. At that point, your first impulse might be to look for a way to get the tenant out of your building, particularly if the conviction is for a recent, violent crime. With a month-to-month tenant, it's easiest to just give the regular, required amount of notice to move out. (But there's an exception if the conviction was for drug use, and the tenant is currently not using illegal drugs—such a tenant is protected from termination under federal fair housing laws.)

TIP

Your "tenant screening" report may not have told you everything. "I ordered a background report on a prospective tenant," said Alex, a landlord in Cleveland. "It came back clean—but luckily I didn't stop there. When talking to a prior landlord, I learned that this guy had been convicted of a drug sale, though he didn't end up serving time. That's probably why the report didn't include the conviction. But with that information, I denied the application."

If your tenant has a lease, and is otherwise law- and rule-abiding, you won't be able to terminate the agreement just because you now know about the criminal record, no matter how unsavory or alarming. But it's a different story if your lease or rental agreement states that false and material information on the rental application will be grounds for termination. In that case, you can take steps to terminate the tenancy and evict.

Violations of a tenant's basic legal responsibilities

Virtually every state allows you to end the tenancy of a tenant who has violated basic responsibilities imposed by law. Violations might include grossly deficient housekeeping practices that cause an unhealthy situation, like allowing garbage to pile up; seriously misusing appliances, like defrosting the freezer with an icepick; or substantially damaging the property, perhaps by knocking holes in the walls.

The obligations to keep the property liveable and to refrain from damaging it should already be set out in your leases or rental agreements. But even if they're not, tenants are still legally bound to observe them.

USA TODAY Snapshots®

Garbage time
Top five foods thrown away by U.S. consumers because of spoilage:

Fresh vegetables and bagged salad — 58%
Fresh fruit — 49%
Bread — 49%
Milk, yogurt and cheese — 48%
Pre-packaged sandwich meat, hot dogs, bacon — 29%
19%

Source: DuPont Ipsos Public Affairs
Note: Margin of error ±3% percentage points.

By David Stuckey and Marcy E. Mullins, USA TODAY
2005

If a tenant or guest substantially damages the premises, you'll be within your rights to use an Unconditional Quit notice. The law does not require you to give tenants accused of serious misbehavior a second chance. Tenants who have earned this type of termination notice generally get only five to ten days to move out.

Tenant's illegal activity on the premises

In recent years, many states have responded aggressively to drug dealing in residential neighborhoods by making it easier for landlords to evict based on these or other illegal activities. You don't always have to wait until the tenant is convicted of a crime or even arrested—you may be able to evict based on your fact-based suspicion that illegal activity is afoot. But first, check your state's law to learn what level of proof you'll need to support this termination.

Evictions based on criminal activity are often called "expedited evictions," because they take less time than a normal eviction. Expedited evictions are preceded by an Unconditional Quit notice that tells the tenant to move out (and do it quickly). If the tenant stays, you can go to court and file for eviction. The court hearing on the eviction is typically held within a few days, and, if you win, the tenant is given very little time to move.

Resolving Disputes

If you have a problem tenant who won't listen to reason, but eviction doesn't seem like your best option (or perhaps you don't have solid legal grounds for it), there are other means for settling your dispute. Here are some ideas.

Try to negotiate a settlement

Because fighting a court battle costs time and money, you're almost always better off trying to settle any dispute first—whether it's over the acceptable noise level at your tenant's next party (some concrete guidelines specifying days, times, and decibel levels would help), or whether the tenant was justified in repainting the living room without your approval. Your goal should be to achieve the best result at the lowest cost. If instead you act on conviction or principle (whether right or wrong), chances are you'll spend far too much time and money.

USA TODAY Snapshots®

Secondhand smoke in America

126 million
Non-smoking
Americans exposed to
secondhand smoke

45 million
Number of adult
cigarette smokers

22 million
Children ages 3
to 11 exposed
to secondhand
smoke

Source: Centers for Disease Control and Prevention

By David Stuckey and Karl Gelles, USA TODAY
2007

Your first step in working toward a compromise with a problem tenant is to call and arrange a time to meet. Dropping over unannounced to talk may work in some circumstances, but is generally not a good idea, because the tenant may feel threatened and react defensively. Writing a letter first, offering to meet with the tenant to work something out, is a good way to let the tenant know you want to settle the matter. Here are some negotiating pointers:

- **Ask to hear the tenant's point of view.** Once the tenant starts talking, listen closely and don't interrupt.

- **Acknowledge hearing key points, even if you disagree with them.** Sometimes it's even a good idea to repeat the tenant's concerns, to demonstrate that you know what they are.

- **Avoid personal attacks.** This only raises the level of hostility and makes settlement more difficult.

- **Be courteous, but not weak.** Let the tenant know you have the resources and evidence to fight and win if you can't reach a settlement.

- **If possible, try to structure the negotiation as a mutual attempt to solve a problem.** For example, if a tenant's guests have been disturbing the neighbors, seek solutions that recognize the interests of both parties.

- **Put yourself in the tenant's shoes.** What would you want to get out of the settlement? Let the tenant have at least a partial sense of victory.

- **When you propose settlement terms, make it clear that you're compromising.** Offers of settlement (clearly labeled as such) can't be introduced against you if you ever end up in court.

- **For a powerful incentive, try money.** To avoid later costs, be willing to pay—perhaps by reducing rent for a short period, lowering the amount owed for damages to the premises, or offering an outright cash settlement for the tenant to leave (with payment made only when the tenant hands you the keys). Many tenants may settle at a surprisingly low figure if they can walk away from the bargaining table a little richer.

- **If you reach an understanding, promptly write it down and have all parties sign it.** You or your lawyer should volunteer to prepare the first draft. If you're paying the tenant some money as part of your agreement, make sure the tenant acknowledges in writing that your payment fully satisfies the claim.

Send a warning notice

Giving the tenant a written notice to cease the disruptive activity can be effective. Even if your oral warning or attempts to negotiate have been unsuccessful, people tend to take written notices a bit more seriously.

Your letter should include:

- details of the problem behavior, including dates and times of the occurrence

- what exactly you want the tenant to do (such as stop having noisy parties, pay for damage to the rental unit, or get rid of a long-term guest)

- the specific lease or rental agreement provision that prohibits this behavior, such as a clause requiring tenants to repair damaged property, or a lease restriction on guests, and

- the consequences for the tenant's failure to comply (such as termination or eviction proceedings).

TIP

Involve the cosigner when you send your warning notice.
Jim, who rented to three college students in Boston, insisted that
each student's parents cosign the lease. When Jim learned that the
students had brought in two unauthorized occupants, he wrote to
them, pointing out that their lease forbade unapproved residents; and
he cc'd their parents. That did the trick. "Once the parents realized
that they could be financially responsible for damage caused by these
newcomers, they apparently got on the phone, and the newcomers
were gone within a couple of days."

What if the tenant doesn't reform, despite your reminder? If you
want to get the tenant out, you certainly have grounds for terminating.
However, in a sense, you'll have to start over, by giving the tenant
a formal termination notice that meets your state's requirements.
(Termination notices are explained further below.)

Try mediating

If your settlement efforts don't work out, you may wish to try bringing
in a neutral third party to mediate. Mediation is often available at little
or no cost from a publicly funded program. A mediator has no power
to impose a decision, but simply helps both sides work out a mutually
acceptable solution.

Mediation can make good sense, especially if any of the following are
true:

- You've had otherwise positive experiences with the tenant, who
  seems worth dealing with in the future.

- The tenant agrees to split the cost (if any) of mediation.

- The tenant wants to avoid eviction and the expense and delay of
  litigation.

- The tenant is up to date on rent (or has cooperated by putting the
  rent money into some type of escrow account).

Mediation in landlord-tenant disputes is usually fairly informal. The mediator will ordinarily have everyone sit down and express all their issues—even emotional ones. This often cools people off and results in a quick compromise. If not, however, the mediator may talk to each person sequentially to try and determine his or her bottom line. Then, shuttling back and forth, the mediator helps the parties structure an acceptable solution. At some point, everyone has to get back together to sign off.

RESOURCE
Need information on local mediation programs? Call your mayor's or city manager's office, and ask for the staff member who handles "landlord-tenant mediation matters" or "housing disputes." That person should refer you to the public office or business or community group that attempts to resolve these disputes informally, and at little or no cost. Most local courts also provide referrals to community mediation services. For lists of professional mediators and extensive information on mediation, see www.mediate.com.

Represent yourself in small claims court

If your attempts at settling a dispute fail, you may end up having to sue. Fortunately, if the dispute is over a relatively small amount of money (less than $10,000 in most states), you can cost-efficiently represent yourself in small claims court. A few states call small claims courts by other names (such as landlord-tenant court), but the purpose is the same: to provide a speedy, inexpensive resolution of disputes. In a few states, eviction suits can be filed in small claims court.

Small claims court procedures are relatively simple and don't normally require a lawyer's help. You pay a small fee, file your lawsuit with the court clerk, have the papers served on your opponent, show up on the appointed day, tell the judge your story, and present any witnesses and other evidence. The evidence you bring with you is usually the most important part of your case—for example, a photograph of a damaged house and the convincing testimony of someone who helped you fix it are usually all you need to prevail and recover money over and above the tenant's deposit.

Don't immediately head for small claims court just because it's relatively easy and you're sure you have a good case. If you suspect you won't be able to collect the money owed—from your tenant's paycheck, bank account, or other financial resource—small claims court will be a waste of time. A judgment you can't collect is worthless.

Avoiding Retaliation Charges

Tenants have a number of legal rights, such as the right to complain to governmental authorities about health or safety problems or the right to be free from illegal discrimination. To ensure that these rights protect tenants, most states forbid landlords from retaliating against a tenant who asserts them.

A tenant who is avoiding eviction or legal liability may claim your legitimate actions are retaliatory. To counter such claims:

- Establish a paper trail to document important facts of your relationship. For example, set up clear, easy-to-follow procedures for tenants to ask for repairs, and respond.

- Demonstrate that you have a good reason to end the tenancy. In other words, be prepared to prove that your reasons were valid and not retaliatory.

- Have legitimate business reasons for any rent increase or other change in the conditions of the tenancy, and make the changes reasonable. In theory, you may not need a reason to increase the rent (unless you live in a rent-controlled area), but if you have no plausible business reason—such as evidence that local rents have risen—you'll have a harder time countering a tenant's claim that the increase was illegal.

- If a tenant files a complaint with a government agency just before you were going to raise the rent or give the month-to-month tenant a termination notice anyway, wait. In some states, if a landlord's negative act occurs within a certain time from the date of a tenant's complaint, the landlord will have a harder time countering the claim of retaliation. Wait until that time period is up.

RESOURCE

For more information on small claims court, see *Everybody's Guide to Small Claims Court,* by Ralph Warner (Nolo), which covers court procedures, legal theories and strategies, and collection methods for all 50 states.

When All Else Fails: Terminations and Evictions

Unfortunately, even the most sincere and professional attempts at conscientious landlording sometimes fail, and you need to get rid of a troublesome tenant. The key to winning an eviction lawsuit (sometimes called an unlawful detainer, or UD, lawsuit) is properly terminating the tenancy before you go to court. Otherwise, you can't proceed with your lawsuit, let alone get a judgment for possession of your property or for unpaid rent. In order to properly terminate, you must give your tenant adequate written notice, in a specified way and form. If after that the tenant doesn't move (or reform), you can file a lawsuit to evict.

Because an eviction judgment means the tenant won't have a roof over his head, state laws are usually very demanding of landlords. Each state, and even some localities, such as those with rent control, have their own procedures as to how termination notices and eviction papers must be written and delivered ("served"). Different types of notices are often required for different situations. You must follow the rules and procedures exactly. Otherwise, you'll run into delays in evicting the tenant—and maybe even lose your lawsuit—even if your tenant has bounced rent checks from here to Mandalay.

No matter how solid your reasons for evicting, get ready for the tenant to mount a defense—and possibly win. For one thing, the way that you've conducted business with the tenant may affect the outcome. If the tenant can point a finger at you, such as for acting in retaliation, it may shift attention away from the tenant's wrongdoing and sour your chances of victory.

Eviction itself—that is, physically removing the tenant and possessions from your property—can't be done until you've gone to court and proven that the tenant did something wrong that justifies ending the tenancy. And even then, you can't just move the tenant's stuff out onto the sidewalk and say goodbye. In most states, you must hire the sheriff or marshal to perform that task.

Sending termination notices

For a month-to-month tenancy, termination is theoretically easy: Simply give the proper amount of notice (30 days in most states). You don't usually need to give a reason. For a tenancy governed by a lease, you'll have to wait until it expires on its own at the end of the lease term. You generally aren't required to renew a lease.

But if your tenant has done something wrong, you may not want to wait the 30 days or until the lease expires. State laws allow you to terminate by serving the tenant with one of three different types of notices. Although terminology varies somewhat from state to state, the substance of these notices is remarkably the same. Most states set standards for the content and look of a termination notice, requiring certain language and specifying the size and appearance of type.

- Pay Rent or Quit notices are typically used when the tenant hasn't paid the rent. They give the tenant a few days to pay or move out ("quit").

- Cure or Quit notices are typically given after a violation of a term or condition of the lease or rental agreement, such as a no-pets clause or the promise to refrain from making excessive noise. Typically, the tenant has a set amount of time in which to correct, or "cure," the violation; a tenant who fails to do so must move or face an eviction lawsuit.

- Unconditional Quit notices are the harshest of all. They order the tenant to vacate the premises with no chance to pay the rent or correct the lease or rental agreement violation. In most states, Unconditional Quit notices are allowed only when the tenant has repeatedly violated a lease or rental agreement clause, has been chronically late with the rent, has seriously damaged the premises, or has engaged in illegal activity.

Many states have all three types of notices on the books. But in some states, Unconditional Quit notices are the only notice statutes on the books. This means that you are free to give your tenants a number of days to pay up, fix the problem, or cease the violation, but you don't have to—you can demand that they just leave.

Terminating for late rent payments

Not surprisingly, the top reason landlords terminate a tenancy is nonpayment of rent. In most states, this is grounds for immediately sending a termination notice, giving the tenant a few days—usually three to five—to pay up. The exact number of days varies from state to state. In some states, you don't even need to give the tenant a chance to pay up, but can go straight to using an Unconditional Quit notice.

> CAUTION
>
> **Is your property in Connecticut, Delaware, Maine, Oregon, or Rhode Island?** These states won't let you send a termination notice (either a Pay Rent or Quit notice or an Unconditional Quit notice) until the rent is a certain number of days late. Instead, tenants enjoy a statutory "grace period," plus the time specified in the Pay Rent or Quit notice, in which to come up with the rent. (In other states, you may provide this benefit in your lease.)

If the tenant is late with the rent and you deliver a termination notice—whether or not it gives the tenant a few days to pay the rent—expect a phone call or a visit from your tenant, hoping to work something out. If you accept rent for the entire rental term, you have canceled the termination notice for that period. In most states, it's as if the tenant had paid on time in the first place.

After all this, what if the tenant is late again with the rent? Check your state's law. In several states, you don't have to give such tenants a second chance—or at least not a third chance, within a certain time period.

If you accept even a partial amount of rent a tenant owes—whether for past months or even just the current month—you will, in most states, cancel the effect of a Pay Rent or Quit notice. But you can still go ahead with your attempts to get the tenant out—just pocket your tenant's payment with one hand and hand over a new termination notice with the other, demanding that the tenant pay the new balance or leave.

> **WARNING**
>
> **If your tenant is in the military or the activated reserves, special rules apply.** Federal law requires a court to stay (postpone) an eviction for up to three months unless the judge decides that military service does not materially affect the tenant's ability to pay the rent. The law applies only to evictions for nonpayment of rent, not other reasons, such as keeping pets in violation of the lease. Nor does it apply if you've terminated a rental agreement with a 30-day notice.

How eviction lawsuits work

When the deadline in the termination notice passes, your tenant is supposed to pack up and leave. Unfortunately, that doesn't always happen. Nor can you just call the police and have them escort the person out. Instead, you must file and win an eviction lawsuit. The resulting court order will give you the right to call a sheriff or marshal and arrange to physically evict a tenant who refuses to leave. The whole process may take weeks—or months—depending on whether the tenant contests the eviction in court.

Eviction lawsuits are filed in a formal trial court (called "municipal," "county," or "justice") or in small claims court. A few states have separate landlord-tenant courts in larger cities, specifically set up to handle evictions. Some states give landlords a choice of where to file; others confine eviction lawsuits to one court or the other. Call the clerk of your local small claims court to find out whether it handles evictions.

If small claims is an option, it's usually best for an eviction, because of its speed and simple procedures. And you can, if you really want to (or if the court won't allow attorneys there anyway) go without a lawyer and save on those fees. Your main job will be to gather evidence to persuade the court to believe your side of the story. But if lawyers are allowed in small claims court in your state, you might want to use one. As described just below, eviction lawsuits are rather tricky, and it may be more effective to hire a pro. (By the way, you can always consult with an attorney; what some states don't allow is for litigants to actually bring lawyers to small claims court to present their cases for them.)

If small claims court isn't an option, you'll have even more reason to hire a lawyer. Regular court is far more complex, with more rules about what kind of evidence can be submitted, and more procedural steps to get to a resolution.

> **RESOURCE**
>
> **Really don't want to hire a lawyer?** *Represent Yourself in Court: How to Prepare & Try a Winning Case*, by Paul Bergman and Sara Berman (Nolo), explains what happens in a regular trial court and how to present evidence and arguments yourself.

To get an eviction lawsuit going (in any court), you'll have to follow these steps:

- **File a complaint.** This legal document lists the facts that you think justify the eviction. It also asks the court to order the tenant to leave the property and pay back any rent, any damages directly caused by having unlawfully remained on the property, court costs, and possibly attorney fees. Your complaint doesn't need to be long or complex—in fact, in some states, landlords use a preprinted complaint form, prepared by the court.

- **Serve the tenant.** When you file a complaint, the clerk will assign a date on which the case will be heard by the court. That date is entered on the "summons," a piece of paper that tells the tenant he or she is being sued and must answer your charges in writing and appear in court within a specified number of days or lose the lawsuit. You must then arrange for the tenant to be given the complaint and the summons. In legal jargon, this is called "service of process." State laws are quite detailed as to the proper way to deliver, or "serve," court papers. Most critically, neither you (including anyone who has an ownership interest in your business) nor your employees (if you have any) can serve these papers. The method of delivery is specified as well: Normally, the preferred way is "personal" service, which means that a law enforcement officer or professional process server personally hands the tenant the papers. Failure to properly serve the tenant is one of the most common errors landlords make, and may result in court dismissal of your lawsuit even before trial. Even a seemingly minor mistake—such as forgetting to check a box, checking one you shouldn't, or filling in contradictory information—will increase the chances of your tenant successfully contesting the lawsuit.

Tips on Dealing With a Tenant During an Eviction

To keep things businesslike:

- Avoid all unnecessary personal contact with the tenant during the eviction process unless it occurs in a structured setting, such as a mediation.
- Keep your written communications to the point and as neutral as you can.
- Treat the tenant like he or she has a right to remain on the premises, even though you're trying to prove the opposite. Until the day the sheriff or marshal shows up to evict, the tenant's home is legally his or her castle.

- **The tenant answers.** The tenant must file a document called an "answer" on or before the date printed on the summons. (If the tenant doesn't, and then doesn't show up in court, you'll usually win the lawsuit automatically.) Like your complaint, the answer need not be a complex document, and may be a preprinted form.

The tenant may dispute that what you say is true. Alternatively, the tenant may try to put forth a good legal reason (such as discrimination or retaliation) to excuse what would otherwise be grounds for eviction. This is called an affirmative defense.

Once you're done with these preliminaries, you'll proceed with your lawsuit. Many eviction cases never end up in trial—for example, because the tenant moves out or negotiates a settlement with the landlord. But each case that does go to trial will have its own unpredictable twists and turns, which can greatly affect trial preparation and tactics. For this reason, you'll probably need to hire a lawyer, if you haven't done so already.

> **WARNING**
> **Complete your lawsuit, even if you think you've won already.** Never walk away from a lawsuit without formally ending it, even if the tenant moves out or pays what's owed without going to court. Doing so preserves your reputation as someone who uses the courts with respect. If you're simply a no-show, expect a chilly reception the next time you appear in court. In addition, if you don't appear for trial but the tenant does, the tenant may win and be entitled to move back in and collect court costs and attorney fees.

Eviction lawsuits are typically decided on the spot or very soon thereafter, after the judge has heard the witnesses and reviewed any relevant laws. If you win, you get an order from the judge (a "judgment") declaring that you're entitled to possession of the property. You may get a money judgment for back rent and court costs and attorney fees, too.

You'll need to take the order to the local law enforcement official, along with the appropriate fee, which the tenant will be expected to pay back as part of your costs. The sheriff or marshal will give the tenant a notice saying that the official will be back, sometimes within just a few days, to physically remove the tenant if necessary.

Unfortunately, having a judgment for the payment of money isn't the same as having the money itself. Your tenant may be unable (or unwilling) to pay you, despite the fact that you have a formal court order. Unless the tenant voluntarily pays up, you will have to collect the debt—for example, by using the tenant's security deposit or hiring a collection agency.

If you lose the eviction case, your tenant can stay, and you'll likely end up paying for your tenant's court costs and fees. You may also be hit with money damages if the judge decides you acted illegally, as in the case of discrimination or retaliation.

How Tenants May Stop or Postpone an Eviction

In rare instances, a tenant may be able to get a judge to stop an eviction that's already been ordered, but only by convincing the court of two things:

- Eviction would cause a severe hardship for the tenant or family.
- The tenant is willing and able to pay any back rent owed (and your costs to bring the lawsuit) and future rent, as well.

It's very unusual for a judge to stop an eviction—after all, if the tenant's sympathetic predicament (and sufficient monetary reserves) weren't persuasive enough to win the case in the first place, these arguments probably won't be given new weight after the trial.

The tenant may instead ask for a postponement of the eviction. Typically, evictions are postponed in three situations:

- **Pending an appeal.** A tenant who files an appeal may ask the trial judge to postpone ("stay") the eviction until a higher court decides the case.
- **Until the tenant's circumstances improve.** A tenant may be able to persuade a judge to allow a little more time to find a new home.
- **Until the weather improves.** In most states, judges are not required to postpone an eviction on frigid days, but there's nothing to stop a tenant from asking.

How not to evict: Illegal "self-help"

As any experienced landlord will attest, there are occasional tenants who do things so outrageous that the landlord is tempted to bypass normal legal protections and take direct and immediate action to protect the property. For example, one landlord with whom we spoke said, "Out of desperation, I asked two tough-looking, armed friends of mine to come over and tell the tenant it was long past time to go."

Don't do anything like this. Shortcuts such as threats, intimidation, utility shutoffs, or attempts to physically remove a tenant are illegal and dangerous. Today, virtually every state forbids these "self-help" evictions. If you resort to them, you may well find yourself on the other end of a lawsuit.

Even if your state hasn't legislated against self-help evictions, throwing your tenant out on your own is highly risky and likely to land you in more legal entanglements than if you had gone to court for an eviction judgment in the first place. The potential for nastiness and violence is great; the last thing you want is a patrol car at the curb while you and your tenant wrestle on the lawn. And you can almost count on a lawsuit over the "disappearance" of your tenant's valuable possessions, which the tenant will claim were lost or taken when you removed them. Using a neutral law enforcement officer to enforce a judge's eviction order will avoid these potential problems.

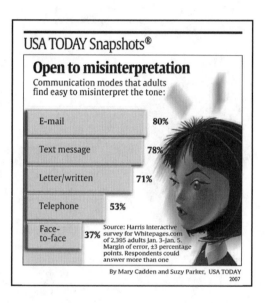

USA TODAY Snapshots®

Open to misinterpretation

Communication modes that adults find easy to misinterpret the tone:

E-mail	80%
Text message	78%
Letter/written	71%
Telephone	53%
Face-to-face	37%

Source: Harris Interactive survey for Whitepages.com of 2,395 adults Jan. 3–Jan. 5. Margin of error, ±3 percentage points. Respondents could answer more than one

By Mary Cadden and Suzy Parker, USA TODAY 2007

Don't Want to Do It Alone? Hiring a Property Manager

Being a landlord can, at times, turn into a busy job. In the words of Sarah, a San Francisco landlord who rents out half her duplex, "You don't get something for nothing." If your time is already stretched super-thin, you might consider getting help. Fortunately, lots of people make it their business to work as a stand-in rental property owner—they're property managers, and if you find the right one, your rental business will get a lot simpler.

A property manager focuses on renting and maintaining property, by handling tasks from finding and screening tenants to maintaining the property to cleaning it up after a tenant moves out. Of course, there's a catch: Property managers normally charge about 10% of your monthly rental income for their services. And that doesn't count any additional tasks, such as handling terminations or evictions, for which you'll pay extra.

In this chapter, we'll help you decide whether paying to hire a property manager is right for you, by explaining:

- what a property manager does
- when hiring a property manager makes the most financial sense
- how to find and choose a property manager, and
- what to include in your signed agreement with a property manager.

What a Professional Property Manager Does

If managing a rental property sounds like a lot of hassle, hiring a property manager may be just the ticket. Here are some tasks you'll be able to offload:

- **Setting the rental price.** Although the final figure will be up to you, a good property manager should research the going rate for local rentals like yours. Setting a realistic rental price will help keep vacancies low and your income stable.
- **Advertising the property.** A good property manager will know how to best advertise your rental, and will make the most of

different methods (Internet, local papers, or flyers) to distribute the information.

- **Preparing the property.** When you're between tenants, the property manager will clean the place up, and arrange for any necessary maintenance work like painting, replacing fixtures, and more. Instead of you trying to cram these tasks into your after-work and weekend schedule, the property manager will bring in professionals to handle them all at once. That means faster results and shorter vacancy periods.

- **Screening tenants.** Your property manager may take phone calls from applicants, show them the property, have them fill out applications, interview them, run credit or criminal background checks, and verify employment and rental history. The property manager uses this information to find the best tenant (though you may have a say in the final selection).

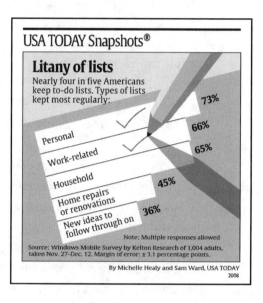

USA TODAY Snapshots®

Litany of lists

Nearly four in five Americans keep to-do lists. Types of lists kept most regularly:

Personal — 73%

Work-related — 66%

Household — 65%

Home repairs or renovations — 45%

New ideas to follow through on — 36%

Note: Multiple responses allowed

Source: Windows Mobile Survey by Kelton Research of 1,004 adults, taken Nov. 27-Dec. 12. Margin of error: ± 3.1 percentage points.

By Michelle Healy and Sam Ward, USA TODAY 2008

- **Moving tenants in.** Once you find an appropriate tenant, the property manager will negotiate the lease or rental agreement, coordinate the tenant's move and provide keys, give the tenant a move-in checklist, and handle any other move-in responsibilities.

- **Collecting rent.** The property manager will collect monthly rent and, depending on the terms of your contract with the manager, deal with problems if a tenant doesn't pay. In most cases, managers will be motivated to collect the rent because their pay is a percentage of the rental income—if there's no income, they don't get a penny.

- **Handling tenant problems.** Late rent isn't the only tenant problem that may crop up (as discussed in Chapter 9). Your property manager will work on resolving all manner of problems and deal with tenant complaints or concerns (though they will not handle an eviction for you). As Rosario, a landlord in El Paso, Texas, says, "I've found that tenants feel more comfortable approaching the property manager than me about issues with the property—maybe they think I'll take it personally if they complain. Anyway, it all works out, because that way they don't wait until the small problems turn into big ones."

At Least You're Not Dealing With Property Managers in China

A seat on the Gold Land Green Town homeowners association in Beijing offers a chance to weigh in on fees for utilities and garbage pickup, to schedule yoga classes, and to set rules for use of the plush clubhouse.

But it's becoming a jungle in the big city. The Communist Party's decision to empower homeowners groups is partly recognition that property owners have become prey for corrupt bureaucrats and unscrupulous developers—and need to channel their anger when they are victimized.

Typical is a high-profile case that began with a parking-fee dispute between property managers and homeowners at the Peaceful and Tranquil Home, an apartment development in northeast Beijing. The conflict has escalated into frequent violence.

Li Youcheng, head of the homeowners committee, says he was attacked by goons working for Jiaren, the property management company. "They wanted to kill me," says Li, who has scars on his back and head from ax and knife wounds he received in the attack in June. "The property company uses the underworld to scare the homeowners."

At Least You're Not Dealing With Property Managers in China, cont'd

The day after the attack, Li left the hospital in a wheelchair to attend the meeting of homeowners that voted by a two-thirds majority to replace Jiaren with a new firm. "It was the first public referendum in Beijing," he says proudly.

The putsch failed. After confrontations with Jiaren's guards, many residents have moved out. Li and other holdouts had their electricity cut off after they stopped paying utility fees to the company, which also removed the benches where elderly residents congregated.

"Ten of us have been beaten since 2004. I have to carry a knife at all times," says Feng Juanjuan, who serves as treasurer on the homeowners committee.

Liu Mingwei, manager of Jiaren, denies the accusations. "We are a company, not the underworld. We have never sent people to beat others," he says. "The residents blame us for everything. I wish they wouldn't make so much trouble."

"The property managers here aren't here to manage me but to serve me," says Lei Xia, a resident at Beautiful Garden in west Beijing. "And the government is also moving this way, becoming more service-oriented and democratic. This is a gradual change. It won't happen overnight."

 "China's homeowners get small taste of democracy; In country's housing developments, residents elect their own leaders," by Calum MacLeod, April 18, 2006.

- **Keeping the property in good condition.** This means taking care of all repairs and maintenance (described in Chapter 8), as well as regular, general upkeep like mowing and pruning the yard. Usually, a property manager has someone on staff or on call—such as a handyperson—to handle immediate problems, and a list of seasoned professionals to call for more serious issues.

CAUTION

Your maintenance and repair costs may go up. The fees you pay to a property manager probably mean any maintenance problems will be identified quickly—and you'll end up paying someone for even simple tasks (like fixing a broken door lock or tightening a loose hinge), which you might otherwise have been able to handle on your own. When a property manager hires someone to fix a problem, you'll pay not only that worker, but also the manager, for setting up (and possibly supervising) the job.

- **Performing inspections.** A property manager can handle the regular inspections that every property requires, to make sure there's no major damage or problem that needs repair.
- **Managing finances.** Your property manager should also perform certain financial tasks, including collecting, holding, and returning deposits; tracking income and expenses; and sending you regular (monthly or quarterly) reports on these items.
- **Complying with laws and regulations.** A good property management company will know applicable federal, state, and local laws and regulations like those governing security deposits, rent control, and evictions. This will save you having to study and figure out how to comply with these laws.

CAUTION

Lesson learned the hard way: Don't expect regular monitoring from the property manager. As Darla, who rented out her former home in Seattle, explains: "Because I lived several hours away, I relied on the property managers for regular maintenance. Mostly I was happy with them, but they didn't catch the fact that my tenants were keeping dogs—and that the dogs were ruining the carpets. Worse yet, before I sold the place and asked the tenants to move, they sprayed the carpets with some oily substance—perhaps to mask the dog odors—which cost me $400 to remove and clean. If I'd lived locally, I could have driven by occasionally, and probably would have spotted the dogs."

Is Property Management Right For You?

If you're not sure whether you're ready to pay someone a relatively large amount of cash to manage your property, consider two things: whether you're in a good position to manage the property yourself, and whether property management makes financial sense.

Are you ready to take care of the property yourself?

Having just read about the process of managing a property, you know the basics of what's involved—selecting and managing tenants, keeping the property in good repair, making sure your tenants don't cause trouble in the neighborhood, and handling tenants' departures and the return of their deposits, for example.

Even if you think you're able to handle the serious tasks, there are situations in which hiring a property manager makes good sense. Here are some of them:

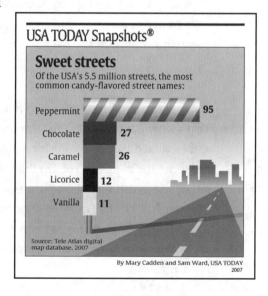

USA TODAY Snapshots®

Sweet streets

Of the USA's 5.5 million streets, the most common candy-flavored street names:

Peppermint — 95
Chocolate — 27
Caramel — 26
Licorice — 12
Vanilla — 11

Source: Tele Atlas digital map database, 2007

By Mary Cadden and Sam Ward, USA TODAY 2007

- **You live far away.** Maybe you're renting out a vacation home in a remote part of the state, or maybe it's an investment property across the country. Whatever the case, if you can't be right there to handle management tasks, you'll waste a lot of time trying to do so remotely—and your property will probably suffer without someone there to see how the tenants are treating it, handle emergencies, and so forth.

- **You don't want to study the ins and outs.** If you're not interested in learning about and complying with federal and state laws, understanding how to find and screen tenants, or figuring out at least the basics of home repair and maintenance, hiring a property manager is a good idea.

- **You don't have time to spare.** Maybe your successful career is more lucrative than your time spent managing a property could ever be, or maybe you've got your hands full caring for children or an elderly parent. If your life is already jam-packed, adding the stress of managing a rental property may simply be too much to deal with.

- **You own multiple properties.** If you own a multi-unit property or several different properties, the amount of time you'll spend being a landlord will go up—but so will the income you'll get from the rent, so hiring a property manager may become more affordable. Even if you aren't at that sweet spot yet, if you plan to be, it's worth keeping in the back of your mind.

 TIP

You can hire a property manager for a short period of time. That's what Laura, a landlord with properties in Washington, Nevada, and Florida, did in preparing for a month-long trip to Europe. It allowed her some stress-free travel. On the other hand, she discovered that, "I'd rather work with tenants myself, especially when it comes to choosing new tenants. I think I'm more concerned than the property manager about finding someone who's easy to deal with. I ended up with an angry tenant (chosen by the company) who tried to get out of paying for damage."

How much does property management cost?

Typically, you'll pay between 6% and 12% of the rental income to the manager. Single-family homes are almost always on the higher end of this percentage scale, because it's more costly to deal with them, per unit, than multi-family properties. To get an idea of what property managers in your area cost, call a few and ask.

CAUTION

High-maintenance properties mean higher management fees.
If your property isn't in good shape, expect to pay more—not only
in repairs, but in the property manager's fee. A manager will rightfully
assume that it's going to take more time and effort to manage your
property than it would to handle a similar property in good condition.

Of course, an advantage to paying a percentage-based fee out of your
monthly income is that the property manager will be highly motivated
to keep the place occupied. Still, you might also need to factor in
various add-on costs, such as:

- **Extra fees to find a new tenant.** Some property managers charge an
  extra fee to advertise, screen, and move a new tenant in, such as
  one half the first month's
  rent. While your initial
  reaction might be, "Whoa,
  I'm not paying for that!"
  take a closer look at the
  numbers first: The man-
  ager might negotiate by
  setting your monthly fee
  comparatively lower. And
  if the manager helps you
  find a stable tenant who
  stays several years, wouldn't
  it be better to pay 8% per
  month plus a leasing fee
  rather than 10% a month

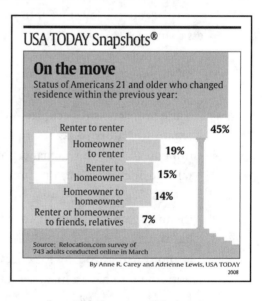

USA TODAY Snapshots®

On the move

Status of Americans 21 and older who changed
residence within the previous year:

Renter to renter — 45%
Homeowner to renter — 19%
Renter to homeowner — 15%
Homeowner to homeowner — 14%
Renter or homeowner to friends, relatives — 7%

Source: Relocation.com survey of
743 adults conducted online in March

By Anne R. Carey and Adrienne Lewis, USA TODAY
2008

  without a leasing fee? (Then again, if you don't see an adjustment
  in the manager's prices to account for this fee, this argument loses
  its luster.)

- **Administrative fees for repairs and maintenance.** You'll need the
  property manager to hire outsiders—plumbers, electricians, and
  other repairpeople. What you don't need or want is for your

manager to tack on a fee for doing this, so negotiate that ahead of time. Find out also whether you'll have to pay any extra fees if the company buys supplies on your behalf, like paint or carpeting.

TIP

If your homeowners' association maintains the property, don't pay your property manager to do it. If you live in a condominium or other common interest development, your homeowners' association may take care of communal areas, such as garden areas and shared hallways. Make sure your property manager knows what the association is responsible for: You don't want the manager to handle and charge you for repairs you weren't responsible for in the first place. Instead, the property management company should notify the association when it receives a tenant complaint concerning a common area. You may be able to negotiate a lower fee with your property manager because there's less to manage.

- **Minimum monthly fees for unoccupied property.** Some property managers set a baseline monthly fee that they'll get paid even if the property isn't occupied—or if it's occupied by a deadbeat tenant who doesn't pay the rent. This decreases the manager's impetus to find you a tenant, not to mention to choose a good, reliable one who'll pay on time.

- **Full fees regardless of whether the tenant pays the rent.** Allowing the management company to collect its fee even if the tenant hasn't paid on time is a bad idea. You want the property manager as motivated as you are to collect the rent, which means you'll want them to have a financial stake in the tenant's timely payment.

- **Late fees going to the property manager.** Some property managers specify that they get to keep any late fees. Again, this isn't ideal, because it reduces their motivation to make sure the rent is collected on time. You'll also want to be certain late fees don't exceed legal maximums—if they do, look for another property manager.

Will the costs undo your profits?

A 6%–12% fee can seem pretty steep if you're just trying to eke out a small profit. To decide whether it makes financial sense, add it to the expense portion of your Monthly Property Expense Estimate in Chapter 1, and then rerun the numbers to show your expected profits.

Also adjust the other expenses on your worksheet, where appropriate—a slight bump upward in your repair and maintenance costs, but (unless the property manager charges you extra), removal of the costs to market your property. Take a close look at what's included in any prospective property manager's fees,

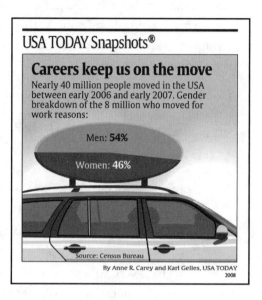

USA TODAY Snapshots®

Careers keep us on the move

Nearly 40 million people moved in the USA between early 2006 and early 2007. Gender breakdown of the 8 million who moved for work reasons:

Men: **54%**

Women: **46%**

Source: Census Bureau

By Anne R. Carey and Karl Gelles, USA TODAY 2008

and make additional expense adjustments—for example, if lawn care is part of the package, remove your expected weekly payment to the mowing service.

> **TIP**
>
> **The property manager's fee is tax-deductible.** We discussed various tax deductions in Chapter 6—and this is one of them.

Even if the fees for property management will wipe out all or much of your rental income, you don't have to rule it out entirely. You may find a property manager who will provide limited services for a lower fee— for example, agree that you'll find your own tenants, but the manager will collect the rent and coordinate repairs. The expense may be worth it if it frees you of whichever parts of your responsibilities are hardest to juggle or handle at a distance.

As you study your adjusted numbers, keep in mind that a property is usually its least profitable in the early years. If you wait a couple years more—either paying for property management and losing money, or managing the property yourself until you turn a profit—you may be in a better financial position. At that time, paying for a management company may fit more comfortably within your budget, especially if you can increase rents.

Comparing Pros and Cons

Use this checklist to help you decide whether the benefits of hiring a property manager outweigh the costs. The more boxes you check in each category, the more you should lean toward that choice.

On the plus side of hiring a manager (check every box that describes you):

❑ I have very little free time to take care of maintenance, tenant communications, and other tasks.

❑ I don't relish the idea of interacting with tenants personally.

❑ I live far from the property.

❑ I can earn enough from rents to comfortably pay the property manager's fees, leaving me free to spend my time elsewhere.

On the minus side of hiring a manager (check every box that describes you):

❑ I have enough free time to spend managing the property, or it's so close to my current house that the time requirements will be reduced.

❑ I'm handy myself, or know a lot of good repairpeople, so there wouldn't be much point in delegating those tasks.

❑ I enjoy the idea of earning money by taking an active role as a landlord.

❑ The fees for high-quality local property managers would all but obliterate my profits anyway.

How to Find the Best Property Manager

Anyone can manage a property for you—but that doesn't mean you should let them. Instead, you're looking for a professional manager who knows the business. Many professional property managers are licensed real estate brokers or work for them (as some states require). But it's better if the company is dedicated to property management, not buying and selling real estate. The skills required are very different, and you want someone who is focused on management, not doing it as a side business in the hopes that you, the landlord, will decide to sell the property and use the broker as your selling agent.

Several trade organizations offer education and training leading to designations such as "Certified Property Manager." (These designations are not, however, legal licenses.) The best program is probably offered by the Institute of Real Estate Management (IREM), which offers three designations: Certified Property Manager (CPM), Accredited Residential Manager (ARM), and Accredited Management Organization (AMO—and for the management firm, not the individual manager). To find out more about what these designations mean, visit the IREM's website at www.irem.org.

Getting recommendations

You may already know of several reputable property managers in your area, but if not, you'll need to start looking for one. Here are some likely resources:

- **Ask friends and family.** Of course, you want to talk to people who are familiar with the rental property market in the area you're looking to hire. Neighbors can be another good resource, especially if you're in an area with a lot of rentals, such as a condo complex.

- **Talk to colleagues and your local apartment association.** Other owners of properties similar to yours are probably your best bet— your needs won't have much in common with those of a landlord for a 50-unit building, for example. However, you might find out whether those large owners belong to an apartment owners' association, and ask whether the association has a "small owners" group.

- **Search professional directories on the Internet.** Visit the website of the Institute of Real Estate Management (IREM) at www.irem. org and click "Find a Member." Or visit the National Association of Residential Property Managers' (NARPM) website at www. narpm.org and click "Search Property Managers." To find a local or state member of the National Apartment Association, visit the NAA website at www.naahq.org.

With a list of a handful of names, do a quick Internet search to find out whether these managers have websites. If so, you might find out whether a firm specializes in any particular area of residential property management, or whether it's located in close enough physical proximity to handle your property.

Meeting and choosing among potential managers

Once you've narrowed down your list of potential hires, call three or four of them and arrange to meet and discuss working together. Be prepared to ask some targeted questions, such as:

- **Do you hold any licenses?** Find out whether the agent is a licensed real estate agent (required in some states), and whether he or she has earned any special certifications, like the Certified Property Manager designation through the Institute of Real Estate Management (IREM).

- **How long have you been in the property management business?** You're looking for someone with at least several years' experience.

- **Who will handle my property?** Make sure you meet with the person who will actually be responsible for managing your property (if it's one person). Then find out that particular person's experience level, and make sure you get along—remember, you could be working together quite a bit. Finally, make sure you know who's going to help you out if that person isn't available.

- **How many properties do you manage?** You're looking for someone who's not too busy to comfortably deal with you. If you're working with an individual manager, find out not only how many clients the company has, but how many properties that individual is responsible for. Also find out what type of properties the company deals with—be sure they have experience with properties similar to yours.

- **What are the fees?** You want to know all fees—your monthly fees and any add-ons for things like finding a new tenant, cleaning a property after a tenant moves out, or delivering a termination notice. Also ask whether you'll be charged, and how much, if the place is vacant.

- **How will you advertise the property?** You want to know that your property manager is using effective advertising methods, especially ones you might not have access to (anyone can put a posting on Craigslist).

- **How do you screen tenants?** Take a look at the written application form (and ensure it doesn't violate any laws on its face, such as those prohibiting discrimination) and find out what background checks the company will conduct and how. Make sure the company is as focused on finding a reliable tenant as you are—despite the fact that the company might be all too happy to receive extra payments for late fees or tenant turnover.

- **How do you handle repairs and maintenance?** Make sure someone will be available to handle any problems, 24 hours a day, seven days a week. Refer to Chapter 8 for a full list of repair and maintenance issues to discuss with your property manager.

- **Do you have a standard property management agreement?** Most management companies do, and as we'll explain below, they're written to benefit the company, not you. Make sure the standard agreement can be altered if necessary. Most companies will resist this, but it's not impossible to find one that will make reasonable adjustments.

- **Do you have a standard lease?** Most property management companies do, and you want to take a look before signing on. As with a property management agreement, a lease agreement will be written to benefit the company first, not you or the tenant. Make sure the lease is fair and legal. In particular, check that the late fees don't exceed the maximum allowed in your state.

Things You Wish Your Property Manager Would Do

Thinking of renting a luxury home this summer? Luxury leader Abercrombie & Kent is betting you'll pay extra for one that comes with a helper on call.

The company is the first to go nationwide with the concept of "concierge villas"—luxury rental homes that come with a private concierge who will handle everything from buying groceries to picking up ski lift tickets to arranging an in-house massage.

"Going on vacation in a private residence always felt like a do-it-yourself vacation," says Larry Andreini, president of Abercrombie & Kent Concierge Villas, which launched this week in 21 destinations including Aspen, Colorado, Naples, Florida, and Maui. "Somebody had to buy the groceries, clean the house, and run errands, (which means) one of the people on vacation never got to do the vacation."

Abercrombie is following a growing number of local and regional rental companies that have begun offering luxury homes with concierges on call.

"So many property management companies are nothing more than a check-in desk," says San Sophia owner Keith Hampton. "We wanted a standard more akin to a four-star hotel."

 "Rental homes give travelers white-glove treatment; Concierge service spreads to vacation villas," by Gene Sloan, May 21, 2004.

- **How will you send financial information?** Your property manager should provide you a regular report that details income and expenses. You'll want to know how often you can expect to receive the report and what format it will be in. Ask for a sample.

- **What kind of insurance do you carry?** It's important that the company carry comprehensive general liability insurance, workers' compensation insurance (to pay for any injuries sustained by employees), automobile insurance, and errors and omissions insurance (in less legal terms, malpractice insurance). Ask to see proof (a "certificate of insurance," on an "ACORD" standard form).

- **Do you have a fidelity bond?** Property managers handle a lot of money—and it isn't unheard of for a less-than-honest employee to skim some off the top. A fidelity bond (in the $1,000,000 range) will protect you if someone makes off with some of yours.

- **Do you have references?** Get and call two or three, and make sure they own properties similar to yours. Find out whether they're satisfied with the service they've received, how long they've been working together, and specifics like how long it takes the property manager to respond to inquires, requests, or complaints—both the owner's and the tenant's.

Once your questions have been answered satisfactorily, drive by the properties owned by the references of any manager you're considering hiring, and any other properties you know the manager handles. Take a close look at how well they're maintained. If you have a chance, talk to the tenants—they're likely to give you a non-biased answer on what it's like to deal with the management company. Once you've made your decision, get ready for the next step: signing a property management agreement.

Put It in Writing: Drafting An Agreement With Your Property Manager

For convenience' sake, your property manager's company doubtless has a standard agreement that it will ask you to sign. Every agreement will include some basic provisions, which you'll want to review carefully. Make sure the agreement:

- **Identifies the parties.** This should be fairly straightforward—you and any co-owners should be named, as should the property management company. However, if it's important to you to work with a specific employee, you might want that spelled out in the agreement.

- **Specifies the property.** Make sure the property is sufficiently identified, particularly if it's in a multi-unit building or complex.

- **Details the fees you'll pay.** You want the fees very clearly spelled out—the regular fee ("10% of the monthly rent") as well as any add-on fees, or minimum monthly fees paid even if the property is vacant. How often you'll have to pay the fees is also important to see spelled out—often, they're deducted from the rent payment, with the rest of the payment forwarded to you (be sure the agreement specifies how quickly the company must forward the rent to you, minus its fee). Also be sure you know where and how your rent money is held before it's divvied up—ideally, in an individual trust account.

- **Explains the manager's responsibilities.** Look back to the list of responsibilities at the beginning of this chapter. Are they all covered in the agreement? If not, you'll have a hard time getting the manager to take care of them.

- **Explains your responsibilities.** Your list of responsibilities should be short—making timely reimbursements to the management company for repair expenditures is probably the most important one. But if you've agreed to hire a property manager for limited services only, it will be important to clearly list what you'll still be responsible for handling.

- **Includes the contract's duration.** You don't want a management agreement with an end date in the far future—it decreases the manager's motivation to make sure you're a satisfied customer. On the other hand, you shouldn't expect the contract to be significantly shorter than the tenant's lease period—it wouldn't be fair to the property manager to bring a tenant in, only to have you take over managing the property. No matter how long you agree to continue the management relationship, make sure it's spelled out in the agreement, as well as how much notice will be needed if you or the management company want to end the relationship early (for example, 30 days' written notice). Avoid an agreement that allows you to terminate only for specified reasons.

- **Addresses how much the manager can spend without your authorization.** You'll probably create a reserve account into which you'll deposit money that the manager can use for necessary expenses like repairs. Make sure your agreement specifies how much the manager can spend without prior approval—as well as where and how the money will be held.

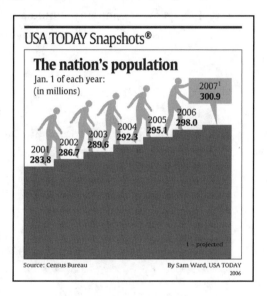

USA TODAY Snapshots®

The nation's population

Jan. 1 of each year: (in millions)

2001 283.8
2002 286.7
2003 289.6
2004 292.3
2005 295.1
2006 298.0
2007[1] 300.9

1 – projected

Source: Census Bureau

By Sam Ward, USA TODAY 2006

- **Doesn't disclaim responsibility.** In many contracts, you'll find a provision in which the property management company attempts to hold itself harmless if its own errors and those of its employees cause you harm or injury. You may also see a related clause, called an indemnity clause, in which you promise to reimburse the company for any losses it suffers as a result of its negligence. Obviously, these are onerous clauses and you should get rid of them if you can. If you can't, you can take some solace if both you and the company have adequate insurance—with insurance properly in place, these clauses will seldom come into play.

- **Is signed.** Both you and a representative of the property management company should sign and date the agreement.

CAUTION

What happens if there's a dispute between you and the property manager? Your agreement should specify whether you must resolve any legal disputes through specific avenues, like mediation or arbitration.

If you find that any of the provisions of an agreement are unacceptable, you'll have to decide whether to challenge them or sign anyway. A property management company should agree to alter an agreement, if your request is reasonable. If not, you may want to consider going elsewhere.

Ready to Quit? Exiting the Rental Property Business

No matter how much you enjoy being a landlord or how profitable it is, at some point, you may be ready to give it up. Maybe you're ready to spend your time on other projects, or spend your money on other investments. Or perhaps you're simply ready to enjoy the benefits of selling the property—the appreciation that's accumulated, in part thanks to your conscientious maintenance.

In this chapter, we'll discuss the decision to stop being a landlord. We'll cover:

- identifying your objectives so you can develop an exit plan that meets them
- deciding when the time is right to get out
- exploring different ways to exit the business, and
- getting the property ready to sell.

What's the Driving Force? Identifying Your Exit Plan Objectives

People have lots of different objectives when they decide it's time to stop being a landlord. Here are some of the most common ones:

- **Realizing profit.** Over the years, you may have watched the value of your property rise. While that looks good on paper, it won't pay your son's college tuition or buy you the sailboat you've always wanted. You may be interested in cashing in on that gain.

- **Avoiding taxes.** The downside to ongoing increases in your property's value is that the taxes you'll owe on profits when you sell are going up, too. Many landlords are hoping to avoid, or at least limit, this tax liability.

- **Reducing workload.** For some, dealing with a rental property simply gets to be too much bother, or interferes too much with their day job.

- **Passing money to heirs.** Lots of landlords want to make sure they have adequate assets to pass on. They may worry that leaving property to their heirs is more complicated and stressful for these heirs than leaving money.
- **Keeping a property that you want to use yourself.** Some landlords may be done with the business—but not the property. For example, you may have inherited a cottage that you're now ready to retire in.

As you read through this chapter, keep your own objectives in mind, and see which of the options here best meets them.

What Are Your Options? Exploring Opportunities

There are many ways you can stop being a landlord. It may be as simple as putting the house on the market, or as complex as executing a tax-deferred exchange to buy another investment property. We'll explain the details of these and other strategies, below.

Sell the property

The most straightforward way to get out of the rental property business is to sell the property. Selling your property has the advantage of being relatively simple to do—you may have done it before with a personal residence—and it gives you an immediate (and often large) amount of cash to spend any way you please.

But selling your home has some disadvantages, too. First of all, it involves high transaction costs. If you hire a real estate agent, you'll pay a commission (usually 5%–6%). That doesn't count the cost of getting the property ready for sale, or any of the other transaction costs that are commonly paid by the seller (which customarily vary by geographic area). Altogether, you could spend up to 10% of the sale price just on these costs.

But the transaction costs won't be your biggest expenses—they'll probably pale in comparison to your capital gains tax bill. For example, if you bought a house four years ago for $200,000 and you sell it now for $300,000, you'll pay taxes on approximately $100,000 (though probably a bit less after adjusting the basis, which we'll explain further below). With a current long-term federal capital gains tax rate of 15%, that's $15,000 to the federal government alone. States also collect capital gains taxes.

> **CAUTION**
> **Short-term capital gains are taxed at ordinary income tax rates.** If you've owned your property for a year or less and are selling it at a gain, you'll be taxed at your ordinary income tax rate—probably much higher than 15%! You might be better off waiting to sell until you've held the property for more than one year.

In addition to taxes on your gain, you'll have to pay taxes on the "recapture" of depreciation you took over the years. As explained in Chapter 6, the IRS requires you to take annual deductions to account for the decreased value of your rental building (but not the land it sits on) caused by normal wear and tear.

On residential property, the IRS arbitrarily set the "life" of the property at 27.5 years. That means that over 27.5 years, you're allowed to deduct the purchase price of the property (minus the land) in equal amounts. So if you bought a property with a house on it worth $100,000, each year you probably deducted around $2,750.

This works great while you're a landlord and are taking the deduction, but when you're ready to sell, you must pay tax on any profits that essentially paid you back for the depreciation deductions you took. The tax rate depends on when you bought the property, but if it was after May 6, 1997, it's fairly safe to say you'll pay a 25% capital gains tax.

How to Estimate Your Capital Gains Tax

Worried about how much you're going to pay in capital gains taxes? Do some rough calculations first. Your capital gains tax liability is based on your purchase price, but you're allowed to increase that amount (called the "basis") to account for certain expenses, decreasing your taxable gain. Include these adjustments when you calculate your tax liability.

Step 1: Start with your purchase price. Then add your closing costs, such as title fees, escrow fees, and recording fees. Add only the costs you paid, and don't count any amounts in escrow for future payment, like taxes or insurance premiums. (If you're not sure whether an expense qualifies, look at IRS Publication 551, *Basis of Assets*, available at www.irs.gov.)

Step 2: Did you make any improvements to the property? If they have a useful life of more than one year, you can add those costs to the basis. There are a few other expenses that can adjust your basis, but they won't apply to most people. These include things like zoning fees and legal fees—for example, for defending a challenge to title. See Publication 551, above, if you think one of these exceptions may apply to you.

Step 3: Estimate how much you think you can sell your home for, based on an honest assessment of its fair market value.

Step 4: Reduce the sale price by the cost of your sale expenses, such as broker fees, title fees, and escrow fees.

Step 5: Subtract the Step 2 figure—the adjusted purchase price—from the Step 4 figure—the adjusted sales price. This is the amount you will be taxed on as a capital gain, not counting the depreciation you must recapture (at a higher tax rate).

As you can see, selling the property can be expensive. But although these tax rates seem high, they're considerably lower than most of us pay on our regular income. Also, the 15% rate is set to expire at the end of 2010; after that, it will go up to 20% for most people. Relatively speaking, the current rate is still a pretty good deal.

Avoid taxes with a 1031 exchange

If you read the information above and are horrified at the tax bill that might accompany a sale, you might be interested in the "1031," "like-kind," or "Starker" exchange. In a 1031 exchange, you can defer paying taxes on the sale of a business or investment property when you reinvest your gain in other business or investment property.

Despite the name, you don't literally swap one property for another—you can sell your property to any buyer and find a property you want to purchase from any seller. But to qualify as an exchange, you must meet certain requirements. Most importantly, you have 45 days from the sale of the first property to find and identify potential properties to purchase. Within 180 days of the sale, you must actually purchase one or more of those properties. During that time, the sale proceeds can never be in your hands, or the transaction won't be considered an exchange. Instead, all the cash from the sale must be held in an escrow account. (You'll usually hire a third party, called a qualified intermediary, to hold the cash for you—your transaction costs will be a little bit higher as a result.)

USA TODAY Snapshots®

Not-so-humble abodes

States with the highest percentage of homes with four or more bedrooms:

39.2% Utah
28% Maryland
26.5% Virginia
26.2% Colorado
26.2% Minnesota

Source: Census Bureau By David Stuckey and Marcy E. Mullins, USA TODAY 2008

Although this arrangement allows you to defer capital gains taxes from the sale, you'll have to pay tax eventually, when you sell the property bought in the exchange. (The exception would be if you do another exchange, in which case your taxes will be deferred again.) However, to fully defer your taxes, the new property you buy has to be worth the same as or more than the old property you are selling. You can also defer the taxes on the recapture of depreciation you've taken on your current property, discussed above.

Exchanging property provides other advantages, too. For example:

- **You can leverage your investment into a higher value property.** If the value of the property you currently own increases significantly, you may want to trade up to a more expensive property or properties that yield higher rents. For example, if the rental house you bought for $100,000 is now worth $500,000, you may use your gain to purchase an eight-unit building that costs $900,000. Because you aren't paying taxes, you have more cash available for such a leveraged investment.

- **If you're tired of the day-to-day management of being a landlord, you can buy a lower-maintenance property.** For example, you can exchange an active rental property for undeveloped land you think will appreciate soon. Or you can purchase a fractional share in an investment property (known as a tenancy in common). In the most sophisticated arrangements, you own a part of a large commercial property, with a professional company managing it and distributing rent payments to you, with very little other responsibility.

- **You can buy multiple properties.** While there are some rules about the number and types of properties you can buy, you can exchange a single property for several different investment properties.

- **You can continue to depreciate property.** If you have depreciated your current property to or near the maximum amount allowed, a 1031 exchange gives you the opportunity to start fresh with a new property. However, the adjusted basis of the current property transfers to the replacement property. That means you can take depreciation deductions only on the new property reduced by the depreciation you've already taken on the old one.

Because 1031 exchanges have very technical requirements, see your tax or legal adviser if you're considering one.

Offer seller financing to home buyers

If you're ready to sell your property but aren't interested in reinvesting in another business or investment property, you have another option to help soften the tax blow: an installment sale, sometimes called "seller financing." With an installment sale, you act as a lender as well as a seller, letting the buyer pay you over time. You may be the primary mortgage holder or a secondary mortgage holder.

Buyers are attracted to installment sales because they avoid the expense or hassle of dealing with a traditional lender, and because installment sales offer flexibility.

For example, a buyer who is self-employed, and can't show regular income despite a profitable business, may have a hard time getting a traditional loan. Or maybe the buyer needs a lower monthly payment than the bank will offer, and you're able to offer more creative financing.

But installment sales aren't just good for buyers—you may benefit, too. First of all, you'll earn interest on the money lent to the buyer, receiving a stable, steady return on your investment. Additionally, you can spread out payment of your capital gains taxes, which need to be paid only in the year you receive the actual gain. And your gain will be partly the loan principal, so in the early years, when most of each payment is usually interest, your capital gains tax bill will be low. (You will still be taxed on the interest income, at ordinary income tax rates.) This frees more money for other investments or uses.

> **TIP**
>
> **Need expert help with preparing and recording the mortgage and related legal documents?** Check out Virgin Money (www. virginmoneyus.com). The company specializes in person-to-person loans, between relatives, friends, and other parties.

Of course, there are drawbacks to the installment sale. Perhaps the biggest is the risk if the buyer doesn't pay. As a secured lender (one who has filed a mortgage or deed of trust), you'd have the right to seek payment through a foreclosure, but that's an expensive and time-consuming process. And if you were the second mortgage holder, you'd be paid only after the first mortgage holder is paid.

The other major drawback is the risk that the buyer will pay the loan off early. If this happens, you'd have all the remaining taxable gain due in that year, which could wreak havoc on a well-planned tax strategy. Although you might be able to limit this possibility by including prepayment penalties on the loan, many states limit the amount of any prepayment penalty.

TIP
You can combine a 1031 exchange with an installment sale. This topic is beyond the scope of this book, but if you're interested, speak with a financial or tax adviser.

Move into the property yourself

Perhaps you've been holding onto your property so that you can someday retire or move into it. This approach offers certain tax benefits.

As of January 1, 2009, if you convert a property you own to your main home and live there for two out of the five years before its sale, you don't have to pay tax on the portion of your gain that's attributable to your personal use. The maximum exclusion under this provision is $250,000, or $500,000 if you're married and filing jointly. (If that sounds different from the way you thought the capital gains tax exclusion worked, you're right: In 2008, Congress changed the calculation method in order to collect more taxes.) If you own and live in a multi-unit property, you can use the exclusion on a fractional basis, excluding gain on the portion of the property that was your principal residence.

For example, if you buy a house in 2009 and rent it out for four years, then live in it for an additional six years, you can exclude 60% of your gain, and will have to pay taxes on only 40%. But this won't help you avoid taxes on your recaptured depreciation deductions.

For more information, see IRS Publication 523, *Selling Your Home,* available at www.irs.gov.

> **CAUTION**
>
> **Did you acquire your property in a 1031 exchange?** If so, you must live in it for five years, not two, before you can take the primary residence exclusion.

Bring in a co-owner

If you're tired of being the sole owner and caretaker of your property, you could ask someone to buy in. Legally speaking, you'd turn the ownership into a tenancy in common—a form of joint ownership that allows you and co-owners to hold property in unequal shares. Neither of you needs the other's permission to sell your interest, and you can decide how to divide up the use and care of the property.

You may be able to find a buyer who's interested in this arrangement, and is willing to manage the property. If you also act as the mortgage holder, you'll have monthly income at the same time. See a legal or tax adviser for details.

Donate the property to a charitable remainder trust

Though donating your property to a charity may seem like a money-losing proposition, it can have significant tax advantages. You can name yourself and your spouse as beneficiaries of the trust, creating an income stream for the rest of your life, then donate the remainder to a charity of your choice.

You can also take a significant tax deduction, based on the projected value of the benefit the charity will receive (after your death) and the type of charity you donate the property to. For more information on this and other estate planning strategies, see *Plan Your Estate,* by Denis Clifford (Nolo).

What Rights Does the Tenant Have If You Sell?

If you have tenants living on your property at the time you decide to put it on the market, you'll need to understand their rights (and yours) during the selling process and beyond. (If the property is vacant, you can skip this section.) Dealing with current tenants can be a challenge (and a possible hindrance to a sale), which is why many owners wait until the property is vacant before selling.

Tenants with leases will continue to have the right to live on the property until the lease ends, despite the change in ownership. In other words, the new owner will step into your shoes, and must honor the lease just as you did. This doesn't mean, however, that you or a prospective owner can't approach tenants and ask to buy them out of their leases. Tenants have no obligation to negotiate with you or the buyer, but many will, seeing an opportunity to make some money.

Tenants who rent on a month-to-month basis present you and the new owner much more flexibility. As you know, you can terminate month-to-month tenants with proper

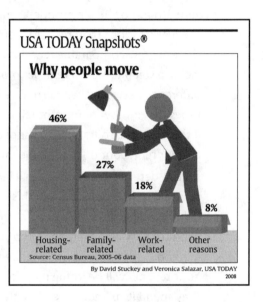

USA TODAY Snapshots®

Why people move

46% Housing-related
27% Family-related
18% Work-related
8% Other reasons

Source: Census Bureau, 2005-06 data

By David Stuckey and Veronica Salazar, USA TODAY 2008

notice, 30 days in most states. While you may not terminate for an illegal (retaliatory or discriminatory) reason, ending a tenancy in order to prepare and show the property (which you would do), or to live in it once it's purchased (which the new owner would do) is legal in every state. Some long-term monthly tenants are entitled to slightly more notice in some states, but the general rule is the same—you can end their tenancies with relative ease.

What Does a Buy-Out Cost?

When deciding how much rent to charge, you looked at the state of the market—was it hot or cold, and what were the rents for properties like yours? You'll use the same approach, and add in some individual factors, if you decide to try to end a current tenancy early by buying out your lease-holding tenants.

First, understand that the tenants will have to find another place to live. What rent will they have to pay to find a comparable unit? If they are long-term, good tenants, whom you've wisely kept around by making modest rent increases over the years, if the market is hot (and rents for comparable rentals are high), and there are few comparable rentals available, your tenants will be facing a steep uptick in rent per month. Expect to pay at least the difference between their current rent and the expected new rent, times the number of months left on the lease. On the other hand, if the market is soft and the cost of a similar rental is close to their current rent, your offer could be much lower.

Next, determine whether you'll include help on moving costs. You might be inclined to skip this—after all, you wouldn't be helping them move at the end of the lease. But here is where you need to think creatively and keep your goal—a vacant property— in mind. Suppose you're asking them to leave six months early. Your tenants will be losing interest on the moving money when they spend it six months early. Offer at least to cover this sum. Throw in a bit more to compensate them for the inconvenience this sudden move entails—and keep in mind that disruptions that involve kids' schooling, commuting, and loss of a familiar neighborhood are hard to quantify but mighty important to the people involved.

If You Decide to Sell: Getting Ready

If you decide to sell the property, even in a 1031 exchange or install-ment sale, you'll have to deal with putting your house on the market and finding a buyer. A little advance planning will help you maximize your return.

Is now a good time to sell?

Many factors affect whether it's a good time to sell your rental property. Unless you have no choice in the matter—for example, you need the cash, or a life change has made managing a property impossible—it's worth considering whether now is the best time to put your place on the market. Consider these factors:

- **Your local real estate market.** Real estate markets fluctuate—and they're often intensely local. What's happening can vary by city, neighborhood, block, or even street, so make sure you understand what's being sold nearby and at what price. If you know the market is cold—that there are more houses on the market than there are buyers—you can't expect to command the same price for your property as you would if the market were hot (if there were more buyers than available houses). In a cold market, consider whether you'd rather wait to see if prices increase. (But keep in mind—if the property isn't producing income, this could end up costing you more in the long run, as you continue to make regular monthly payments.)

- **The condition of the property.** Over the years, you've worked to conscientiously maintain the property. But you can't necessarily say the same for your tenants. And if you have long-term tenants, you may not have made a lot of improvements or accounted for regular wear and tear, either. You might need to wait until you can invest some cash upfront before putting the property on the market.

- **Whether the property is currently occupied.** Whether you want a property occupied when you sell may depend on who you expect your buyer to be—an individual looking for a home, or an investor looking for an income-producing property. Either way, it may be easiest to show the property when it's empty, so if you are between tenants, this may provide you an easy opportunity to make a sale. (On the other hand, some buyers will be happy to find a property with a stable, income-producing tenant—particularly if they themselves are first-time landlords, perhaps buying your duplex.)

- **What effect selling will have on your tax liability.** As discussed above, when you sell can significantly impact your tax liability. Make sure you understand the consequences—for example, if you sell at a gain after owning a property less than a year, any gain will be a short-term capital gain, taxed at your current income tax rate. If that's higher than the current long-term capital gains rate of 15%, you might want to hold off to qualify for the lower rate.

Hire an agent or sell it yourself?

The vast majority of property owners enlist real estate agents to help them sell. Real estate agents serve many functions: They help set a realistic price for the property, prepare it for sale, advertise it, find and show it to prospective buyers, negotiate and close the sale, and handle paperwork to make sure the whole process goes smoothly.

Of course, these services come at a cost—typically 5% to 6% of the sale price. And you, as the seller, will normally be expected to pay the full cost, with your agent splitting the commission with the buyer's agent.

Some sellers instead choose to sell the property themselves. They reason that they can handle a lot of the basic tasks an agent takes care of, and that the biggest challenge—marketing the property—should be no problem, because many buyers look at properties on the Internet. Having saved the cost of the commission, they can easily afford to hire an attorney or title officer to help with the closing. Other expenses may include the cost of online listing services like forsalebyowner.com or fsbo.com, which help increase exposure and traffic to the property.

The Internet Changes Everything

For six months, Nancy Teer-Sims tried selling her parents' home in Durham, North Carolina, with a real estate agent. The results: few showings, no bids. So when the agent's contract expired in December, Teer-Sims dumped the agent, cut the asking price, and listed the home on five websites, including eBay, Craigslist, and ForSaleByOwner.com.

"By selling it ourselves, we could lower the price by $50,000," she says, because she wouldn't have to pay the standard 6% commission. In four months, she's shown the house ten times and had three offers.

Though the offers so far were too low, she's amazed by the flood of responses: 1,400 visitors to her website (www.43beverly.com) and dozens of email inquiries from people interested in the property.

Her story illustrates how the breadth of information now available on the Internet is shifting the balance of power in the real estate industry, giving home buyers and sellers more control over the deal than ever before and fueling competition among agents.

Gone are the days when real estate agents could guard the information about homes for sale in their Multiple Listing Service. Now, buyers and sellers can see all the homes for sale on 800 regional multiple listing services on the Web. They can see thousands of newly built homes for sale and apartments for rent nationwide. They can view aerial photos of homes and neighborhoods. They can get appraisals or see how much the house down the block fetched. They can shop for loans and compare mortgage rates. They can check out local schools and community features for towns across America. They can ask questions and get answers in online forums.

The Internet Changes Everything, cont'd

In 1995, just 2% of home buyers used the Internet to look for a home. By 2007, 84% of home shoppers went house-hunting online, and nearly one-fourth of buyers first found the property they bought on the Internet, according to the National Association of Realtors (NAR).

Armed with more information, sellers are bargaining down agents' commissions, and buyers are asking for rebates. They are turning to a growing number of brokers who offer discounted or *a la carte* services. And some are even cutting out the agent altogether and forging deals directly on the Internet. These factors have pushed commissions to an average of 5.1%, down from the long-standing 6%, according to Real Trends, a real estate newsletter.

The gravest threat of all to Realtors is probably the rise of discount brokers, who dangle rebates or charge low flat fees or reduced commissions.

The Internet lets home buyers and sellers do almost all the house hunting themselves. And that means there will be less need for traditional real estate agents, says Steven Levitt, a University of Chicago economics professor and co-author of the best-seller *Freakonomics: A Rogue Economist Explores the Hidden Side of Everything.*

"I predict there will be a shakeout in real estate," he says. "I would not be surprised if there are one-third less of the traditional real estate agents a decade from now than there are today."

 "Realtors fight for business model; Traditional agents lobby against discount brokers," by Noelle Knox, July 13, 2006.

RESOURCE
Thinking of selling yourself? For more information, read
For Sale By Owner in California, by George Devine (Nolo). Although
the book has California-specific legal forms, it also includes general
information about the pros and cons of selling yourself, along with lots
of useful tips for marketing the property, evaluating an offer, negotiating
a sale, and more.

But selling a property yourself can be harder than it looks. First,
you've got to do enough research to set your starting price just right—
too high, and you may drive away potential buyers, who are unlikely to
return after your house goes stale on the market. Also expect to spend
large amounts of time on tasks like coordinating visits by prospective
buyers, evaluating offers and deciding whether to accept or counteroffer,
and making sure all the formalities that lead to a closing—title
insurance, removing contingencies, and more—are properly handled.

If you instead decide to work with an agent, you'll want to choose
the best (especially because you won't pay a premium to do so—the
standard commission remains the same). You're looking for someone
who is experienced, trustworthy, and professional. Ideally, this means
someone who's been operating in the area where you're selling for at least
three years, has handled many transactions involving rental properties,
and promptly returns calls and schedules appointments with interested
buyers. If you're doing a 1031 exchange or an installment sale, find an
agent experienced in that field.

Ask other rental property owners in the area for recommendations,
and interview at least three potential agents. Below are some questions
you can ask:

Real Estate Agent Interview Questions

❑ Do you work full time as a real estate agent? (Best answer: Yes.)

❑ How long have you been in the real estate business? (The longer the better, but at least three years.)

❑ Do you have additional certifications beyond your general real estate license? If so, what are they? (More certifications show a commitment by the agent to professional development.)

❑ How many residential investment real estate transactions have you been a part of in the past year? (Should be a minimum of ten.)

❑ In how many of those did you represent the seller? (Best answer is "all of them"; should be at least half.)

❑ What was the price range of homes you sold in the last year? What was the average price? (Should be about your price range.)

❑ Do you specialize in certain types of property? (Should be the type of property you're selling, like a single-family house or condo.)

❑ Do you specialize in a certain geographic area? (Should be the geographic area where you're looking to sell.)

❑ Do you partner with other agents or use assistants? (If so, find out whom you'll be working with, what their real estate experience is, and what they'll be doing.)

❑ How will I reach you? Are there days or times you're unavailable, or do you have vacations planned? (Make sure you can reach the agent when you need to. If you plan to sell soon, make sure the agent will be readily available.)

❑ Can you provide at least three names of landlords who are recent clients and sold their investment properties with you, who will serve as references? (Only acceptable answer is "Yes.")

Will the buyer be an investor or a homebuyer?

Whether you expect to sell your house to an investor or to someone who will live in the property is very important. The two have very different objectives. A homebuyer looking for a place to live will walk in and say, "Can I imagine myself living here?" But a shrewd investor will want to know, "Will I make money renting this property out?" And the situation may be mixed if, for example, you're selling a duplex that the buyer will live in part and rent out the other part.

Of course, you won't always know who the buyer will be, and you'll want to be prepared in any case. But you may be able to make an educated guess. For example, if you've been the only rental on the block in a desirable neighborhood for the last several years, it's highly likely an interested buyer will consider moving into the place. On the other hand, if you own a condo in a development in which more than half the units are rented, investors may come around looking.

If there's any possibility you'll sell to an investor, part of your sales preparation should involve showing that the property is capable of delivering a healthy return. Your real estate agent, if

USA TODAY Snapshots®

Homes holding steady

Cities with the lowest percentage of homes purchased in 2007 that are now worth less than is owed on them:

Corvallis, Ore.	9%
Bridgeport-Stamford-Norwalk, Conn.	12%
Durham, N.C.	12%
Burlington, N.C.	12%
Austin-Round Rock, Texas	16%

Source: Zillow.com

By Jae Yang and Julie Snider, USA TODAY 2008

you work with one, will likely help you prepare a brochure, "pro forma," or similar document that shows prospective buyers the property's potential profitability. This document will include much of the same information you may have had access to when you bought, including the number of units (in your case, probably only one or two) and how much each one rents for each year. This figure—the income—is reduced by the vacancy rate and normal operating expenses.

Your agent will probably encourage you to present these numbers in the best possible light. In fact, the numbers will probably be based on the property's potential, even if you're not realizing that full potential (but make it clear that the numbers are potential, to avoid a charge later that you misled the buyer). For example, even though you've rented your house for $1,000 per month to the same reliable tenant for the last six years, the new owner may actually be able to ask $1,200 per month if it's clear that the market for a property like yours has gone up. Or, perhaps you spent $15,000 replacing the roof last year, which made your expenses unusually high—call this out as an unusual and long-lasting improvement, and note if you can that you don't anticipate significant spending in the next year.

> ⓘ **CAUTION**
>
> **It may be time to cut expenses.** Because investors may ask how much you actually spent on maintenance and improvements in the previous year, try to keep these numbers reasonable in the months before you sell. Don't defer needed maintenance—it will cost you more in the long run—but consider holding off on non-necessary improvements.

The savviest investors will want to know what you've actually spent, and will base their own profitability calculations on these numbers. If you get a lower offer as a result, be prepared to justify a higher asking price. For example, you may tell a prospective purchaser, "Because I live far away and didn't have a lot of time to deal with this property, I rented it to a reliable tenant at a below-market rate, even after rents went up in the area. But in this great neighborhood, with low vacancy rates, you could easily find a tenant willing to pay $200 more per month."

If you anticipate selling to someone who plans to live in the house, you'll have a whole different set of objectives. Most important will be making the property physically attractive, as discussed below under "Preparing the property for sale."

Of course, it's difficult to make a house sparkle if a tenant is still living there. You can't control the tenant's taste in furniture or level of cleanliness. Here are some possible ways to reach your goals without getting resistance from the tenant:

- **Negotiate a move out.** As explained above, if the tenant is on a lease, you may be able to work out an early termination. For example, you could offer to pay moving expenses, pay the tenant a small fee, or reduce the rent for a short period in exchange for moving out more quickly.

- **Pay for a cleaning service.** If you don't want or can't get your tenant to move out, you could instead hire someone to clean the place—maybe once for a thorough cleaning, then regularly to maintain it in good condition. Don't expect the tenant to pay for this. It will still be worth the cost, if it presents your property in the best possible light.

- **Offer to pay for the spruce ups.** If your tenant has a lot of stuff cluttering the place up, offer to pay for a storage facility, or provide onsite storage if available. You might also want to buy inexpensive items—a new comforter, shower curtain, and so forth—to enhance the appearance of the place.

CAUTION

Be sure to follow state law when showing an occupied property. Most states regulate the reasons you may enter rented property, and how to give notice to your tenants. Check your state's entry laws and be sure to give adequate notice. Uncooperative or hostile tenants can ruin a showing or open house, so it pays to get your tenants on your side with, for instance, an offer to reduce the rent for the time the property is on the market.

Small Improvements Can Bring the Biggest Return

Thomas A. Fogarty of USA TODAY spoke with Bradley Inman, founder of Internet realty company HomeGain, about the value of dealing with minor home issues—even if the house has some major shortcomings.

As Inman says, a common mistake by those preparing a house for sale is excessive spending on improvements.

Sellers are better advised to deal with major shortcomings of a house in negotiations rather than try to fix them.

A HomeGain survey of 2,000 realty agents found that small upgrades can have a big payback at sale time.

For example, a $470 yard clean-up and landscaping job can be expected to add about four times that sum to the eventual sales price, the survey says. Painting, floor repairs, and carpet replacement in preparation for a sale also carry big returns.

 "Upgrades can raise home's value; Some improvements have a bit more price-boosting potential than others," by Thomas A. Fogarty, April 26, 2002.

Preparing the property for sale

Whether you're moving a tenant out or dealing with a vacant property, you'll want to take some active steps to make things look their best in preparation for sale. You're looking to appeal to the broadest spectrum of buyers so that you can sell quickly at a competitive price. Our advice in Chapter 3 on sprucing up a rental property applies also to preparing a house for sale.

But before you start sprucing up, you may have some deferred maintenance to deal with—repairing dry rot or fixing leaking windows, for example. As much as you may have tried to stay on top of such problems, some may have escaped the tenant's and your notice (or been caused by the tenant).

"Staging" Can Bring Faster Sale, Higher Price

Sellers must work harder these days to attract buyers. Yet oddly enough, the trick to making your home stand out is often to make both the interior and exterior look generic, almost bland. And that's where home staging comes in.

"The philosophy is the buyer must be able to picture themselves living in your home," says Fran Freedman, 65, a lawyer in Philadelphia. "The decor should be understated so they can say, 'This would be the perfect place for my...'"

Does it work? When Coldwell Banker Residential Brokerage in Los Altos, California, looked at nearly 2,800 properties in eight U.S. cities in 2004, they found that the staged homes, on average, sold in half the time that the non-staged homes did. The sellers with staged homes ended up with 6.3% more than their asking price, on average, while sellers with non-staged homes sold for 1.6% more.

The cost of hiring a company to stage your home tends to range from $1,800 to $3,800 but can go much higher, depending on the size of the house and the amount of work involved.

Judee von Seldeneck put her staged home in Philadelphia on the market in 2006; it sold in one day, for $700,000.

From moving shrubs to planting flowers, to replacing the knobs on kitchen cabinets and ripping up the carpet on the stairs, every change was made to accentuate the house's best features. There were even pumpkins on the porch to lend a homey, inviting look.

Inside, the stagers "put furniture that looked comfortable but not too heavy, not cluttered," says von Seldeneck, CEO of an executive search firm. The books on shelves, colors of the rug, the furniture—all were "geared more toward younger people."

She spent $8,000 on the job and says, "It was the best money I ever spent."

Short of hiring a company to do the work, there are some simple steps any seller can take to stage a home:

"Staging" Can Bring Faster Sale, Higher Price, cont'd

- **Cleaning.** The house should be Q-tip clean. Every surface should sparkle; every groove should be dirt-free.
- **Color.** Dark walls make the house look smaller. Walls should be off-white, or have earthy tones if the room has lots of light. Ideally, the carpet would be "real estate beige."
- **Focal point.** To think like a professional stager, stand at the doorway of each room. What features do you want to accentuate? Where's the focal point? (A room should have only one.) Arrange the furniture so the eye is drawn to the focal point.
- **Dining room.** Take out the leaves from your dining table and put no more than four chairs around it. Set the table as if for a meal, and put an appealing centerpiece in the middle.
- **Kitchen.** The exterior of the refrigerator should be bare. Store any appliances out of sight. Hide the trash can, and put the sponge and soap under the sink. You can spruce up an outdated kitchen simply by changing the knobs and hinges.
- **Master bedroom.** Buy a new bedspread, if necessary.
- **Bathroom.** Replace bar soap with liquid. Coordinate all towels using one or two colors. Fold them in thirds and hang them neatly. Clean or replace the shower curtain. Make sure all grout is clean and in good condition.
- **Outside.** Keep the lawn mowed and the edges neat. Trim shrubs, especially around windows. Put flowering plants near the front door. Does the house need painting? Consider painting or staining the front door; it's one of the least expensive ways to spruce up the entry. If there's furniture on the porch, make sure it isn't plastic but rather good wicker or wrought iron. Power-wash or stain the deck.

 "'Staging' results in faster sale, richer price," by Noelle Knox, October 27, 2006.

Leaving minor maintenance matters for the next owner to deal with is usually a mistake. For one thing, in most states, you'll have to disclose problems that you know about, and you'll be in a weaker bargaining position as you and the buyer argue over each necessary change. Ultimately, your house value will go down.

For another, signs of deferred maintenance are a big red flag for potential buyers. They may worry that the property has other hidden problems. If they plan to rent the property out, especially if they plan to keep the same tenants, they may be concerned that your poor maintenance means the current tenants are unhappy or unlikely to stay. Still, if something major like the roof is old but still functional, you may be best off reducing your price accordingly, or offering a "credit" to the buyer to make the change. This will save you the effort of either taking care of it yourself or negotiating it in the purchase agreement. If a buyer says, "I'm knocking $15,000 off the offer price to replace the roof," you can confidently reply, "Actually, the asking price was set based on comparable properties, but discounted for the cost of a new roof."

USA TODAY Snapshots®

Homeowners' perceptions vs. actual home values

What homeowners think and actual U.S. home value changes:
■ Think
▢ Actual

74%
51%
32%
21%
17% 5%

Home value has increased in the past year

Home value has decreased in the past year

Home value has stayed the same

Source: Zillow.com

By Jae Yang and Alejandro Gonzalez, USA TODAY 2008

Index

NOLO Bestsellers

Plan Your Estate

$44.99

How to File for Chapter 7 Bankruptcy

$29.99

Form Your Own Limited Liability Company

$44.99

Deduct It! Lower Your Small Business Taxes

$34.99

Retire Happy

$19.99

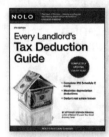

Every Landlord's Tax Deduction Guide

$34.99

Get the Latest in the Law

Nolo's Legal Updater
We'll send you an email whenever a new edition of your book is published! Sign up at **www.nolo.com/legalupdater**.

Updates at Nolo.com
Check **www.nolo.com/update** to find recent changes in the law that affect the current edition of your book.

Nolo Customer Service
To make sure that this edition of the book is the most recent one, call us at **800-728-3555** and ask one of our friendly customer service representatives (7:00 am to 6:00 pm PST, weekdays only). Or find out at **www.nolo.com**.

Complete the Registration & Comment Card ...
... and we'll do the work for you! Just indicate your preferences below:

Registration & Comment Card

NAME	DATE

ADDRESS

CITY	STATE	ZIP

PHONE	EMAIL

COMMENTS

WAS THIS BOOK EASY TO USE?   (VERY EASY)   5   4   3   2   1   (VERY DIFFICULT)

☐ Yes, you can quote me in future Nolo promotional materials. *Please include phone number above.*

☐ Yes, send me **Nolo's Legal Updater** via email when a new edition of this book is available.

Yes, I want to sign up for the following email newsletters:

   ☐ **NoloBriefs** (monthly)
   ☐ **Nolo's Special Offer** (monthly)
   ☐ **Nolo's BizBriefs** (monthly)
   ☐ **Every Landlord's Quarterly** (four times a year)

☐ Yes, you can give my contact info to carefully selected partners whose products may be of interest to me.

Send to: **Nolo** 950 Parker Street Berkeley, CA 94710-9867,
       Fax: (800) 645-0895, or include all of the above
       information in an email to regcard@nolo.com with
       the subject line "US-FTL1."

US-FTL1

NOLO and USA TODAY

Cutting-Edge Content, Unparalleled Expertise

The Busy Family's Guide to Money
by Sandra Block, Kathy Chu & John Waggoner

Drawing on the experience of three respected USA TODAY financial writers, *The Busy Family's Guide to Money* will help you make the most of your income, handle major one-time expenses, figure children into the budget—and much more. **$19.99**

The Work From Home Handbook
Flex Your Time, Improve Your Life
by Diana Fitzpatrick & Stephen Fishman

If you're one of those people who need to (or simply want to) work from home, let this concise and powerful book help you come up with a plan that both you and your boss can embrace! **$19.99**

Retire Happy
What You Can Do NOW to Guarantee a Great Retirement
by Richard Stim & Ralph Warner

You don't need a million dollars to retire well, but you do need friends, hobbies and an active lifestyle. This book covers all the financial and personal necessities that can make retirement the best time of your life. **$19.99**

Easy Ways to Lower Your Taxes
Simple Strategies Every Taxpayer Should Know
by Sandra Block & Stephen Fishman

Provides useful insights and tactics to help lower your taxes. Learn how to boost tax-free income, get a lower tax rate, defer paying taxes, make the most of deductions—and more! **$19.99**

Stopping Identity Theft
10 Easy Steps to Security
by Scott Mitic, CEO, TrustedID, Inc.

Don't let an empty bank account be your first warning sign. Prevent theft of personal information with this book's ten strategies. Learn how to scrutinize credit reports, prevent medical ID theft and more. **$19.99**

800-728-3555 or www.nolo.com